MW00767894

CiTY·SMaRT™
GUIDEBOOK

Salt Lake City

Margaret Sandberg Godfrey

John Muir Publications
Santa Fe, New Mexico

John Muir Publications, P.O. Box 613, Santa Fe, New Mexico 87504

Printed in the United States of America.
First edition. First printing May 1999.

ISBN: 1-56261-469-X
ISSN: 1522-8525

Editors: Sarah Baldwin, Elaine Robbins
Graphics Editors: Heather Pool, John Lyons-Gould
Production: Marie J.T. Vigil
Design: Janine Lehmann
Cover design: Suzanne Rush
Typesetter: Laurel Avery
Map production: Julie Felton
Printer: Edwards Brothers
Front cover photo: © Leo de Wys, Inc./J. Goebel—Mormon Temple on Temple Square
Back cover photo: © Frank Jensen—Skiing near Salt Lake City

Distributed to the book trade by
Publishers Group West
Berkeley, California

CONTENTS

How to Use This Book   V

1 Welcome to Salt Lake City   1
Getting to Know Salt Lake City 2 • A Brief History of Salt Lake City 5 • The People of Salt Lake City 9 • When to Visit 11 • Calendar of Events 11 • About the Weather 13 • Dressing in Salt Lake City 14 • Business and Economy 15 • Schools 16

2 Getting Around Salt Lake City   17
City Layout 17 • Public Transportation 19 • Driving in Salt Lake City 21 • Biking in Salt Lake City 22 • Salt Lake City International Airport 23 • Train Service 24 • Interstate and Regional Bus Service 24

3 Where to Stay   25
Downtown 26 • Southeastern Valley 38 • University Area 42 • Western Valley 43 • Cottonwood Canyons and Environs 45

4 Where to Eat   49
Restaurants by Food Type 50 • Downtown 51 • Southeastern Valley 62 • University Area 68 • Western Valley 70 • Cottonwood Canyons and Environs 71

5 Sights and Attractions   75
Temple Square 75 • Downtown 79 • Southeastern Valley 92 • University Area 93 • Western Valley 96 • Cottonwood Canyons and Environs 99

6 Museums and Galleries   100
Fine Art Museums and Public Galleries 100 • Science and History Museums 102 • Specialty Museums 103 • Galleries 105 • Public Art 107

7 Kids' Stuff   110
Animals and the Great Outdoors 110 • Museums and Libraries 112 • Theater 116 • Stores Kids Love 117 • Fun Centers 118 • Within a Short Drive 119

8 Parks, Gardens, and Recreation Areas   121

9 Shopping   129
Shopping Districts 129 • Other Notable Stores 136 • Notable Bookstores 138 • Department Stores 139 • Shopping Malls 140 • Factory Outlets 142

10 Sports and Recreation   144
Professional Sports 144 • Olympic Winter Games of 2002 Venues 148 • Recreation 151

11 Performing Arts   161
Theater 161 • Music and Opera 164 • Dance 166 • Concert Venues 168

12 Nightlife   **170**
Dance Clubs 171 • Music Clubs 172 • Pubs and Bars 175 • Social Clubs 177 • Movie Houses of Note 179

13 Day Trips from Salt Lake City   **181**
Antelope Island State Park 181 • Bear Lake 183 • Park City 184 • Weekend Trip: Dinosaurland 186 • Weekend Trips: Southern Utah's National Parks and Monuments 187

Appendix: City•Smart Basics   **190**
Emergency Phone Numbers 190 • Hospitals and Emergency Medical Centers 190 • Visitor Information 190 • Recorded Information 190 • Ski Information 190 • City Tours 191 • Car Rental 191 • Resources for New Residents 191 • Multicultural Resources 191 • Disabled Services 191 • Other Community Organizations 191 • Main Post Office 191 • City Media 191–192 • Bookstores 192–193

Index   **194**

MAP CONTENTS

Greater Salt Lake City Zones   vi

2 Getting Around Salt Lake City
Light Rail   20

3 Where to Stay
Downtown Salt Lake City   28–29
Greater Salt Lake City   40–41

4 Where to Eat
Downtown Salt Lake City   54–55
Greater Salt Lake City   64–65

5 Sights and Attractions
Temple Square   77
Downtown Salt Lake City   82–83
Greater Salt Lake City   94–95

10 Sports and Recreation
Winter Games Venues   149

13 Day Trips from Salt Lake City
Salt Lake City Region   182

See Salt Lake City the CiTY·SMaRT™ Way

The Guide for Salt Lake City Natives, New Residents, and Visitors

In *City•Smart Guidebook: Salt Lake City*, local author Margaret Sandberg Godfrey tells it like it is. Residents will learn things they never knew about their city, new residents will get an insider's view of their new hometown, and visitors will be guided to the very best Salt Lake City has to offer—whether they're on a weekend getaway or staying a week or more.

Opinionated Recommendations Save You Time and Money

From shopping to nightlife to museums, the author is opinionated about what she likes and dislikes. You'll learn the great and the not-so-great things about Salt Lake City's sights, restaurants, and accommodations. So you can decide what's worth your time and what's not; which hotel is worth the splurge and which is the best choice for budget travelers.

Easy-to-Use Format Makes Planning Your Trip a Cinch

City•Smart Guidebook: Salt Lake City is user-friendly—you'll quickly find exactly what you're looking for. Chapters are organized by travelers' interests or needs, from Where to Stay and Where to Eat, to Sights and Attractions, Kids' Stuff, Sports and Recreation, Nightlife, and even Day Trips.

Includes Maps and Quick Location-Finding Features

At the end of every listing in this book is a geographic zone designation (see the following pages for zone details) that tells you what part of town the listing can be found in. Staying close to the University of Utah and wondering about nearby sights and restaurants? Look for the "University Area" label at the end of the listings and you'll know that statue or café is not far away. Or maybe you're looking for the Family History Library. Along with its address, you'll see a "Downtown" label in parentheses at the end of the description, so you'll know just where to find it.

All That and Fun to Read, Too!

Every City•Smart chapter includes fun-to-read (and fun-to-use) tips to help you get more out of Salt Lake City, local trivia (did you know that Temple Square has 5 million visitors every year?), and illuminating sidebars (to learn about the Great Salt Lake, for example, see page 3).

SALT LAKE CITY ZONES

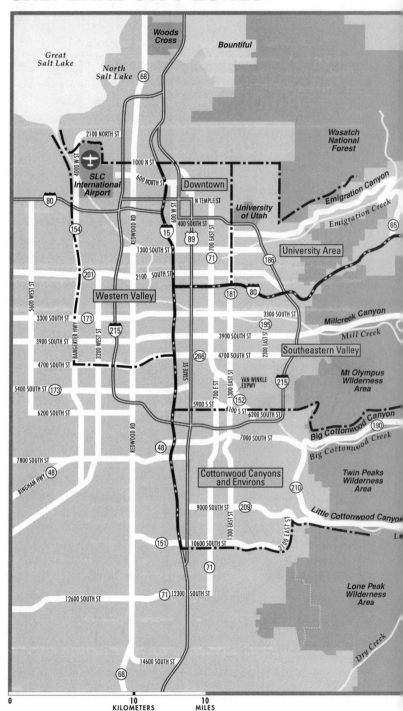

Great
Salt Lake

Woods
Cross

Bountiful

North
Salt Lake (68)

2100 NORTH ST

Wasatch
National
Forest

4000 W ST

SLC
International
Airport

1000 N ST

600 NORTH ST

Downtown

Emigration Canyon

(80)

N TEMPLE ST

Emigration Creek

(154)

600 W ST

University
of Utah

400 SOUTH ST

(65)

(15)

(89)

700 EAST ST

University Area

REDWOOD RD

1300 SOUTH ST

(71)

(186)

(201)

2100   SOUTH ST

5600 WEST ST

Western Valley

(181)

(80)

Millcreek Canyon

3300 SOUTH ST

(171)

3300 SOUTH ST

Mill Creek

BANGERTER HWY

(215)

3200 WEST ST

3900 SOUTH ST

(195)

3900 SOUTH ST

Southeastern Valley

2300 EAST ST

4700 SOUTH ST

(266)

4700 SOUTH ST

Mt Olympus
Wilderness
Area

5400 SOUTH ST (173)

700 E ST

1300 EAST ST

VAN WINKLE
EXPWY

(215)

STATE ST

5900 S ST

(152)

6100 S ST

6200 SOUTH ST

6200 SOUTH ST

Big Cottonwood Canyon

(190)

(48)

7000 SOUTH ST

Big Cottonwood Creek

7800 SOUTH ST

REDWOOD RD

Twin Peaks
Wilderness
Area

BINGHAM HWY (48)

Cottonwood Canyons
and Environs

(210)

Little Cottonwood Canyon

9000 SOUTH ST (209)

1300 EAST ST

(151)

10600 SOUTH ST

2700 EAST ST

L

Lone Peak
Wilderness
Area

(71)

12600 SOUTH ST

(71) 12300 SOUTH ST

14600 SOUTH ST

(68)

Dry Creek

0   10   10
        KILOMETERS   MILES

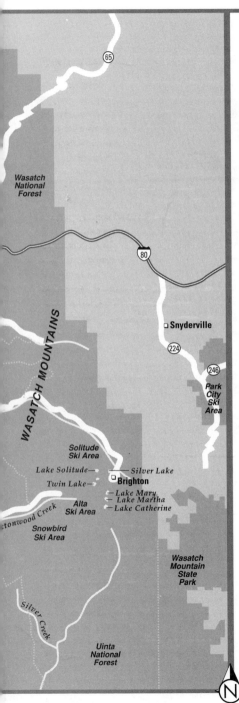

SALT LAKE CITY ZONES

Downtown (DT)
The area east of I-15 to 1300 East Street and the area south of 1000 North Street to I-80. Includes Temple Square and the majority of sights in this book.

Southeastern Valley (SV)
The area east of I-15 to the foothills of the Wasatch Mountains and the area south from I-80 to 6200 South Street. Includes Salt Lake Community College and Millcreek Canyon.

University Area (UA)
The area east of 1300 East Street to the foothills of the Wasatch Mountains, and the area south of 1000 North Street to I-80. Includes the University of Utah and Emigration Canyon.

Western Valley (WV)
The area east of Bangerter Hwy to I-15 and the area south of 1000 North Street to 4700 South. Includes Great Salt Lake and Bonneville Salt Flats.

Cottonwood Canyons and Environs (CC)
The area east of I-15 to the canyon's terminus and the area south from 6200 South Street to 10600 South Street. Includes Brighton, Solitude, Alta, and Snowbird resorts.

Utah Travel Council

1

WELCOME TO
SALT LAKE CITY

Situated against the northeast foothills of the Salt Lake Valley and close to the canyon streams that provided water for the first pioneer settlers, Salt Lake City's 90 square miles make up just a small portion of the valley. Views to the south and west show the sweep of the Wasatch and Oquirrh Mountains, and the 800-square-mile valley that lies in between. A generation ago most people lived in the city proper, but the valley towns have since grown exponentially, and now the entire area flows as a continuous population base. Though Salt Lake City remains the valley's cultural and financial headquarters—where most valley residents spend their working days and their nights on the town—the descriptions in this book cover the wider area commonly referred to as "Salt Lake."

Many guidebooks to Salt Lake City, especially those written by non-residents, portray it in modest terms—the city is "safe" and "clean," the citizens "wholesome," the skyline "easily digestible." Though these descriptions are true enough, they don't capture the more exciting aspects of the area. Here you'll find world-class recreation possibilities in the Rocky Mountains to the east, and the desert and Great Salt Lake to the west. Salt Lake City supports a lively performing arts scene and the hugely popular Utah Jazz NBA team. On certain fine days, the sky has an exotic hue—a psychedelic blue found only in this 4,300-foot pocket of the Rocky Mountains. In addition to these attractions, an increasing ethnic population has made the city more culturally diverse than is often supposed.

Some locals may not be so quick to defend their city, perhaps because they prefer to keep Salt Lake City to themselves. The city's puritan reputation has staved off the masses and caused the urbane and sophisticated—along with the strip mall developers and asphalt layers—to go elsewhere in search of a hip and colorful lifestyle. Salt Lake City is lovely and real . . . and perhaps a tad boring. And what a wonderful thing that is for the people who live here.

Getting to Know Salt Lake City

The first thing that many visitors to the area notice is the mountains that rise dramatically from the valley floor, forming an almost perfect circle around Salt Lake City. To the east are the Wasatch Mountains—11,000-foot peaks that form the western boundary of the Rocky Mountains. The steep, granite slopes of the Wasatch catch most of the snowfall that sweeps across the valley floor, and they are home to the world-class ski resorts of which Utahns are so proud. To the west are the more humble Oquirrh Mountains, and just farther north and west is the Stansbury range, which shields Salt Lake City from the deserts beyond.

The second thing that most visitors notice is that there is no lake in the middle of Salt Lake City. Indeed, some Salt Lakers who have navigated the city their entire lives have never even visited the Great Salt Lake. Its shores lie northwest of the city, and the best view of the water from inside city boundaries requires a drive or a hike to the foothills of the Wasatch Mountains.

It seems visitors also notice the wide, tree-lined streets that criss-cross the city; they were originally designed so that a wagon and team of oxen could easily turn around. In most tourist polls, "clean streets" make the top ten list.

Salt Lake City's skyline

Utah Travel Council/Frank Jensen

The Great Salt Lake

The Great Salt Lake earns its name by being both big and salty. Its shores span 2,000 square miles, making it the largest lake west of the Mississippi River and the second-largest inland sea in the world (the first is the Dead Sea, on the Israel–Jordan border). Its salt content rises and falls with its waterline, but it is approximately five times saltier than ocean water. The reason for this size and salinity is dictated by geography. The lake sits in the bottom of a huge basin, into which three major rivers flow. There is no outlet for the water, and thousands of years of evaporation have left a high concentration of minerals. The ebb and flow of the water formed the vast salt crystal desert on its western shore.

Though the Great Salt Lake doesn't flow through the boundaries of the city proper, its waters still manage to affect many aspects of city life. It creates its own weather; the "lake effect" is often blamed for the unexpected storms that periodically dump snow and rain on Salt Lake City and surprise every weather forecaster in town. Winter inversions that lure and trap low cloud covers over the city can be traced to the Salt Lake Valley's basin geography, which was in part created by the lake. The lake is also a source of wealth; mining its various salts is a multimillion-dollar business, and the brine shrimp that exist only in the lake's peculiar ecosystem are responsible for adding about $30 million dollars to Utah's tax base each year—the shrimps' eggs are shipped all over the world for fish food.

Neighborhoods

Salt Lake City has a number of distinct neighborhoods. Located just west and north of the state capitol grounds, the Marmalade District—named after its streets, which include Quince and Apricot—is a residential pocket with narrow streets and cliff-steep hills. The area's architecture was adapted to accommodate its verticality, and some clever and unique housing is the result.

Just north of South Temple Street, the Avenues is a collection of numbered and lettered streets. A century ago, when Salt Lake City's wealthiest citizens lived on South Temple Street, the working classes built their homes on narrow streets "hidden" behind the grand mansions. These Avenues are a wild, eclectic mix of styles.

In the northwestern section of the city, Rose Park was one of the first "subdivisions" anywhere, built in the late 1940s. Its symmetrical streets are named after rose varieties, and many of its small homes and

For the Birds

The California seagull earned a place in Utahns' hearts and history books 150 years ago by saving a crop of grain. The story goes that the Mormon pioneers had been in the Salt Lake Valley several years and were just about to harvest their first abundant crop. The previous winters had been hard and food-scarce, but the pioneers felt hopeful that adequate provisions would make the coming winter easier to bear. One bright day that hope was severely tested when an infestation of millions of grasshoppers darkened the sky and descended on their fields. The insects marched as a single, endless unit across the landscape, devouring everything in their path. The pioneers' attempts at staving off the grasshoppers were futile, and it looked as though all was lost.

Then, in what can only be described as a miracle, seagulls began to arrive. First one at a time, then in pairs, and finally in great flocks, seagulls flew down and ate the grasshoppers. They reportedly ate and ate and ate, not stopping until every last grasshopper was gone. The crop and the future of the pioneers was saved. A statue memorializing this event is found inside Temple Square, and the seagull is further honored with the title of Utah State Bird.

Meanwhile, grasshopper infestations, though uncommon, continue to this day. In rural areas their marauding numbers have stopped traffic as they walk across roads and fields by the millions, eating everything in their path.

Utah Travel Council/Frank Jensen

This Is the Place Monument, where Brigham Young first viewed the Salt Lake Valley.

lots are perfectly manicured. St. Mary's and Indian Hills are newer, upscale neighborhoods built in the eastern foothills of Salt Lake City. Both feature wide, curving streets, large houses, and excellent valley-wide views.

Federal Heights, near the University of Utah, is the grande dame of Salt Lake City's residential neighborhoods, reserved for the city's wealthy elite. Its tree-canopied streets are lined with stately homes built a century ago.

Outlying Areas

Business, farming, and ranch districts that once stood separate and apart from Salt Lake City have in the last century melded into each other's borders and become part of a continuous population flow across the Salt Lake Valley. Sugarhouse, named after a former sugar mill, has been absorbed by the city's southeastern borders and remains a commercial district filled with small shops and businesses. Holladay, named after its founder, John Holladay, borders Salt Lake City directly to the south. It was once an unpopulated farm area; now it is a desirable residential area filled with ranch-style homes on large lots.

In recent decades the western valley has traded in large ranches for sprawling subdivisions and has incorporated into its own bustling city, known as West Valley City. Kearns, Murray, and Midvale, located mid-valley, are smaller cities that are fast losing their status as bedroom communities and becoming busy commercial districts. Sandy and Draper are full-fledged, fast-growing large cities located in the most beautiful part of the valley—the foothills just below the Cottonwood Canyons.

A Brief History of Salt Lake City

In the mid-1700s Spanish priests were the first Europeans to explore and chart the region that would become Utah. In search of a trade route from Santa Fe, New Mexico, to Monterey, California, Fathers Dominguez and Escalante made their way to the tip of the Salt Lake Valley before turning back to avoid winter weather.

The priests made note of several of the Native American tribes they encountered, including the Shoshoni, Goshute, Paiute, and Ute tribes, which had lived in northern Utah for centuries, subsisting on small mammals and native plants. The largest tribe in Utah, the Navajo, lived farther to the south. Much earlier, before recorded history, the Anasazi and Fremont people hunted and gathered in Utah. Flint points, bone awls, and other evidence of their 10,000-year-old culture have been found in caves near the shores of the Great Salt Lake, and their rock art can still be seen in many areas throughout the state.

By the 1820s trappers had discovered the area, with its plentiful supply of beaver and other fur-bearing animals. Perhaps the most famous of these is Jim Bridger, who is frequently credited with discovering the Great Salt Lake. In 1824 he made a bet with another trapper on the course of the Bear River and floated downstream to its junction with the lake. He thought he had discovered an arm of the Pacific Ocean.

Even the most faithful of the Mormon pioneers must have harbored doubts when they first glimpsed the Salt Lake Valley—the home chosen for them by their leader, Brigham Young. In July of 1847, after months of traveling through the fertile grasslands of the Midwest and an arduous climb over the verdant Rocky Mountains, Young looked down into a desolate basin filled with sagebrush and brackish water, and declared he had found "the right place." He had envisioned just such a valley for his flock, a secluded land where they could practice their religion in peace—a desert quickly passed over by earlier westbound emigrants; a place, in fact, that nobody else wanted.

Yet the day after their arrival, the pioneers began irrigating their land with water from the canyon streams, and within a few months they had begun to turn their desert bowl into a green valley. Within a year crops were harvested, permanent houses were built, and schools were established. Over the next decades thousands more of Brigham Young's followers would join the pioneers in the Salt Lake Valley.

Construction of a transcontinental railroad was begun during Abraham Lincoln's administration, and by 1869 the joining of separate lines from the east and west coasts was almost complete. On May 10 of that year, workers laid the final rail in Promontory, Utah, and with much ceremony dignitaries struck a symbolic golden spike to join the first coast-to-coast railway.

Ogden, a city 45 miles north of Salt Lake City, was the primary stop for railroad traffic in Utah, but the effect on all of northern Utah was immediate. A lucrative mining industry, a non-Mormon enterprise, took hold in Salt Lake City, and within a short time city politics were no longer decided exclusively by the LDS Church. Fierce business competition and trade wars arose between Mormons and "gentiles." A non-Mormon newspaper, the *Salt Lake Tribune*, competed with the church-owned *Deseret News*. New laws and recriminations were made against the decades-old practice of polygamous marriage.

Years of bitter fighting between the federal government and the LDS church finally ended when polygamy was officially abandoned as a

Entertainment at Old Deseret Village commemorating the city's history

church tenet in 1890. By the end of the century, Mormons and non-Mormons had reached a sort of truce, and business and politics in Salt Lake City accommodated both groups. This reconciliation was partly responsible for Utah's long-denied grant of statehood in 1896.

During the next two decades Salt Lake City's thriving economy altered the city's appearance. Imposing buildings were built downtown to house banks and other commercial industries. South Temple Street became a showcase of mansions for wealthy citizens. Streets were paved and trolley service was available throughout downtown. Migration from rural areas doubled the city's population.

World War I continued the economic boom for the city, since mining and agriculture were important for the war effort. Both industries collapsed, however, during the Great Depression, and at its height over one-third of Utahns were unemployed. The federal programs of Roosevelt's New Deal began an economic ascent in Salt Lake City that was further boosted by World War II, when local industries were again in demand.

Salt Lake City has experienced exponential growth in the last half of the twentieth century. The farms and ranches that once surrounded the city limits have become suburbs and shopping malls, and the once uninhabited Salt Lake Valley now has only pockets of open space. Though growth has brought unprecedented prosperity to the city, its rapidity has sparked new interest in city planning and environmental protection. Small parks and wild areas have been created throughout the city, and older buildings are being renovated rather than torn down. Salt Lakers are especially protective of the canyons that radiate from the eastern city limits—in recent years limits have been placed on development in the mountain areas.

SALT LAKE CITY TIMELINE

Prehistory	Anasazi and Fremont cultures hunt and gather in Utah. Ute, Paiute, Goshute, and Shoshoni tribes settle in Utah.
1776	Fathers Dominguez and Escalante explore and chart Utah as they search for a trade route from New Mexico to California.
1824	Fur trappers from the Eastern states carve trails through Utah's mountain passes.
1830	The LDS Church organizes in New York state.
1843	Captain John C. Fremont explores the area surrounding the Great Salt Lake.
1847	The first wagon train of Mormon pioneers arrives. Brigham Young is named president of the LDS Church.
1848	The Utah area acquires U.S. sovereignty.
1849	Thousands of adventurers pass through Salt Lake City on their way to the promise of gold in California.
1850	Congress creates the Territory of Utah.
1852	Polygamy becomes an official, public tenet of the LDS Church.
1856	Mormon hand-cart parties begin migration to Utah.
1857	U.S. government sends troops to Salt Lake City to quell the "Mormon Rebellion." Peace is established the next year.
1860	Pony Express establishes stations crossing Salt Lake City.
1868	Zion's Mercantile Cooperative Institution (ZCMI) is established as the nation's first department store. It continues to thrive 130 years later.
1869	The "golden spike" is driven at Promontory, 40 miles north of Salt Lake City, creating the first union of a transcontinental railroad.
1877	Brigham Young dies.
1880	Electric lights and telephones installed.
1890	Polygamy is made illegal.
1893	Construction of Salt Lake City Mormon Temple completed.
1895	Utah women granted the right to vote.
1896	Utah becomes the 45th state of the union on January 4.
1915	State Capitol building completed.
1922	First radio station, KSL, begins broadcasting.
1940	Utah Symphony established.
1948	First television station, KDYL, begins broadcasting.

Craig Breedlove drives to speeds of 601 mph on the Bonneville Salt Flats.	1965
The LDS Church president announces that all male church members are equal, reversing earlier doctrine that had excluded African Americans.	1978
Record snowfall inundates the Wasatch Front mountains, sending spring floods into the streets of downtown.	1984
A committee is formed to pursue the Olympic Winter Games.	1985
The International Olympic Committee chooses Salt Lake City as host for the Olympic Winter Games of 2002.	1995
Utah celebrates its centennial year of statehood.	1996
Gateway project commences, with the goal of renovating and redeveloping the western half of Salt Lake City.	1997
Construction of city light rail transportation system begins.	1998

The People of Salt Lake City

Salt Lake City's population of 175,000 is just a fraction of the larger metro area of Salt Lake County, which has a population of 830,000. Nearly three-fourths of the population is Caucasian. The second largest ethnic group is Hispanic, which makes up less than 10 percent. Other population groups, in descending order, are Asian and Pacific Islanders, African Americans, and Native Americans. The fastest growing group is Asian and Pacific Islanders, who now number 29,000. This group migrates to Utah mostly as converts to the LDS Church, and their growth rate since 1990 is 46.7 percent. The Caucasian population's growth rate is just 5.5 percent in the same time frame, dramatically slower than all of the other groups. Since 1990 the Hispanic population of 60,000 grew 40 percent; the African American population of 7,100 grew 39 percent, and the Native American population of 7,000 grew 29 percent. In the year 2020, Salt Lake City's population is expected to grow to 190,000 residents.

Utah is both blessed and cursed with the lowest median age in the country—the average age for Salt Lakers is just 28 years. Part of the reason for this is that Salt Lake City has a higher birth rate and more family members per household than the national average, and one of the largest percentage of citizens under five years of age. This young population base creates a safe, friendly, and vibrant environment in which to live; Salt Lake City is consistently rated as "the best place to

A Mormon City

As many people know, Salt Lake City is the world headquarters of the Church of Jesus Christ of Latter-Day Saints. Perhaps only Rome or Mecca is so inextricably linked with its predominant religion. Even though in recent decades migration from other states has reduced the ratio of Mormons to non-Mormons, Salt Lake City remains famous as a religious center.

The church's long name is shortened to "the LDS Church" in most publications, and its members—the Mormons—are named after one of their sacred texts, The Book of Mormon. Joseph Smith was the founder and first president of the LDS Church, while Brigham Young was the second president and the leader who oversaw the settlement of the Salt Lake Valley. There are various memorials to the two men throughout the city.

The church's religious philosophy includes large families, conservative politics, and a strict moral code prohibiting the ingestion of alcohol, tobacco, and caffeine. Mormons' love of documenting history is evident in the church's famous genealogy archives; their passion for the fine arts is reflected in Salt Lake City's world-class symphony, dance, opera, and theater companies.

Much of the central downtown area is owned by the LDS Church, notably Temple Square and the blocks surrounding it, which are home to church offices and public attractions. The LDS Temple, found inside the walled, 10-acre square, is an architectural landmark. Only faithful Mormons who receive permission from their leaders are allowed inside the Temple building. All of the other buildings in the square, including two visitor centers, are open to the public.

raise a family" in national surveys. Conversely, the unbalanced population strains the city's school systems, with per-student spending lower in Utah than in most other states in the nation. A recent poll of Utahns showed "population growth" as one of the chief quality-of-life concerns for the future.

July 24—Utah's State Holiday

The first wagon train of Mormon pioneers entered the Salt Lake Valley in several groups—arriving on July 21, 22, and 23 of 1847. Brigham Young, the leader of the Mormons, was delayed by sickness from making his entrance until July 24. Ever since, July 24 has been a holiday in Utah, and celebrations now rival any other holiday. All government and most business operations suspend for the day. For weeks preceding the 24th, rodeos, fairs, races, and community celebrations serve as a countdown. The annual 24th of July Parade and the rodeo in Salt Lake City are known as two of the largest events in the West.

When to Visit

Each of Salt Lake City's four seasons has a separate but equal appeal. Winter is beloved by skiers, snowmobilers, and sledders, who prize the dry, fluffy snow conditions found only on the Wasatch Front. Snow and ski events in the mountain resorts take place nearly every weekend. This is fine arts season in Utah as well, when opera, symphony, ballet, modern dance, and theater companies perform at various venues. Utah Jazz basketball and Utah Grizzlies hockey teams compete at the Delta Center and E Center, respectively, from December through February.

Spring brings soft skies and the first blooming flowers, along with garden shows and Salt Lake Buzz baseball at Franklin Covey Field. Summer is festival season in Utah, with dozens of events—including rodeos and craft fairs—almost every day of the week. Albion Basin at the top of Little Cottonwood Canyon is world famous for its display of wildflowers, at its peak in June and July. Autumn offers fabulous leaf displays in the Wasatch canyons, along with cooler weather ideal for hiking and other outdoor activities.

Calendar of Events

January
International Auto Expo, Salt Palace; Jazz at the Hilton (through spring); Sundance Film Festival, Downtown (also in Park City).

February
Wasatch Telemark Fun Race, Alta; Chili Open Golf Tournament, Wheeler Farm.

March
International Sportsmen's Expo, Salt Palace; NFL Celebrity Ski Classic, Snowbird; St. Patrick's Day Parade, Downtown.

April
Easter Sunrise Service, Snowbird; Semiannual Conference of the LDS Church, Temple Square; Arbor Day Ceremony, Red Butte Garden and Arboretum.

May
Sailing Festival, Great Salt Lake; Beach Fest, Great Salt Lake State Park; Living Traditions Festival, Washington Square; Dino Dash 5K, University of Utah.

June
Utah Arts Festival, Downtown; Salt Lake City Classic Run, Downtown; Gina Bachauer Piano Competition, Abravanel Hall; Antelope Island By Moonlight Bike Ride, Antelope Island.

Salt Lake City's Weather

	Average Daily High/Low Temps (°F)	Average Monthly Precipitation (inches)
January	37/19	1.3
February	43/24	1.2
March	52/31	1.8
April	62/38	2.0
May	72/46	1.7
June	83/54	0.9
July	93/62	0.8
August	90/61	0.9
September	80/51	1.1
October	66/40	1.3
November	50/30	1.3
December	38/22	1.4

Source: National Weather Service

July

Pioneer Day events, including parade and 10-day rodeo, throughout Utah; Speed Opener, Bonneville Salt Flats; Japanese Obon Festival, Japanese Church of Christ; Twilight Concert Series, Gallivan Center.

August

Belly Dance Festival, Snowbird; Mondays in the Park Concert Series, Liberty Park; Speed Week, Bonneville Salt Flats; International Festival, Jordan Park; Twins' Day, Hogle Zoo.

September

Utah State Fair, Utah State Fairgrounds; Greek Festival, Holy Trinity Greek Orthodox Church; Oktoberfest weekends, Snowbird (through October).

October

Semiannual Conference of the LDS Church, Temple Square; Utah Flute Festival, Downtown.

November

Christmas Lighting of Temple Square (through December); Lights On, Gallivan Center; Holiday Quilt Show, Downtown; Dickens' Christmas Festival, Downtown.

December

Festival of Trees, Salt Palace; Vivaldi Candlelight Concert, St. Mark's Cathedral; Christmas at Temple Square (nightly programs); First Night New Year's Eve Celebration, Downtown.

About the Weather

Salt Lake City receives the full force of all four seasons, and each faithfully follows the calendar for a three-month reign. November brings the first storms of winter, and by January the city is generally covered with a winter-long layer of snow. In April the city is awash in blooms, and by July the temperatures hover near the century mark. By late August the heat has abated, and in late September the turning leaf colors, especially in the surrounding canyons, are magnificent. Summer is hot, with an average July high of 93 degrees, and winter is cold, with an average January low of 18 degrees, but extreme temperatures are rare.

The city's altitude is 4,300 feet above sea level, and the climate is labeled as "high desert." The sun shines 7 days out of 10, and some rain falls about 2 days out of 10. Precipitation in the Salt Lake area ranges from just 5 annual inches in the Great Salt Lake Desert to 16 inches in Salt Lake City, with a snow depth of 10 feet or more in the Wasatch

Mountains. Humidity is less than 30 percent, which accounts for the unusually light and fluffy snowfall both in the valley and the neighboring mountains. The dry air also makes the summer heat much more bearable than in more humid parts of the world.

In all seasons, Salt Lakers depend on the nearby mountains for relief from the weather. In winter, when occasional inversions create a low cloud cover over the city, a drive up a mountain canyon can offer sun and warmer temperatures. On summer weekends, Salt Lakers often pack their cars and head for the canyons, where the daytime temperatures can be as much as 20 degrees cooler and midsummer nights often require a jacket.

Dressing in Salt Lake City

The typical closet of a Salt Lake City resident holds everything from shorts and sandals to down jackets and lined waterproof boots—and the changeable weather in spring and fall can mean that all of them might be worn within a week's span. With temperatures ranging from the 90s in summer to the low teens in winter, clothes to fit every season are a necessity. A safe rule for a day spent out of doors, in any season, is to dress in layers that can be added to or shed as changing conditions require. Early mornings and evenings can be much cooler than midday.

Once the protective layers have been established, the primary emphasis for most Salt Lakers is comfort. Casual dress is accepted almost everywhere in town for shopping, dining, and most social events. During the workday, downtown street wear consists mostly of skirts, slacks, and sport coats. Salt Lakers do like to dress up for evening concerts and nights on the town; however, everything from jeans to sequins are seen at opera and ballet premieres.

Twice a year, in October and April, the LDS Church hosts a worldwide religious conference at Temple Square in the heart of downtown. During conference weekends thousands of Mormons congregate in Salt Lake City. If visitors would like to know how Mormons dress, these weekends provide a prime viewing opportunity. But, in truth, Mormons dress just like everyone else, albeit a tad more conservatively. Mormon women generally cover their arms, and both men and women wear clothes that come to the knee or below.

Western wear and cowboy boots are commonly seen on city streets, but much of it is worn only for show, since most of the real cowboy work in Utah is done in areas north and south of Salt Lake City. Utah's official dance is the square dance, and periodically large groups of revelers will stage a hoedown and parade the streets in their costumes. Square-dance couples usually wear twin outfits, with the man's shirt matching the woman's costume. Women dancers seem to love myriad petticoats, which show off their twirling techniques.

Another staple of city dress is that of the dedicated recreationalist.

Clothes designed for skiers, rock climbers, runners, and cyclists are standard outfits for those who take advantage of Salt Lake City's outdoor lifestyle, as well as for those who wish to look as if they do.

Business and Economy

In contrast to its casual, relaxed atmosphere, Salt Lake City's economy moves at a fast and furious pace. Utah is consistently ranked by national media as one of the top 10 places to do business in the United States. In 1997 job growth in Utah was second highest in the country, with the unemployment rate of 3.2

Some of Salt Lake City's many children at Snowbird resort

Salt Lake Convention & Visitors Bureau

percent near the nation's low. A Utah Office and Planning and Budget report states, "Utah enters 1998 with the longest sustained economic expansion in modern economic history and continues to record population and job growth rates that are twice the national average." Despite its booming economy, Utah's per capita income ranks 44th out of the 50 states at $27,500 (the state's young population is a contributing factor).

The construction industry is a primary force in Salt Lake City's economy. New construction for a city light rail system, Olympic facilities, and Interstate 15 renovation are primary current projects. High-tech industries are another mainstay of the economy, especially in the areas of biomedical and medical products and software systems. Salt Lake City's diversity of industries is credited for its ability to withstand fluctuations in the marketplace. Mining, government, manufacturing, tourism, and the service industries are all major contributors to Salt Lake City's tax base.

Cost of Living
Salt Lake City follows the pattern of most midsize western cities as a relatively inexpensive place to live. Money magazine recently ranked Salt Lake City against 300 other U.S. cities and found its cost of living to be about 5 percent lower than the national average. The prices listed below show the median cost for visitor services.
- 5-mile taxi ride: $10
- Average dinner: $10–$17
- Daily newspaper: 50¢
- Hotel double room: $85
- Movie admission: $6

Housing

Food, clothing, and education in Utah are considered a value. Housing costs, however, have shown a dramatic rise in the last decade, mostly as a result of an even more dramatic rise in the population. In 1995 the average price of a Salt Lake City home was $133,000; in 1998 that same home sold for $194,000. Rental housing can be expensive and difficult to find, especially in the downtown area and the city's desirable eastside neighborhoods.

Taxes

Property taxes are levied locally by elected assessors and fluctuate annually according to a neighborhood's desirability and turnover. Salt Lake City residents pay a 6.35 percent sales tax. Motor vehicles are taxed according to individual cars' age and selling price. State income taxes are calculated by deducting a portion of federal tax and then applying a 7 percent rate.

Schools

Within the boundaries of Salt Lake City proper, all public schools belong to the Salt Lake City School District. Its 25,000 students attend 36 schools, most of which have special programs for both gifted and challenged students. The outlying valley, much of which is included in this book's description, is home to a much larger population and is divided into three school districts: Murray with 6,400 students, Jordan with 72,000 students, and Granite with 76,000 students. Four-year colleges include the University of Utah and Westminster College.

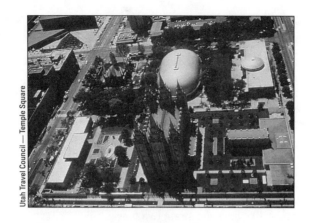

2

GETTING AROUND SALT LAKE CITY

Salt Lake City is relatively easy to navigate, especially if you keep a couple of key landmarks in mind. Mountains (and the Great Salt Lake) completely encircle the Salt Lake Valley, and the geography of the different ranges makes a compass unnecessary. The Wasatch Mountains—the western-most range of the Rocky Mountains—are east of the city. Their dramatic peaks and sweeping elevations are visible from all parts of the valley. The more rounded but still mighty Oquirrh Range is to the west of the city, pro-viding a distinct directional vision for travelers heading to Nevada, Califor-nia, or just to the west side of town.

City Layout

Salt Lake City streets maintain a strict grid system designed 150 years ago by Mormon leader Brigham Young. The system requires a few min-utes of orientation, but once mastered it proves a fail-safe location device. All streets run in true lines, checkerboard fashion—east, west, north, and south—radiating from Temple Square. Indeed, a historic marker on the southeast corner of the temple grounds marks the dead center of town. The streets that line up from the south side of the temple begin as South Temple Street and follow as 100 South, 200 South, etc. The same goes for the streets in other directions—North Temple is located just north of Temple Square, with successive streets 100 North, 200 North, and so forth. Some streets have both a name and number (300 South is also called Broadway). All numbered streets are given

Three of the four streets that border Salt Lake City's Temple Square are named for their location—South Temple, North Temple, and West Temple. In a break with symmetrics, the fourth offshoot from Temple Square, to the east, is Main Street. In early pioneer accounts, it is labeled "East Temple." Its change to "Main" was most likely a means of identifying it as the primary business and retail corridor in Salt Lake City.

increments of 100; thus, the street two blocks south of Temple Square becomes 200 South, while the street 30 blocks east becomes 3000 East.

Now comes the tricky part—all addresses have two directional names. Finding 653 East 800 South Street, for example, means heading six blocks east of the Salt Lake Temple and then another eight blocks south. The building "653" will be halfway between 600 and 700 East Streets, but actually located on 800 South Street. Named streets are based on numbered streets; finding "1264 Green Street" requires knowing that Green Street is also 640 East Street. All street names and their directional locations are found in the front section of the local Yellow Pages, which also contains a detailed street map. Rather than puzzle over this written description, visitors should hit the pavement and test the system on their own. It's easy—really!

Two major interstate freeways intersect Salt Lake City. The first is I-15, which runs north and south through the area just west of the business district. North of the city, I-15 travels through the major city of Ogden and on through rural Utah to Idaho. South of the city I-15 travels through Provo and Orem, over a vast expanse of the state to Utah's southwesternmost city, St. George, and on to Arizona and Nevada. The second major inter-

Day Tours

The following bus companies offer day and half-day sightseeing and orientation tours of Salt Lake City:

Executors of SLC, 801/898-8564

Gray Line Motor Tours, 801/521-7060

Lewis Bros. Tours, 801/359-8677

Passage To Utah, 801/519-2400

state is I-80, which runs east and west through the city, roughly along the borders of 2100 South Street. I-80 continues west to Nevada and east to Colorado. A belt route, I-215, forms a circle around the Salt Lake Valley, with connections to I-15 and I-80.

Public Transportation

City Buses
Salt Lake City's public bus transportation is provided by Utah Transit Authority, known locally as UTA. The company has provided transportation in Utah for over 25 years, and currently operates with 550 buses and 1,200 employees. Ninety separate routes cover the Salt Lake Valley, and the rotation of schedules allows commuters to travel all over Salt Lake Valley's metropolitan area, and to destinations outside of the valley, in Davis, Weber, and Utah Counties, as well. Full bus service is confined to weekdays between the hours of 6 a.m. and 7 p.m. Nighttime and Sunday service is limited. Fares are $1 for local service and $2 for express routes. For more information about UTA, call 801/596-0337. For bus route and scheduling information, call 801/287-4636.

Ski Buses
During the winter months, Utah Transit Authority operates bus routes from the Salt Lake Valley to Little Cottonwood Canyon and Big Cottonwood Canyon, servicing the ski resorts of Alta, Snowbird, Brighton, and Solitude. Ski bus stops are located valley-wide, from North Temple Street in central downtown, to 10600 South in Sandy. The buses run seven days a week, on approximate hourly rotations, between the hours of 6 a.m. to 5 p.m. for up canyon routes, and 7:45 a.m. to 8 p.m. for down canyon routes. Fares are $4.50 for trips to and from the central downtown area, and $1.75 for trips that begin and end closer to the canyons.

T I P

The largest road construction project in the United States is currently underway in Salt Lake City. Seventeen continuous miles of I-15, the freeway that runs north and south along the Wasatch Front just west of the city, is being completely rebuilt to include state-of-the-art traffic monitoring and to accommodate additional traffic. The project is scheduled for completion in autumn of 2001. In the meantime, travel on I-15 can be slow and circuitous.

LIGHT RAIL

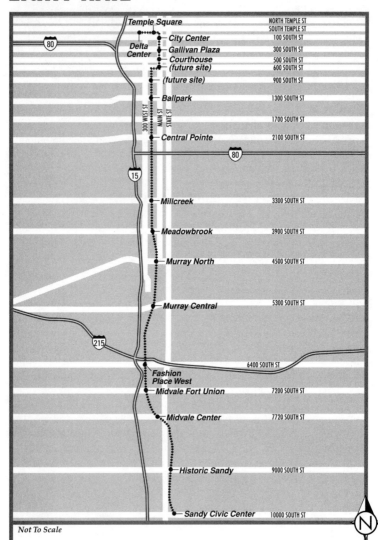

Temple Square
City Center
Delta Center
Gallivan Plaza
Courthouse
(future site)
(future site)
Ballpark
Central Pointe
Millcreek
Meadowbrook
Murray North
Murray Central
Fashion Place West
Midvale Fort Union
Midvale Center
Historic Sandy
Sandy Civic Center

NORTH TEMPLE ST
SOUTH TEMPLE ST
100 SOUTH ST
300 SOUTH ST
500 SOUTH ST
600 SOUTH ST
900 SOUTH ST
1300 SOUTH ST
1700 SOUTH ST
2100 SOUTH ST
3300 SOUTH ST
3900 SOUTH ST
4500 SOUTH ST
5300 SOUTH ST
6400 SOUTH ST
7200 SOUTH ST
7720 SOUTH ST
9000 SOUTH ST
10000 SOUTH ST

Not To Scale

Salt Lake City's TRAX

TRAX (the name designated by the Utah Transit Authority for the new light rail transit line) will be fully operational March 2000. A one-way trip from Sandy to downtown will take about 30 minutes, including all 16 stops. The system will operate from 5:30 am to midnight on weekdays, and 6:30 am to midnight on Saturdays. During peak hours, TRAX vehicles will stop at stations every 10 minutes (or less), and every 20 to 30 minutes during off-peak hours.

The cost of riding TRAX will be the same as taking a bus, and transfers will be issued upon request. Bikes will be allowed on TRAX vehicles during certain off-peak hours of operation.

Light Rail

Utah Transit Authority is currently in the midst of a major construction project that will result in a north–south light rail system for the Salt Lake Valley, with an anticipated completion date of March 2000. The tracks will cover 15 miles, from 10000 South in Sandy to the Delta Center at 300 South in Salt Lake City, with 16 stops along the way. At 55 mph, the trip will take about 30 minutes. The light rail system will be called TRAX, a nickname taken from Transit Express. TRAX tickets will cost the same rate as bus fares, and both will be interchangeable. This project is the first of many phases that will eventually traverse

Horse-drawn carriage rides in the downtown area

the entire valley with light rail. A second phase of construction, which will run from the airport through downtown to the University of Utah, will begin in 1999 and is scheduled for completion in 2002.

Taxis

Three major taxi companies operate in metropolitan Salt Lake City. Yellow Cab (801/521-2100), Ute Cab (801/359-7788), and City Cab (801/363-5550) have 24-hour dispatched service and ferry passengers from the Salt Lake City International Airport, throughout Salt Lake City, and to Wasatch Front ski resorts. Taxi service is in demand especially after dark, as the city's bus service ends at 7 p.m. Smaller cab companies service the outlying areas of the Salt Lake Valley, including Murray Cab Company (801/328-5704) and West Valley Taxicab Company (801/328-5705).

Driving in Salt Lake City

Driving in Salt Lake City is, most of the time, a fairly straightforward proposition. The streets are consecutively numbered in both directions, and the distance from here to there is easy to navigate. The years before the Olympic Winter Games of 2002, however, are dedicated to transportation improvements that are wreaking havoc on normal auto routes. As described above, both the major interstate that runs just west of town and the thoroughfares that are being prepared for light rail are major construction zones. A consequence is an ever-changing maze of rerouted traffic and a rush hour comparable with much bigger cities. Drivers are

TIP

Virtually all of downtown Salt Lake City's streets are outfitted with parking meters, which generally are limited to two hours. Both Crossroads Mall and ZCMI Mall have vast parking areas, with fees of approximately one dollar per hour. Once drivers are outside the downtown area, parking on side streets is mostly free.

advised to travel during off-peak hours, and to listen to local radio stations, most of which provide frequent traffic updates.

Biking in Salt Lake City

Salt Lake City has designated several secondary auto routes to double as commuter bicycle paths. Though still in the development process, many of these lanes are marked with bicycle logos, both to direct bicyclists and to alert drivers of their proximity. These roads include 1500 East between 2100

Major Airlines Servicing
Salt Lake City International Airport

American, 800/321-2121
America West, 800/235-9292
Continental, 800/523-3273
Delta, 800/221-1212
Frontier, 800/432-1359
Northwest, 800/225-2525
Southwest, 800/435-9792 or 801/359-1221
Trans World, 800/221-2000
United, 800/241-6522

Commuter Airlines

Alpine Air, 801/575-2839
Skywest, 800/453-9417

South and 900 South, 11th Avenue between "B" Street and Virginia Street, and a network of routes in and around the University of Utah campus.

Salt Lake City International Airport

Salt Lake City's International Airport is ranked as the 36th busiest in the world. Its two terminals are serviced by nine major airlines and two commuter airlines, with 337 daily departures to 68 cities. Delta Air Lines has established one of its hubs here and has its own concourse servicing 164 flights each day.

Services at the airport include language translation accessed through the phone system, foreign money exchange in both terminals, a barbershop and a beauty shop, infant care stations, two major gift shops and satellite gift shops throughout the airport, two cocktail lounges and a brew pub, and over a dozen food-service areas.

Long-term parking lots are serviced by shuttles that ferry passengers to the main terminals. A short-term parking structure, with space for over 2,000 cars, has direct access into both terminals. Arrangements for taxis, limousines, and shuttles can be made at ground transportation desks, which are found near baggage claim areas. All major rental-car companies have offices at the airport.

Private airplane facilities are just east of the Salt Lake City International Airport, and satellite general aviation facilities are in other areas of Utah.

An observation area for the general public is located at the far south end of the airport complex, just north of the Wingpointe Golf Course clubhouse. A grassy area has picnic tables, signage that illustrates different types of aircraft, and radios that broadcast communications between pilots and the control tower. A parking area situates cars perfectly to see takeoffs and landings.

Salt Lake City International Airport

Airport Express

Most major hotels in Salt Lake City offer shuttle services to and from the airport. Commercial shuttle services, including Affordable Airport Shuttle (801/561-2090) and Airport Xpress (801/269-9977), charge approximately $20 for express service from the airport to downtown areas, with $5 for each additional passenger.

Utah Travel Council/Frank Jensen

Play It Safe

Salt Lakers consider their city a safe place to live, and they walk and drive through all areas of town during all hours of the day. A rising crime rate, however, warrants some cautionary measures. The heart of downtown, which includes the blocks bordered by South Temple Street, State Street, 300 South, and 200 West, can be walked safely most hours of the day. The majority of nightspots close by 2 a.m., and taxi or car travel is advised after that hour. Visitors should avoid walking the blocks just south of 300 South and west of 200 West after dark. Salt Lake City's public bus system operates between 6 a.m. and 7 p.m., with limited after-hours services.

Train Service

Amtrak's California Zephyr runs from Sacramento, California, to Chicago, Illinois, stopping to pick up passengers twice a day at Salt Lake City's Rio Grande Train Depot, 320 South Rio Grande Street (450 West). The westbound train leaves at 1:15 a.m., and the eastbound train departs at 4:35 a.m., seven days a week. For station information, call 801/531-0188. For Amtrak information and reservations, call 800/872-7245.

Interstate and Regional Bus Service

Greyhound Bus Lines operates a nationwide transportation system from its terminal at 160 West South Temple Street. For local terminal information, call 801/355-9579. For reservations, call 800/231-2222.

Salt Lake Convention & Visitors Bureau – Cliff Lodge

3

WHERE TO STAY

Salt Lake City's visitor accommodations are generally found in clusters, and their location often defines their purpose. The blocks that flank the Salt Palace Convention Center are home to multistory luxury hotels, equipped with business centers, fitness areas, restaurants, lounges, and other services expected by the executive traveler. Sprinkled around the perimeter of downtown are extended-stay motels catering to families, skiers, trainees, and other groups. The pocket of "express" lodging found near the airport provides a no-fuss means for both coming and going. Facilities near the resorts of the Cottonwood Canyons tend to be of the alpine lodge variety, their primary market being skiers and other outdoor enthusiasts. Salt Lake City's bed-and-breakfast trade has grown significantly in the last few years—a number of historical homes throughout the city now offer overnight stays.

The Salt Lake Valley has a total of 14,000 hotel and motel rooms, most of which have been built in the last 20 years to accommodate the exponential growth of the Salt Lake Valley. Although hotel construction continues at a fast pace (three major hotels are scheduled to open before the end of the century), visitors do well to make reservations as far in advance as possible. Large conventions, major sports events, and LDS Church conferences sometimes converge to fill all available rooms, especially in the central downtown area.

Most published room rates do not include tax. Visitors can expect to pay an additional 10.95 percent tax inside Salt Lake City limits, and an additional 9.85 percent in the outlying valley.

Price rating symbols:
$ $50 and under
$$ $51 to $75
$$$ $76 to $125
$$$$ $126 and up

DOWNTOWN

Hotels and Motels

THE CARLTON HOTEL
140 E. South Temple St.
Salt Lake City
801/355-3418
$$–$$$

The Carlton is a small, European-style hotel that has operated from the same location for decades. Shopping, restaurants, and Temple Square are within a block radius. The Carlton's 55 rooms offer free movies and guests enjoy a hot tub, sauna, exercise room and free breakfast in the Carlton's café. ♿ (Downtown)

CAVANAUGH OLYMPUS HOTEL
161 W. 600 South St.
Salt Lake City
801/521-7373
$$$–$$$$

The 13 floors of the Best Western Olympus Hotel dominate the view of car travelers heading east into downtown Salt Lake City as they exit I-15. From inside, the view from the 13th-floor restaurant is even more compelling as it looks west across the Salt Lake Valley. A second, more casual restaurant is located on the hotel's first floor. Amenities include a barbershop, on-site security, laundry services, and free babysitting.

Guests may purchase tickets to local events and book sightseeing tours from the lobby. ♿ (Downtown)

CROWNE PLAZA
Main and 200 South Sts.
Salt Lake City

At this writing ground construction has begun on a major hotel in the Gallivan Utah Plaza, between Main and State Streets and 200 and 300 South. Scheduled to open in late 1999 or early 2000, the Crowne Plaza will have 370 rooms and rise 12 stories. ♿ (Downtown)

CRYSTAL INN–DOWNTOWN
320 W. 500 South St.
Salt Lake City
801/328-4466
$$$

The Salt Lake City–based chain of Crystal Inns was begun in 1994 and now has eight locations, five of which are in Utah. The inns are named for the owner, Crystal Maggelet, and their mission is to provide the amenities of fine hotels at a low price. This is accomplished with modest exteriors and just-off-center locations. The manager claims that the Crystal Inn–Downtown's 175 rooms are 25 percent larger than the average hotel room. All are equipped with sitting areas, microwave ovens, refrigerators, three telephones, and two phone

---

T i P

Utah Reservation Service, 800/278-8886, offers advance reservation services at hundreds of hotels and motels in the state. The Salt Lake Convention & Visitors Bureau provides accommodation information at 801/521-2822.

lines. Free breakfast is served every morning, and an on-site convenience store is open 24 hours. The fitness center has a heated indoor pool, sauna, and whirlpool spa. Three flexible rooms of meeting space accommodate up to 120 people. ♿ (Downtown)

DOUBLETREE HOTEL
255 S. West Temple St.
Salt Lake City
801/328-2000
$$$–$$$$

The DoubleTree is one of Salt Lake City's nicer hotels, although it has not managed to shed the national-chain syndrome. The large, unremarkable lobby might be found anywhere else in the United States. It is busy most hours of the day, with uniformed valets and bellhops running to and fro, an in-demand concierge desk, and a constant flow of traffic near the registration area. The hotel has 500 rooms, and guests can upgrade to larger rooms in ascending levels of deluxe, business, or executive floors. The DoubleTree is perfectly situated in the center of downtown activity, in walking distance of nightlife, restaurants, museums, shopping, the Delta Center, and the Salt Palace Convention Center. Amenities include an indoor pool, hot tub and sauna, an exercise room, and massage and business centers. The recent remodeling of the lower level has created a terrific Chicago-style steakhouse called Spencer's, which serves the best red-meat-and-martini combination in town. Club Max offers dancing most nights to recorded music. ♿ (Downtown)

EMBASSY SUITES
110 W. 600 South St.
Salt Lake City

801/359-7800
$$$–$$$$

As the name implies, all of the 241 rooms at Embassy Suites are actually two-room suites. All have private bedrooms adjoined to a living area that has a galley kitchen equipped with a refrigerator, microwave, coffeemaker and wet bar. Both rooms in the suite have televisions that access cable, video games, and in-room movies. A work area offers good lighting as well as two telephones with dataports. Free breakfast is served in the atrium lobby, and popcorn and beverages are offered each evening. An informal restaurant is open for lunch and dinner, and a private club called Clouseau's offers drinks and appetizers, as well as a billiards table and sports telecasts. Up to 100 people can be accommodated in the largest of the four meeting rooms. ♿ (Downtown)

HAMPTON INN DOWNTOWN
425 S. 300 West St.
Salt Lake City
801/741-1110
$$$–$$$$

This is one of the new, smaller chain hotels built on the city's western flank, close to freeway access, meant to capture travelers heading north and south between the large Wasatch Front cities. Voicemail, two telephone lines in every room, and private meeting rooms benefit the visitor who wishes to combine business with pleasure. There is no charge for children staying with their parents, and a third or fourth adult can stay in the same room free. Temple Square and two major malls are a short drive away, and the ski resorts are easily reached via Interstate-15. ♿ (Downtown)

DOWNTOWN SALT LAKE CITY

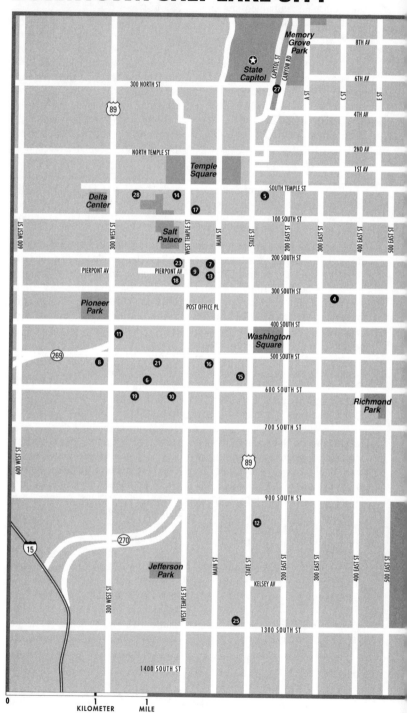

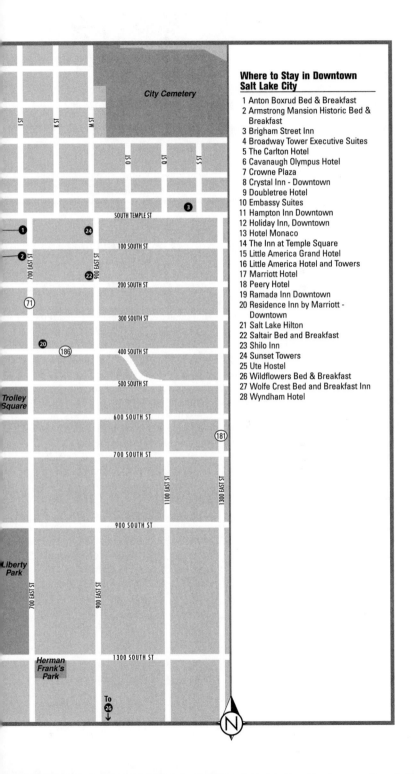

Where to Stay in Downtown Salt Lake City

1 Anton Boxrud Bed & Breakfast
2 Armstrong Mansion Historic Bed & Breakfast
3 Brigham Street Inn
4 Broadway Tower Executive Suites
5 The Carlton Hotel
6 Cavanaugh Olympus Hotel
7 Crowne Plaza
8 Crystal Inn - Downtown
9 Doubletree Hotel
10 Embassy Suites
11 Hampton Inn Downtown
12 Holiday Inn, Downtown
13 Hotel Monaco
14 The Inn at Temple Square
15 Little America Grand Hotel
16 Little America Hotel and Towers
17 Marriott Hotel
18 Peery Hotel
19 Ramada Inn Downtown
20 Residence Inn by Marriott - Downtown
21 Salt Lake Hilton
22 Saltair Bed and Breakfast
23 Shilo Inn
24 Sunset Towers
25 Ute Hostel
26 Wildflowers Bed & Breakfast
27 Wolfe Crest Bed and Breakfast Inn
28 Wyndham Hotel

TRIVIA

An 1869 directory listed a total of six hotels in downtown Salt Lake City. Among them was Mansion House, which carried the following description: "Good rooms well furnished. Table set with every variety the market affords. Cheapest hotel in the city. Attached is a large stable and good corral for teams."

HOLIDAY INN, DOWNTOWN
999 S. Main St.
Salt Lake City
801/359-8600
$$$–$$$$

All of the expected room appointments and extra amenities enjoyed by the Holiday Innophiles of the world are found in this block-long, colonial-style facility. The location is just a bit south of Salt Lake City's grander hotels, but free transportation is provided within a mile radius, and a traveler need not venture outside the hotel to find all of the creature comforts. The 292 rooms have king and double beds, a laundry is available, and workout facilities include a covered pool, hot tub, and sauna. The Main Street Café is open for breakfast, lunch, and dinner. The Key Lounge serves wine and mixed drinks and is named after its grand piano and its keyboardist, who together provide entertainment most nights. よ (Downtown)

HOTEL MONACO
200 S. Main St.
Salt Lake City

At this writing plans are being made to renovate the old Continental Bank Building on the corner of 200 South and State Streets into a "boutique hotel" with an expected four-star rating. The 15-story building will house 225 rooms, many of them luxury suites, as well as restaurant and meeting space. The hotel is scheduled to open in late 1999. よ (Downtown)

THE INN AT TEMPLE SQUARE
71 W. South Temple St.
Salt Lake City
801/531-1000
$$$–$$$$

Don't think you can come to The Inn and sneak a smoke; although Salt Lake City law prohibits smoking in public places, The Inn still asks guests to sign a contract in which they agree not to indulge in cigarettes inside the hotel. The LDS Church–owned facility offers the city's closest proximity to Temple Square, and guests enjoy a 30-second walk to the square's classical concert series and Mormon Tabernacle Choir rehearsals. The public areas are lovely, with a grand piano and lending library among the amenities. Ninety rooms occupy six floors, and all are equipped with four-poster beds and compact refrigerators equipped with free sodas. A breakfast for two is included in the room rate. The Carriage Court on the main level is a public restaurant with a complete breakfast, lunch, and dinner menu. よ (Downtown)

LITTLE AMERICA GRAND HOTEL
State St. between 500 and 600

South Sts.
Salt Lake City
801/596-5800

At this writing, construction is well underway on one of Salt Lake City's largest hotels. Owned and managed by the same group as the Little America Hotel and Towers just a block away, this new hotel is much larger in scope and grandeur. Scheduled to be completed before Fall 2001, it will have 777 rooms and over 100,000 square feet of public areas, including two restaurants and retail space. ⅍ (Downtown)

LITTLE AMERICA HOTEL
AND TOWERS
500 S. Main St.
Salt Lake City
800/453-9450
$$$–$$$$

Perhaps one of the most favored of Salt Lake City's hotels, Little America makes a gallant attempt to create a microcosm of the larger world—or perhaps not the world, merely a "little America." All of the services expected by the executive traveler are found here. The 850 guest rooms range from small "lodge rooms" to an entire tower given over to suites featuring French provincial parlors and Italian marble baths. The huge lobby is domed by an ornate stained-glass window, and a selection of high-end shops are just down the hall. Guests enjoy two swimming pools, a luxurious health club, and the surrounding rolling landscape. Twenty-two meeting rooms accommodate about 100 people each, and a ballroom can seat 1,000 guests for dinner. The two restaurants here are favorites with local residents as well as guests. The coffee shop has excellent breakfasts and the best rye bread in town. The dining room has a daily buffet luncheon, often with an ethnic theme. Two Sunday brunches take place; the one in the ballroom features seafood and flaming desserts, the less pricey brunch in the dining room has a nice omelet bar. ⅍ (Downtown)

MARRIOTT HOTEL
75 S. West Temple St.
Salt Lake City
801/531-0800
$$$$

This deluxe 15-story tower boasts an excellent array of services and a smack-in-the-middle city center location. The Salt Palace Convention Center, Crossroads and ZCMI Malls, and Temple Square are all just a few steps away. The Marriott's large, green-plant-filled lobby is accessible either from the street or from the lower level of the Crossroads Mall. A

T I P

Utah restaurants and bars that offer wine and mixed drinks must have a "private club" license. To enter one of these clubs, a visitor must either purchase a membership ($5 for a temporary two-week card) or be accompanied by a member. Most hotels that have a private club on the premises extend a membership to all of their registered guests at no extra cost.

Marriott Hotel, p. 31

number of large meeting rooms host small business conventions as well as many local social events, and the hotel public rooms are usually a whirl of activity. The suites are perhaps the most extravagant in town, with large living areas and connecting bedrooms. Two sumptuous Presidential Suites are available for $850 per night each. All guests enjoy the health club, whirlpool, sauna, indoor-outdoor heated pool, and seasonal sundeck. JW's Steakhouse serves steak and seafood, and Allie's Family Style Restaurant has salads and sandwiches. A Pizza Hut, coffee bar, and yogurt shop are just off the lobby, and sports fans will find beer and large-screen TVs at the private club called Pitchers. Laundry facilities, dry cleaning and an on-call masseuse are available. & (Downtown)

PEERY HOTEL
110 W. 300 South St.
Salt Lake City
801/521-4300
$$$–$$$$
The Peery is one of Salt Lake City's

first grand hotels. Built in 1910, it catered to upscale travelers debarking at the nearby Rio Grande train station. A few decades later, when the surrounding neighborhood became unfashionable, the Peery fell into disrepair and its beautiful lobby turned shabby and dark. Early in the 1990s a top-to-bottom restoration project was begun, and today the Peery is once again a lovely hotel, with modern amenities including a whirlpool, exercise room, and private meeting rooms. The lobby is especially nice, offering true-to-period furniture and decor. A continental breakfast is included in the room rate, and the on-site Peery Wasatch Pub has a lunch and dinner menu featuring sandwiches, salads, and pasta. & (Downtown)

RAMADA INN DOWNTOWN
230 W. 600 South St.
Salt Lake City
801/364-5200
$$–$$$
The Ramada, located just outside downtown's primary business district, is an affordable alternative to the larger and newer hotels found a few blocks to the north. The Ramada caters to the businessperson, and rooms are available with extra working space and expanded seating areas. Guests enjoy a completely enclosed recreation center with a full-sized pool, sauna, whirlpool, exercise room, and even billiards and miniature golf. A casual diner-style restaurant overlooks the pool. & (Downtown)

RESIDENCE INN BY
MARRIOTT–DOWNTOWN
765 E. 400 South St.
Salt Lake City

The Hotel That Was

For 80 years the Hotel Utah (15 E. South Temple St.) was the undisputed "grande dame" of the city's hotel scene. Built in 1909 at a cost of $2 million, it was important not only for its splendid architecture but also for its service as a bridge between Salt Lake City's LDS religious leaders and its mostly non-LDS business leaders. Businessmen sold shares to finance the hotel's construction, and the LDS Church donated the property, resulting in one of the first successful ventures backed by the entire community. The Hotel Utah was known throughout the Intermountain West for its opulent interiors and first-class service, and it was the setting for many prominent parties as well. Hundreds of the glitterati stayed there over the years; in its time it was visited by every U.S. president, beginning in 1912 with William Howard Taft.

In 1990 the hotel was refitted as an office building for the LDS Church. Although overnight visitors are no longer accommodated, the beautiful lobby remains open to the public, and a small information desk directs tourists to the local attractions offered by the LDS Church. Two restaurants on the 10th floor offer stunning views of the Salt Lake Valley.

801/532-5511
$$–$$$$

Families, ski groups, and business travelers give the Residence Inn top marks. The affordable rooms double as a home-away-from-home, with fully equipped kitchens, fireplaces, mini-office space, and cable TV. Laundry, housekeeping and grocery services are available, and the fitness center includes an outdoor pool, spa and sport court. The on-site Gatehouse hosts a buffet breakfast every morning and snacks and drinks during the cocktail hour. The location is a block from the shopping and restaurants of Trolley Square, a mile from the central business district, and 40 minutes from the ski resorts. ♿ (Downtown)

SALT LAKE HILTON
150 W. 500 South St.
Salt Lake City
801/532-3344
$$$

The Hilton's arrival in the early '70s was greeted with much ceremony by a city that could finally boast the cachet of a large, modern luxury hotel. The Hilton's public rooms still maintain an aura of glamor, and the hotel continues to serve the community well with its huge ballrooms and high-tech meeting rooms. At this writing the Hilton is undergoing a $10 million renovation, which has closed the locally popular Room at the Top lounge along with its killer view of the Salt Lake Valley. The central patio area remains open with a large pool, sauna, and sundeck, and a fitness center is on the hotel's lower level. Other amenities include a beauty salon and a barbershop. A licensed masseuse is on staff. Children (who stay free when accompanied by an adult) enjoy a video game room and free in-room movies. Delta maintains a ticket counter in the lobby, and Ski Utah's information offices are located on the main floor. ♿ (Downtown)

SHILO INN
206 S. West Temple St.
Salt Lake City
801/521-9500
$$$

The Shilo Inn, one of the first big national chain hotels to locate in the heart of downtown, enjoys an ideal location directly across the street from the Salt Palace Convention Center and a block away from Temple Square and the Crossroads Mall. An exterior, glassed-walled elevator offers guests a wonderful city view as they are transported between the lobby and the upper floors. The Shilo has recently been remodeled, and all 200 rooms now boast microwave ovens, refrigerators, and VCRs. A new fitness center offers an indoor pool, spa, and sauna. There's a restaurant, café, lounge, and free continental breakfast. ♿ (Downtown)

UTE HOSTEL
21 E. Kelsey Ave. (1160 South between Main and State Sts.)
Salt Lake City
801/595-1645
$

The Ute is Salt Lake City's only hostel, and its mix of overnight visitors is often the most eclectic in town. Asian, European, and African guests frequent the hostel, as do young Americans from both the North and South continents. Three dorm rooms have rows of bunk beds, and one private room has a king bed, and another a queen bed. In the hostel tradition, baths and showers are shared. Two lounges separate the smokers from the nonsmokers, but both are equal in cable TV and video game services. A full kitchen offers free sodas. Econo rates on bike, ski, skate, and golf rentals are available. (Downtown)

WYNDHAM HOTEL
215 W. South Temple St.
Salt Lake City
801-531-7500
$$$

With an unbeatable location, the Wyndham is flanked on one side by the Salt Palace Convention Center and on the other by the Delta Center, home to the Utah Jazz. Also within a two-block radius are Temple Square, Abravanel Concert Hall, and two major malls. The hotel was built as a DoubleTree, but in 1997 the Double-Tree moved to larger digs a few blocks away, and the Wyndham chain took over the premises, which include a heated indoor pool and a fitness center. All 381 rooms were remodeled at the time of the transfer, and all now feature comfortable chairs, desks, and Wyndham signature amenities including coffeemakers, hair dryers, irons, and ironing boards. The on-site health club has an indoor pool, sauna, whirlpool, and exercise equipment. The City Creek Grill is a full-service restaurant on the lobby level, and its partner, the City Creek Bar, offers a selection of locally microbrewed beers and a huge TV screen for sports lovers. & (Downtown)

Bed-and-Breakfasts

**ANTON BOXRUD
BED & BREAKFAST
57 S. 600 East St.
Salt Lake City
801-363-8035
$$–$$$**

The Anton Boxrud is a gorgeous example of Victorian eclectic style. The home was built by clothing manufacturer Boxrud in 1901 and was a showcase in its time. The current owners have stayed faithful to the original floor plans in their renovation efforts; stained-glass windows, hardwood floors, and unusual sliding pocket doors made of burled walnut remain in their original state. Each of the seven rooms is decorated with antiques, and in each one guests will find chocolates, flowers, and terry robes. Two rooms share a bath, all others have private facilities. Breakfast is a feast here, featuring homemade sticky buns. Meals are served on the My Fair Lady dining table, which movie fans might recognize as the same table at which Audrey Hepburn sat when she was learning to enunciate. Modern amenities include an outdoor hot tub. (Downtown)

**ARMSTRONG MANSION
HISTORIC BED & BREAKFAST
667 E. 100 South St.
Salt Lake City**

**801/531-1333
$$$–$$$$**

This grand old house was built by Francis Armstrong in 1893 as a wedding present for his wife, Isabel; when the pair were courting, their carriage passed the undeveloped site and Armstrong promised his fiancée he would build her a mansion there someday. The current owners have parlayed that romantic notion into 14 private rooms decorated with themes of courtship and love. The February Interlude Room, on the top floor, features a double Jacuzzi in a private turret tower that commands a sweeping view of the city. The June Bride Room has a king-size bed, a large oval Jacuzzi, and a double-headed shower, and is decorated completely in white and taupe. Isabel's wedding dress, which was worn by her mother as well as herself, is displayed on a mannequin in the corner. All rooms have private baths, and all but two have private Jacuzzis. Francis was the first mayor of Salt Lake City and made his fortune in the wood-milling business. His house reflects both his station and his trade, with opulent stained-glass windows and beautiful millwork, including a dazzling oak staircase. The stenciled walls are re-created from original art discovered during a 1980s renovation. & (Downtown)

**BRIGHAM STREET INN
1135 E. South Temple St.
Salt Lake City
801/364-4461
$$$–$$$$**

At the turn of the last century, South Temple was known as Brigham Street (after LDS Leader Brigham Young), and the homes that lined the wide avenue were owned by the trade magnates and society scions of the day. The Brigham Street Inn was one of the most opulent of those residences, and today it remains one of Salt Lake City's architectural jewels. The interior decorations were commissioned by individual designers and feature antiques and original art. All nine rooms represent interpretations of the Victorian era. Most have queen beds, some have fireplaces, and all have private baths. Homemade pastries are the highlight of the continental breakfast. (Downtown)

SALTAIR BED AND BREAKFAST AND ALPINE SUITES
164 S. 900 East St.
Salt Lake City
801/533-8184
$$–$$$$
The main house on this property was built in 1903 and has been faithfully restored to its Victorian origins. Period lamps and furniture, fireplaces, and goose down quilts turn back the clock for guests who wish to escape to a slower-paced era. Two of the five rooms in the house have private baths. A small home next door has been divided into two rental cottages that offer the modern conveniences of cable TV, private phones, kitchens, and private baths. An apartment building nearby has been renovated into five suites with full kitchens and private baths. The suites are intended for extended stays, and guests who are in town to visit a hospitalized family member get a 50 percent discount. A full, homemade breakfast is included for bed-and-breakfast guests, a continental breakfast for cottage and suite guests. (Downtown)

**WILDFLOWERS
BED & BREAKFAST**

Saltair Nostalgia

When the owners of Saltair Bed and Breakfast bought the facility 10 years ago, they chose the name after the elegant dance hall that once graced the shores of the Great Salt Lake. In the late 1800s, until it was destroyed by fire, Saltair was "the" place to be seen on weekends, dancing under the famous salt-dusted roof that sparkled under electric lights. The bed-and-breakfast's name prompted the owners to begin a collection of Saltair memorabilia, which has now taken on a life of its own. Friends have contributed, and returning guests bring items, and the collection now displayed throughout the Saltair numbers in the thousands, and includes photographs, ticket stubs, spoons, steins, dishes, and novelty postcards. Another Saltair building, with architecture meant to re-create the original, is now found on the shores of the lake.

Wyndham Hotel, p. 34

Salt Lake Convention & Visitors Bureau

936 E. 1700 South St.
Salt Lake City
801-466-0600
$$$–$$$$

Wildflowers is named after the beautiful gardens that surround this old home. The owners believe that every flower once was "wild," and their love of the blooms popular a century ago is evident in the beautiful plantings that provide a riot of color and shape during the warm weather months. Inside, an original staircase, chandeliers, and stained-glass windows show off the home's San Francisco–style Victorian origins. Wildflowers is located in one of Salt Lake City's older neighborhoods, and a walk through its residential surroundings offers a glimpse of a number of old, historic homes and some fun shops and boutiques. Four comfortable rooms and one deluxe suite (it takes up the top floor of the house and has a full kitchen as well as dining and living rooms) have private baths and telephones. The word "breakfast" comes in capital letters here;

Southwest-inspired pancakes topped with black beans and salsa, soufflés, fresh fruit, and more are served every morning. (Downtown)

WOLFE CREST BED AND BREAKFAST INN
273 E. Capitol Blvd.
Salt Lake City
801/521-8710
$$$

This bed-and-breakfast is named after Utah Supreme Court Justice James H. Wolfe, for whom the house was originally built. Perched on a curved street overlooking Memory Grove, it was divided into small apartments for several decades. But recently the home has been renovated to its original 1906 floor plan, complete with beautiful grounds. The interiors now offer an elegant and historically correct haven for travelers, with all the modern conveniences. Fourteen suites have business centers, jetted tubs, televisions, VCRs, and spacious sitting rooms. Balconies offer sweeping views of the Salt Lake Valley and the

Wasatch Mountains. A full-service restaurant is available. (Downtown)

Extended Stays

BROADWAY TOWER EXECUTIVE SUITES
230 E. Broadway
Salt Lake City
801/534-1222
$$$$
The Broadway is an extended-stay suites hotel within easy walking distance of Salt Lake City's business district, as well as theaters, restaurants, parks, and a movie house. Suites rent for $1,650 per month for a one-bedroom and $1,850 for a two-bedroom. Each is fully furnished with a complete kitchen and cable TV. All have private sundecks, and the views from the upper floors sweep across the entire Salt Lake Valley. Laundry facilities are available, as are an exercise room, maid service, and covered parking. A lovely meeting area features a large balcony overlooking the valley. & (Downtown)

SUNSET TOWERS
40 S. 900 East St.
Salt Lake City
801/532-6644
$$$$
The Sunset is a combination apartment/extended-stay facility with a 30-day minimum. Its location between the University of Utah and the central downtown area attracts skiers, genealogists, businesspeople, and recovering hospital patients. The corporate suites are fully furnished with kitchens, living rooms, and dining rooms. Laundry facilities and a beauty shop are on-site. The suites on the upper floors of this 15-story building have gorgeous valley and mountain views. & (Downtown)

SOUTHEASTERN VALLEY

Hotels and Motels

QUALITY INN MIDVALLEY
4465 Century Dr.
(4500 South and I-15)
Murray
801/268-2533
$$$
This Quality Inn bills itself as "the skiers' hotel" because of its affordable rates and midpoint location between the resorts of Park City and the Cottonwood Canyons. Arrangements for discounted ski lift tickets, rental, and repairs can be made in the lobby. A "see and ski package" includes lodging, a four-wheel drive vehicle with ski rack, and vouchers for ski-related activities. The largest units sleep six, and an extra $15 buys a room with a microwave/fridge or a jetted tub. All rooms have free cable, and laundry facilities are on-site. & (Southeastern Valley)

RESTON HOTEL
5335 College Dr.
(5300 South and I-15)
Murray
801/264-1054
$$
The big, new Reston has clean, comfortable, no-fuss rooms and reasonable rates. A full-service restaurant, indoor pool and hot tub, and conference and catering facilities attract businesspeople who bring along their skiing families. Vacation packages are available with car and ski discounts. & (Southeastern Valley)

Bed-and-Breakfasts

GRANDMOTHER'S HOUSE BED & BREAKFAST
6401 S. Holladay Blvd.

Holladay
801/943-0909
$$$–$$$$

You would have to follow a fairly circuitous route to go over a river and through some woods to get here, but Grandmother's House does offer the comfort and familiarity of home. All five rooms have private baths and televisions, and a spacious suite has a fireplace and kitchen. Grandmother herself cooks a full ranch breakfast each morning. (Southeastern Valley)

LA EUROPA ROYALE
1135 E. Vine St. (6000 South)
Holladay
801/263-7999
$$$–$$$$

Attention is paid to the smallest details at this lovely home. It was built in the last decade especially as a bed-and-breakfast, and the rooms and common areas have the feel of a luxury hotel. A fountain greets guests as they walk into the lobby, and reproductions of classic statuary are placed throughout the common rooms and the grounds. The living room and dining area both have large windows that look out onto the spacious backyard. The owners did most of the landscaping themselves, including fence building and tree planting, and their labor has yielded a beautiful setting that is sought after for weddings and gala parties. Each of the seven rooms has its own glassed-in gas fireplace, and each is named for a major city of the world. The Dublin Room is typical, with a flowery green decor. A hearty breakfast is served, and guests fetch coffee cups from a heated drawer. Skiers and businesspeople are the targeted audience; however, Salt Lakers have discovered this bed-and-breakfast and locals are regular guests. ⚓ (Southeastern Valley)

LOG CABIN ON THE HILL
BED & BREAKFAST
2275 E. 6200 South St.
Holladay
801/272-2969
$$$

The Log Cabin manages to be both "rustic" and "chic." It is, in fact, a cabin with a rough pine exterior, but the gorgeous surroundings and lovely interiors provide an upscale feel. The building is small, with just four guest rooms; the decor is comfy with a mix of patterns, styles, scattered rugs, and antiques. The proximity to the ski resorts of the Cottonwood Canyons attracts a clientele of skiers, as well as Salt Lakers looking for a getaway. (Southeastern Valley)

THE SPRUCES INN
6151 S. 900 East St.
Murray
801/268-8762
$$–$$$

Little America Hotel and Towers, p. 31

Salt Lake Convention & Visitors Bureau

GREATER SALT LAKE CITY

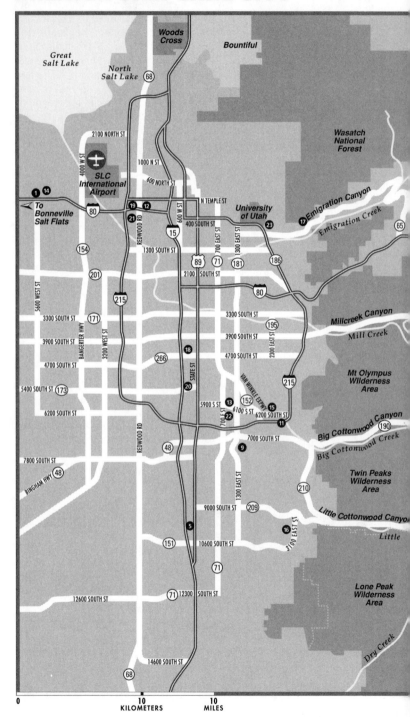

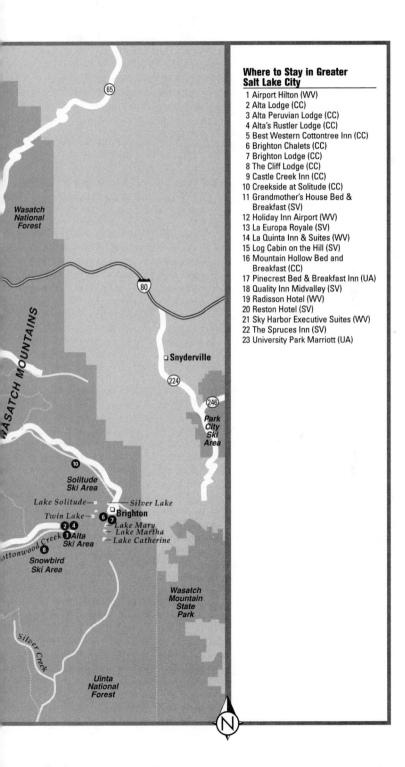

Where to Stay in Greater Salt Lake City

1 Airport Hilton (WV)
2 Alta Lodge (CC)
3 Alta Peruvian Lodge (CC)
4 Alta's Rustler Lodge (CC)
5 Best Western Cottontree Inn (CC)
6 Brighton Chalets (CC)
7 Brighton Lodge (CC)
8 The Cliff Lodge (CC)
9 Castle Creek Inn (CC)
10 Creekside at Solitude (CC)
11 Grandmother's House Bed & Breakfast (SV)
12 Holiday Inn Airport (WV)
13 La Europa Royale (SV)
14 La Quinta Inn & Suites (WV)
15 Log Cabin on the Hill (SV)
16 Mountain Hollow Bed and Breakfast (CC)
17 Pinecrest Bed & Breakfast Inn (UA)
18 Quality Inn Midvalley (SV)
19 Radisson Hotel (WV)
20 Reston Hotel (SV)
21 Sky Harbor Executive Suites (WV)
22 The Spruces Inn (SV)
23 University Park Marriott (UA)

TRIVIA

Rick Majerus, head coach of the University of Utah Runnin' Utes, is beloved for his record as the "winningest" coach in Utah basketball history, as well as for his emphasis on the academic success of his players. When Majerus first came to town for a job interview in 1985, he was put up at the University Park Marriott, just a short walk away from the Huntsman Center, where the Utes play ball. Majerus never left the hotel; a decade and a half later he is still at the University Park— living full-time in a suite of rooms overlooking the Salt Lake Valley.

When The Spruces was built a hundred years ago, it was surrounded by miles of farm and ranch land. The valley has grown and developed into a bustling suburb, and the 16 spruce trees for which the property is named now provide a pocket of shade and green space in the middle of town. Further enhancing the Spruces' appeal is its neighbors: On one side is Wheeler Historic Farm, a county-owned, working farm in the style of the early 1900s; on the other is a small horse operation. From The Spruces' yard, acres of planted fields and dozens of ponies are on view. The house's six rooms are small, unpretentious, and extremely comfortable. (Southeastern Valley)

UNIVERSITY AREA

Hotels and Motels

UNIVERSITY PARK MARRIOTT
480 Wakara Way
Salt Lake City
801/581-1000
$$$$
The University Park has one of the prettiest locations of any hotel in the Salt Lake Valley. Perched on a high bench in the foothills of the Wasatch Mountains, it has 28 suites, half of which boast a view that sweeps across the valley all the way to the Great Salt Lake; the other half look up out at the mighty Wasatch Mountains. A full-service family-style restaurant is located on the atrium level, and a private club/sports bar is one of the best places in town to watch the sunset while enjoying drinks and hors d'oeuvres. The University of Utah campus is directly south of the hotel, and adjoining is Research Park, a many-acred collection of university-supported high-tech companies. Red Butte Arboretum, one of the city's favorite garden areas, is just a few steps away. The hotel specializes in conference facilities with a range of room sizes and seating designs. Some groups opt to conduct their business in the seven-story-high atrium/lobby or outdoors on the beautiful grounds. A lobby gift shop features a package liquor store and made-in-Utah souvenirs. At this writing the hotel is changing ownership and will soon be a part of the Marriott Corporation. & (University Area)

Bed-and-Breakfasts

PINECREST BED & BREAKFAST INN
6211 E. Emigration Canyon
Salt Lake City
801/583-6663
$$$–$$$$

Pinecrest is located in beautiful Emigration Canyon, just a few minutes drive from downtown Salt Lake City but a world away in terms of seclusion and alpine scenery. In the summer months the canyon's cooler temperatures are a welcome relief from the city heat. In winter, it is an ideal base for a ski vacation, with major resorts accessed by driving to the top of the canyon and connecting with I-80. Pinecrest was built in 1915 of locally quarried stone and is tucked away on a six-acre estate, complete with a spring-fed stream and trout pond. The owners take pride in offering guests a romantic and private getaway. Seven theme rooms and cottages include a rustic canyon cabin with a living room, full kitchen, and an upstairs bedroom, and a Jamaican Jacuzzi Room with its own imported-tile sunken tub. The sound of the stream and waterfall just outside the room complete the water-relaxation theme. Most rooms have fireplaces, televisions, and king-size beds. Breakfast is served each morning in the dining room. (University Area)

WESTERN VALLEY

Note: These facilities are located within a three-mile radius of the Salt Lake International Airport, and most provide free transportation to and from the airport, free breakfast service that begins early for the crack-of-dawn traveler, and express check-in/check-out.

Hotels and Motels

AIRPORT HILTON
5151 Wiley Post Way
Salt Lake City
801/539-1515
$$$–$$$$

The setting for the Hilton is the Salt Lake International Center, a business park just west of the airport with spacious, green open areas and an eight-acre manmade lake. The Hilton sits on the shores of the lake, and many guests take advantage of the paddle boats, running paths, and putting green that are located on and around the water. Other amenities are indoor and outdoor swimming pools, a hot tub, fitness center, and sports court. All of the hotel's 287 rooms have been renovated recently, and several levels of suites have been created for business travelers, some with jetted tubs. A restaurant called Grill 114 has a standard American menu and a sunny area that looks out over the lake. The companion Club 114 has cocktails and snacks. ♿ (Western Valley)

HOLIDAY INN AIRPORT
1659 W. North Temple St.
Salt Lake City
801/533-9000
$$$

The amenities and room features are familiar to visitors who have traveled the Holiday Inns of the world, but the difference here is service above and beyond the norm. Staff routinely go out of their way to offer directions, suggest sightseeing trips, and dispense visitor information. Return guests often cite "hospitality" as their reason for a second visit. & (Western Valley)

LA QUINTA INN & SUITES
4905 W. Wiley Post Way
Salt Lake City
801/366-4444
$$$

Just two years old, La Quinta is outfitted with all of the newest amenities for travelers, including heated indoor pool and spa, fitness center, voicemail and free cable TV in every room, and meeting space for groups both large and small. All rooms have big bathrooms and large screen TVs, coffeemakers and dataport phones. & (Western Valley)

RADISSON HOTEL
SALT LAKE CITY AIRPORT
2177 W. North Temple St.
Salt Lake City
801/364-5800
$$$

This Radisson was built to accommodate the overnight air traveler who wants a quick in-and-out from Salt Lake City's international airport (hotel literature boasts that passengers can transport from the airport to the lobby in just three minutes). The hotel's busy location on a main highway belies its quiet interiors and upscale amenities. It is designed to replicate an old-world stone hunting lodge, and all interior rooms are done in a French country style. Twenty-nine suites feature loft sleeping areas, kitchens, fireplaces and whirlpool spas, and 128 guest rooms have a wet bar and refrigerator. An executive workout room is part of the guest package. Meeting rooms for up to 20 people can be reserved. & (Western Valley)

Extended Stays

SKY HARBOR EXECUTIVE SUITES
1876 W. North Temple St.
Salt Lake City
801-539-8420
$$$

The goal here is to make the traveler feel at home, but few homes are

Airport Hilton, p. 43

Salt Lake Convention & Visitors Bureau

equipped with a jogging track, sand volleyball court, and aerobics classes. The long- (or short-) stay traveler also enjoys a tennis court, fitness center, swimming pool, sauna, Jacuzzi, and use of outdoor barbecues. There are four room plans from which to choose, ranging from studios to multi-bedroom executive suites. All are completely furnished with full kitchens, housewares, and cable TV. Laundry facilities are on-site. Sky Harbor is located near the intersection of Salt Lake City's two major freeways, providing easy access to the large cities to the north and south, as well as the ski resorts in the Cottonwood Canyons. The facility's logo features an airplane in flight, which is meant to illustrate the close proximity of the Salt Lake International Airport. ♿ (Western Valley)

COTTONWOOD CANYONS AND ENVIRONS

Hotels and Motels

BEST WESTERN COTTONTREE INN
10695 S. Auto Mall Dr.
Sandy
801/523-8484
$$–$$$

This hotel opened in 1997 and its clean, sunny rooms remain one of the best bargains in the area for families, skiers, and businesspeople. A heated indoor pool and hot tub are open 24 hours a day, a fitness center and laundry services are available most hours, and free breakfast is served every morning. Meeting facilities accommodate up to 250 people. ♿ (Cottonwood Canyons and Environs)

Bed-and-Breakfasts

CASTLE CREEK INN
7391 S. Creek Rd. (1300 East)
Holladay
801/567-9437
$$$–$$$$

The exterior of this large building resembles an ancient European castle, and by stretching the imagination one could almost believe that the surrounding grove of trees were a medieval forest. Ten suites have their own individual decor and title, but none stray too far from the royalty theme. The Romeo and Juliet suite overlooks pastoral Cottonwood Creek, the King's Lodge suite is equipped with a pool table, and The Palace suite is decorated in gold and cream with a four-poster bed. All suites have private baths with whirlpool tubs, fireplaces, large-screen televisions, VCRs, and free movies. Fresh pastries and beverages are served each evening, and morning brings breakfast fit for a king. Castle Creek is just minutes from the ski resorts of the Cottonwood Canyons. ♿ (Cottonwood Canyons and Environs)

MOUNTAIN HOLLOW BED AND BREAKFAST INN
10209 S. Dimple Dell Rd.
(3050 East)
Sandy
801/942-3428
$$$–$$$$

This is a place to really get away from it all. Located in an upscale, easternmost neighborhood of Sandy (once a Salt Lake City suburb, but now one of the fastest growing cities in the state), Mountain Hollow is surrounded by two gorgeous, wooded acres that provide privacy and seclusion. Eleven rooms are decorated in themes of French country and Victoriana. In the winter most of the guests are skiers who take advantage of the close proximity of the resorts in the Cottonwood Canyons. Après-ski guests enjoy the hot tub and complimentary snacks. A continental breakfast buffet is served every morning. (Cottonwood Canyons and Environs)

Alta and Snowbird Resorts (Little Cottonwood Canyon)

Note: These facilities are located at the top of the Cottonwood Canyons, near ski and summer resorts.

ALTA LODGE
Little Cottonwood Canyon Rd.
Alta
801/322-4631
$$$–$$$$
The Alta Lodge has been hosting skiers for over 50 years, and its relaxed atmosphere and friendly service are a tradition. The lodge is built practically into the side of a mountain, and its front rooms look directly out onto the ski hills of the Alta Resort. The lodge has expanded over the years and now has a total of 57 rooms; its newer glass and steel additions hold the more deluxe rooms, while its main building has less expensive dormitory-style rooms. The public rooms are also found in the historic main building and include a lobby with a large fireplace, a family-style dining room, a deck room, and the Sitzmark Club. The lodge has two outdoor saunas and hot pools that look onto the mountains. Rates include breakfast and dinner. (Cottonwood Canyons and Environs)

ALTA PERUVIAN LODGE
Little Cottonwood Canyon Rd.
Alta
800/453-8488
$$–$$$$
Providing optimum service to skiers is the primary goal at the Peruvian. Lift tickets, meals, and tax and service charges are included in the winter rate package. Visitors can book ski lessons, rent and repair skis at the on-site shop, and access all of Alta's base ski lifts from the lower level. The no-frills approach here does not exclude a year-round heated pool (96 degrees in winter—perfect for soaking after a day on the ski hill), a hot tub, and comfortable rooms. In summer the Peruvian is a good base for hiking and wildflower watching. (Cottonwood Canyons and Environs)

ALTA'S RUSTLER LODGE
Little Cottonwood Canyon Rd.
Alta
801/532-ALTA
$$–$$$$
The lodge first opened for business in 1947 to accommodate the brave visitors who had taken up the sport of skiing, and a half-century later it has achieved landmark status in the town of Alta. In the world of ski lodges, this is the real thing; a lovely, rambling, log cabin sort of place, with rustic interiors and Scandinavian decor. In winter the lobby windows, as well as a restaurant and lounge, look directly onto the ski hill, and in summer the view is of green mountains crowded with wildflowers. The older, less expensive rooms are small, with a shared bath down the hall. High-end, newly remodeled rooms feature vista views and spacious sitting areas. The rest of the rooms range between the two, and dorm rooms that sleep six are a bargain for larger groups. A short hill takes skiers to all of Alta's base lifts,

Creekside at Solitude, p. 48

and a complimentary shuttle runs between Alta and neighboring Snowbird Resort. Après-ski activity includes a Jacuzzi, steam room, and year-round, outdoor heated pool. Credit cards are not accepted. (Cottonwood Canyons and Environs)

THE CLIFF LODGE
Little Cottonwood Canyon Rd.
Snowbird
801/521-6040
$$$–$$$$

The Cliff is one of the classier places to stay in the Intermountain West, and one of a handful of top-notch accommodations in northern Utah. The service, rooms, and general surroundings are superior. The Cliff is one of four overnight facilities at Snowbird Resort, and it is generally known as the flagship of the operation. It eschews the typical mountain lodge architecture, opting instead to look like a large concrete box. Inside, the spare concrete walls take on a sophistication and surprising warmth, which compliment the alpine and ski activity out-

side. The furniture is sleek and modern, and a collection of Persian rugs decorate the floors. The 532 rooms all have magnificent views of either the ski mountain or the canyon. An adults-only spa located on the top level has a giant rooftop whirlpool and a fitness and aerobics center. Amenities enjoyed by all ages include a heated pool, saunas, steam room, room service, in-room massage, bellman and valet service, nursery and children's center, retail shops, laundry facilities, ski school and ticket office, and ski rental. Four restaurants feature different themes including fine dining, Southwestern, and natural food. Two lounges often have live music in the evening. ♿ (Cottonwood Canyons and Environs)

Brighton and Solitude Resorts (Big Cottonwood Canyon)

BRIGHTON CHALETS
Brighton Loop
Brighton
801/942-8824
$$$

Brighton Ski Resort is located at the very top of Big Cottonwood Canyon, and the road's terminus is a short, one-way loop dotted with homes decorated in the Scandinavian style. Several of these facilities are available to overnight guests and five are managed together as "chalets." They include buildings called The Manor, The Cottage, and The Studio, and sleep from six to 21 people. All have large kitchens, fireplaces and televisions. (Cottonwood Canyons and Environs)

BRIGHTON LODGE
Star Route
Brighton
801/532-4731
$$–$$$$
The Brighton Lodge is a cozy, family-friendly place to stay, located directly at the base of Brighton's primary ski hill. Twenty rooms come in three varieties: suites, single rooms, and economy/hostel models with twin beds and shared baths. Guests enjoy free continental breakfast, two large hot tubs, and a common area with a fireplace, microwave, and large-screen television. Kids under ten ski free at Brighton (limit two per adult) and they stay free at the Brighton

Lodge as well. Some weeks throughout the winter season are selected as "Snow Weeks," when economical, all-inclusive deals are offered for families. (Cottonwood Canyons and Environs)

CREEKSIDE AT SOLITUDE
Big Cottonwood Canyon Rd.
Solitude
801/534-1400
$$$–$$$$
Solitude Resort has expanded and upgraded its operations in the last few years, and a fine new addition is Creekside Village. Two adjacent facilities accommodate overnight guests. The Inn at Solitude is a 46-room, full-service hotel, with an outdoor heated pool and Jacuzzi. The Creekside Condominiums have 18 units with full kitchens, fireplaces, TVs, and private balconies. Condominium guests are granted use of all hotel facilities. At publication date, two new town home complexes are under construction and six more complexes are in the design stage. Solitude has economical "value seasons" in the spring and fall, with food-and-lodging packages. ♿ (Cottonwood Canyons and Environs)

Tom Anastasian—Market Street Grill

4

WHERE TO EAT

Salt Lake City has no particular food heritage or style, so practically anything goes when selecting a "local" restaurant. The choices are endless and geographic placement is random. A greasy diner run by a shirtless chef is within walking distance of one of the premier restaurants in the state, where tuxedoed waiters hover. There are some rules of thumb: The best pizza in town is found near the University of Utah; the block north of the courthouse complex has a terrific mix of ethnic restaurants; and the central downtown district has the highest concentration of trendy eating spots.

The immigration of Californians is manifested in the growing number of nouvelle eateries, where fresh, herb-infused meals are found. As Utah's ethnic mix becomes more pronounced, South American, Chinese, Vietnamese, Thai, and Mexican restaurants are growing in both number and authenticity. A burgeoning population of all sorts has brought an invasion of chain restaurants to town, many of which have become popular with locals. The best restaurants remain the independent, family-run eateries. These gems may be harder to find, but they are plentiful and worth the effort.

This chapter begins with a list of restaurants organized by the type of food each offers. Each name is followed by a zone abbreviation (see page vii) and the page number where a full description is found. Restaurant descriptions are organized alphabetically within each geographic zone. Dollar symbols indicate the expected rate for a typical entrée.

Price rating symbols:
$ **$10 and under**
$$ **$11 to $20**
$$$ **$21 and up**

RESTAURANTS BY FOOD TYPE

American
Lion House Pantry (DT), p. 57
Ruth's Diner (UA), p. 69

Barbecue
Faces (DT), p. 52
Red Bones (SV), p. 67

Burgers
Busy Bee Lunch (SV), p. 62
Hard Rock Café (DT), p. 53
Hires Big H (DT), p. 53
Snappy Service (DT), p. 60

Chinese/Vietnamese
China Delight (WV), p. 70
Ly Ly Restaurant (WV), p. 70
Xiao Li (DT), p. 61

Contemporary
Hoppers Grill and Brewing Co. (CC), p. 72
Market Street Broiler (UA), p. 68
Market Street Grill (DT), p. 58
Millcreek Inn (SV), p. 66
Porcupine Pub & Grille (CC), p. 73
Red Butte Café (UA), p. 69
Rhino Grille (CC), p. 73
Silver Fork Lodge (CC), p. 73
Urban Bistro Market (DT), p. 61

Delis/Sandwiches
Chuck 'n' Fred's (SV), p. 62
Cucina (DT), p. 52
Cuisine Unlimited (SV), p. 62
Granato's (DT), p. 53
Greek Market and Deli (SV), p. 63
J Burger (DT), p. 56
Piñon Market & Café (SV), p. 68
W. H. Brumby's (UA), p. 70

European
Absolute (DT), p. 51
Café Madrid (SV), p. 62
Lamb's Restaurant (DT), p. 57

Helen's Restaurant and Garden Café (SV), p. 63
The Olympian (SV), p. 67

Fine Dining
The Aerie at Snowbird (CC), p. 71
Baci Trattoria (DT), p. 51
Capitol Café (DT), p. 52
Creekside Restaurant at Solitude (CC), p. 71
Il Sansovino (DT), p. 56
La Caille (CC), p. 72
Log Haven (SV), p. 66
Metropolitan (DT), p. 58
The New Yorker (DT), p. 58
Tuscany (CC), p. 74

Indian
Bombay House (UA), p. 68

Italian
Ciao (CC), p. 71
Il Capriccio (SV), p. 63
Luke's Italian Restaurant (WV), p. 70
Michelangelo Ristorante Italiano (SV), p. 66
Pomodoro (CC), p. 73

Japanese
Ginza Japanese Cuisine & Sushi Bar (DT), p. 52
Koko Kitchen (DT), p. 57
Oh! Bento (DT), p. 59

Mexican
Dos Serranos Beach Grill (CC), p. 72
La Villita Mexican Grill (SV), p. 66
Miramar (DT), p. 58
Red Iguana (WV), p. 71

Middle Eastern
Baba Afghan Restaurant (DT), p. 51

Pizza
The Pie Pizzeria (UA), p. 68
Wasatch Pizza (DT), p. 61

South American
Incantation (DT), p. 56

Southwestern
Chili's Southwest Grill (DT), p. 52
Lakota II (DT), p. 57

Steakhouse
Diamond Lil's (WV), p. 70
Ruby River Steakhouse (DT), p. 60
Sizzler (DT), p. 60
Spencer's Steaks and Chops
(DT), p. 60

Thai
Bangkok Thai (UA), p. 68

Vegetarian
Juice Etc. (SV), p. 63
Oasis Café (DT), p. 59

DOWNTOWN

ABSOLUTE
52 W. 200 South St.
Salt Lake City
801/359-0899
$$
The owners of Absolute operated a group of restaurants in Sweden for a number of years, and they have succeeded in transplanting a bit of their homeland to this hip eatery, located in the midst of Salt Lake City's theater district. The decor is just what patrons might expect from a Swedish restaurant—spare, elegant, and heavy on the teak. The food is also somewhat restrained, but in a sexy sort of way. Schnitzel and saltwater fish steaks pair with pancakes and yellow pea soup for combinations that are so, so Scandinavian. A wonderful salad list and excellent service are noteworthy. Lunch and dinner Mon–Sat. & (Downtown)

BABA AFGHAN RESTAURANT
55 E. 400 South St.
Salt Lake City
801/596-0786
$
Baba Afghan Restaurant specializes in "traditional" dishes, or those prepared the old-fashioned way. First-time visitors to Baba have been known to groan out loud and swoon over the wonderful taste combinations. Everything is made from scratch daily, and the menu is constantly changed to take advantage of the freshest meats, herbs, and fruits. Patrons favor casual clothes and manners, but the service and decor are impeccably formal. Vegetarians are advised to ask about daily specials, as there are always several excellent options, some of which are not on the menu. Lunch and dinner Mon–Fri, dinner only Sat–Sun. & (Downtown)

BACI TRATTORIA
136 W. Pierpont Ave.
Salt Lake City
801/328-1500
$$
This is one of the favored spots in which to "be seen," and why not? Baci is elegantly appointed, the service is mostly terrific, and the menu is ever-changing and fun. The table arrangements assure good views of the other patrons and of the beautiful foods and flowers that are placed about as decoration. The space is divided in half down its length; one side is a private club, and the other, with a second-story balcony, is open to everyone. The food is just what the pampered patrons expect—complicated sauces, simple salads, and entrées with unpronounceable names. Lunch and dinner Mon–Fri, dinner only Sat–Sun. & (Downtown)

CAPITOL CAFÉ
54 W. 200 South St.
Salt Lake City
801/532-7000
$$

Capitol Café, just a few steps from the Capitol Theatre, is a popular spot for ballet and opera fans. The small entry lobby sets the mood—hip and elegant. The walls are boldly painted, and natural light pours through the exterior floor-to-ceiling glass walls, illuminating the patrons seated at the 20 or so small marble tables. The menu, which changes slightly daily, features fresh, nouvelle-inspired entrées. Salads and pizzas are also served all day. True to expectation, the food is beautifully presented and the flavor combinations are complicated and dense. Lunch and dinner Mon–Sat. & (Downtown)

CHILI'S SOUTHWEST GRILL
644 E. 400 South St.
Salt Lake City
801/575-6933
$

Chili's is a 700-member national chain with a half dozen wildly popular restaurants in Utah. The decor is vaguely Spanish and casual, and the waitstaff is young and enthusiastic. The menu is huge, both literally (a laminated trifold over a foot high) and figuratively (about 75 items). Starters include quesadillas and buffalo wings, the salads incorporate a lot of grilled chicken, and the sandwiches feature steak, turkey, and grilled chicken. An entire section is dedicated to yogurt smoothies. Lunch and dinner daily. & (Downtown)

CUCINA
1026 Second Ave.
Salt Lake City
801/322-3055

$

Known far and wide as an Italian gourmet deli extraordinaire, Cucina is packed with lots of good stuff to look at and buy and eat. A passion for detail abounds here, not only in the for-sale items, but in the hand-painted floors, walls, seating areas, and serving dishes. The food setup is deli-style; patrons peruse a glass counter filled with meats, cheeses, prepared pastas, and other delicacies, and custom order their food. Breakfast is popular; it features hot oatmeal and freshly made pastries. Pricey, packaged foods run to the foreign and exotic and include an array of vegan and veggie choices. Breakfast and lunch daily. & (Downtown)

FACES
659 N. 300 West St.
Salt Lake City
801/596-0344
$

Patrons should not be put off by Faces' demeanor. This funky restaurant looks as if it is always closed, its hours are irregular, and once inside, the wait is often longer than anticipated. For lovers of Southern barbecue, however, the food is worth any inconvenience. Owner Ernest Hughes has perfected his skills as a pit man, and his simple menu consists of catfish, wings, and five varieties of barbecue. The many flavors that emanate from his kitchen, however, are the complex manifestation of closely guarded recipes, the fresh ingredients available, and the mood that he happens to be in that day. Lunch and dinner Tue–Fri, dinner only Sat. & (Downtown)

GINZA JAPANESE CUISINE & SUSHI BAR
209 W. 200 South St.

Salt Lake City
801/322-2224
$$

Ginza is a tiny, perfect, sea-green biosphere where calmness and order reign. In this strictly traditional Japanese restaurant, the art of presentation is practiced in decor, menu, and even with the waitstaff, who hover in their mostly green clothes. White-starched sushi chefs are at the ready behind their curvy bar. The food is gorgeous, served on green, ceramic tableware that looks hand-thrown. House specialties include some of the best sushi in town, "box" combination dinners, and excellent tempura. A selection of Japanese beers is available, as well as superior green tea. Lunch and dinner Mon–Fri, dinner only Sat. & (Downtown)

GRANATO'S
1391 S. 300 West St.
Salt Lake City
801/486-5643
$

There aren't that many places in Salt Lake City where you can plunk down $150 for a jar of sun-dried tomatoes. Granato's is one business that offers this opportunity, and more. The large rooms, filled with beautiful, prepared foods, are a food-lover's dream. Deli sandwiches are sold from the back room, and the roster of available ingredients is unusually pleasing. Fresh tomatoes, sun-dried tomatoes, feta cheese, prosciutto, and roasted sweet peppers are among the many offerings, all delivered on excellent bread made at a nearby bakery. A minor letdown is the dining area, which seems to be an afterthought. There's a second location at 4044 South 2700 East, in

Holladay, 277-7700. Lunch Mon–Fri. & (Downtown)

HARD ROCK CAFÉ
Trolley Square (505 S. 600 East St.)
Salt Lake City
801/532-7625
$$

Salt Lakers love the big-city status bestowed by their very own Hard Rock Café, and they show their appreciation by flocking here in droves. Fans of Hard Rockesque won't be surprised—this is a near–carbon copy of the cafés found elsewhere around the world. The dark wood walls are crammed with fascinating rock paraphernalia. The food is just fine. A unique aspect of this café is the display area devoted to the home-grown Osmond Family. Another is the private club section, made necessary by local liquor laws, which segregate alcohol drinkers who do not wish to order a meal. Lunch and dinner daily. & (Downtown)

HIRES BIG H
425 S. 700 East St.
Salt Lake City
801/364-4582
$

Ask anybody where to find the best burger in town, and a majority will answer "Hires." Salt Lakers love this place, and its big indoor seating area is almost always crowded. All of the food is made from scratch, and hamburgers feature fresh buns, homemade sauces, dairy-fresh cheese, and hand-selected beef, which is ground every day right in the store. Almost every variety of burger imaginable is available, including a couple of veggie versions. The fries are hand-cut, and the onion rings are excellent. All of the standard ice-cream

DOWNTOWN SALT LAKE CITY

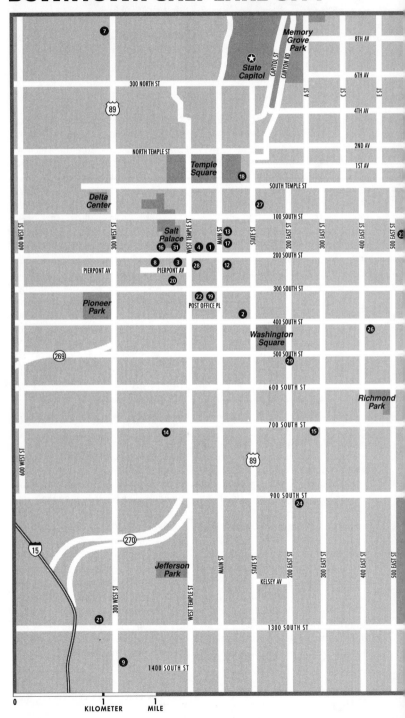

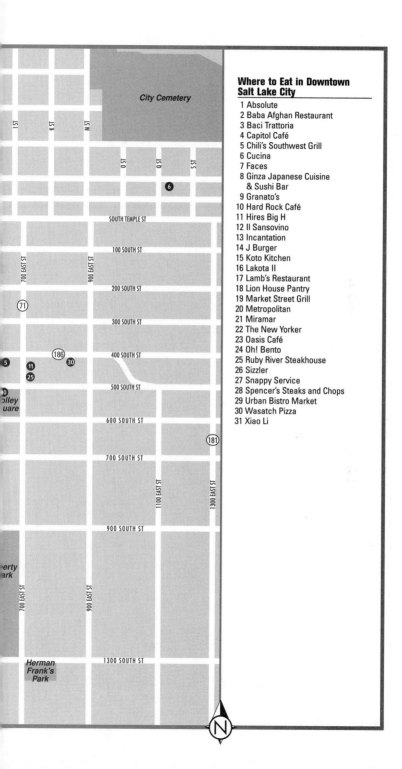

City Cemetery

1 ST
K ST
M ST
O ST
Q ST
S ST

6

SOUTH TEMPLE ST

100 SOUTH ST

700 EAST ST
900 EAST ST

71

200 SOUTH ST

300 SOUTH ST

186 **30**

400 SOUTH ST

5
11
25

500 SOUTH ST

olley
uare

600 SOUTH ST

181

700 SOUTH ST

1100 EAST ST
1300 EAST ST

900 SOUTH ST

erty
ark

700 EAST ST
900 EAST ST

Herman
Frank's
Park

1300 SOUTH ST

N

Where to Eat in Downtown Salt Lake City

1 Absolute
2 Baba Afghan Restaurant
3 Baci Trattoria
4 Capitol Café
5 Chili's Southwest Grill
6 Cucina
7 Faces
8 Ginza Japanese Cuisine
  & Sushi Bar
9 Granato's
10 Hard Rock Café
11 Hires Big H
12 Il Sansovino
13 Incantation
14 J Burger
15 Koto Kitchen
16 Lakota II
17 Lamb's Restaurant
18 Lion House Pantry
19 Market Street Grill
20 Metropolitan
21 Miramar
22 The New Yorker
23 Oasis Café
24 Oh! Bento
25 Ruby River Steakhouse
26 Sizzler
27 Snappy Service
28 Spencer's Steaks and Chops
29 Urban Bistro Market
30 Wasatch Pizza
31 Xiao Li

and beverage choices are available; adventurous diners might consider a cherry root beer. Lunch and dinner Mon–Sat. ♿ (Downtown)

IL SANSOVINO
299 S. Main St.
Salt Lake City
801/533-9999
$$$

If you don't look out the windows, you might believe you are actually in Rome. The pale yellow walls, marble floors, and simple, white-linened tables are reminiscent of the city of fountains. The dining area is divided in two, with a formal decor on one side and a more casual eatery with its own separate menu on the other. Unique-to–Salt Lake City experiences here include a humidor room for after-dinner cigars, a glassed-in table that looks onto the kitchen, and a subterranean room for ultra-private dining. Risotto and pasta dot the menu, but more complicated fare is featured for daily specials. Lunch and dinner Mon–Fri, dinner only Sat. ♿ (Downtown)

INCANTATION
159 S. Main St.
Salt Lake City
801/533-2722
$

Peruvian food is truly distinct from most other ethnic food groups, and at Incantation it is served in its most authentic forms. The restaurant's owner is from Lima, and she creates dishes both from her own region, where potatoes and meat are dominant, as well as from the coastal areas where more fish is consumed. Adventurous eaters will enjoy the ceviche and beef-heart dishes, while more traditional diners will prefer the lamb stew and rice and beans. Everyone should

sample the sauces that cover many of the entrée items. Incantation has not completely shed its former pizza parlor ambience, although displays of native art make an effort. Lunch and dinner Mon–Sat. ♿ (Downtown)

J BURGER
179 W. 700 South St.
Salt Lake City
801-363-2533
$

Don't expect anything fancy at J Burger. The place is clean, noticeably so, but the ceiling sags, the curtains are not new, and the Formica tables have seen a lot of service. But the friendly service and generous servings more than make up for any interior design flaws. Several of the sandwiches merit namesake status: The J Burger, J-Bird, and J-Oink are, respectively, a fancy cheeseburger, a grilled turkey and Swiss, and a grilled ham and cheese. Notable is the nightmare sub; six kinds of meat and cheese that is reportedly a

Oasis Café, p. 59

Oasis Café

nightmare to make, not to eat. Breakfasts are of the huge, stick-to-the-ribs variety. Breakfast and lunch Mon–Fri. ♿ (Downtown)

KOKO KITCHEN
702 S. 300 East St.
Salt Lake City
801/364-4888
$

Local residents might remember the abandoned, inner-city mini-mart that was taken over several years ago by Koko and Hideo Bannai. Their hard work has turned the old building into a bustling restaurant featuring Koko's fresh, low-fat, low-cal Japanese food. Bright yellow walls surround the open kitchen where patrons stand and order their food. Koko's is designed mostly as a take-out restaurant, and inside seating is limited. In warm weather a large, outdoor patio is available. The menu mainstays are chicken and beef teriyaki and chicken, beef, and vegetable curry. Koko is proud of her Japanese-style barbecued spare ribs, naming them the Koko Special. An unusual dish is the Sunny Burger, consisting of a bed of rice, topped with three marinated, meat loaf–like patties, further topped with two sunnyside-up eggs, with mushroom gravy covering all. Lunch and early dinner daily. ♿ (Downtown)

LAKOTA II
380 W. 200 South St.
Salt Lake City
801/519-8300
$$

The second in Utah's series of Lakotas (the first is in Park City) is rugged and stylish and ultra-chic. Its building used to be a warehouse, and most of the multi-stories have been rebuilt as expensive condos. Lakota occupies the bottom floors, Manhattan-style, with a decor that includes exposed metal beams softened by glass and wood touches. Homage is paid to the restaurant's Wild West aspirations (Lakota is a Sioux name) with Southwest colors and a menu that claims to be regional but features New Zealand lamb chops and Greek salads. The bar is wonderful—private and dark and romantic. Lunch and dinner daily. ♿ (Downtown)

LAMB'S RESTAURANT
169 S. Main St.
Salt Lake City
801-364-7166
$$

Lamb's is a throwback to another era, and if there is a theme here, it is continuity. The mud-gray walls and maroon booths have not changed in decades, the dark wood wainscoting has been in place since 1938, and the waitress uniforms have looked the same to several generations of diners. Tables are covered in white linen, and the windowless rooms are softly lit by wall sconces. The Greek bread is wonderful, especially when dipped into one of the homemade soups. Another speciality is Lamb's famous rice pudding. It has been served in the same parfait glasses for years, and the portion is large enough to share with a friend. Breakfast, lunch, and dinner Mon–Sat. ♿ (Downtown)

LION HOUSE PANTRY
63 E. South Temple St.
Salt Lake City
801/363-5466
$

The Lion House dates from the 1850s and was formerly home to the family of Mormon Church Leader Brigham Young. Young reportedly joined his family in these very rooms each day at 2 p.m. for their main meal. Today the Pantry has been restored to its original appearance, albeit with modern kitchens and a cafeteria-style setup, and its goal is to re-create the healthy, homemade food of the pioneer era. (See also Chapter 5, Sights and Attractions.) Lunch only Mon–Thu, lunch and early dinner Fri–Sat. (Downtown)

MARKET STREET GRILL
48 W. Market St.
Salt Lake City
801/322-4668
$$

Market Street Grill's menu and theme is similar to its sister restaurant, the Market Street Broiler (see "University Area" for details). The restaurants are also alike in that they are housed in carefully renovated historic buildings. The Grill is located in an old hotel on a street once known as Market Street, and its interior is retrofitted after the classic grills of coastal cities: black-and-white-checkered tile, open kitchen, formally dressed waiters, lots of noise, and excellent, fresh seafood. Breakfasts are a highlight here, with a long list of huge and reasonably priced specials. Breakfast, lunch, and dinner daily. & (Downtown)

METROPOLITAN
173 W. 300 South St.
Salt Lake City
801/364-3472
$$$

The Metropolitan makes no pretense of catering to small-time spenders, aiming squarely (and sometimes pretentiously) at the upper classes of Salt Lake City society. The food, service, and decor are all exquisite, but many locals are stopped in their tracks when they learn of the $40-to-$75 price of a

meal. Those patrons who are able to throw open their checkbooks are treated to a first-class dining and aesthetic experience. The master chefs create new menus almost every week, featuring the latest food combinations from the most famous cities. The ultramodern decor has received international recognition. Dinner Tue–Sat. & (Downtown)

MIRAMAR
342 W. 1300 South St.
Salt Lake City
801/484-2877
$

Miramar fills the city's Mexican-seafood niche. Patrons who have visited coastal towns south of the border will recognize the service and decor, not to mention the menu. The location used to be a used-car lot, which explains its huge front parking area and glassed-in interior cubicles. The plywood walls and spackled ceilings all manage to jumble into a friendly and casual atmosphere. Besides the seafood dishes, which are mostly very good, the fajitas are the most popular items; served dangerously hot on cast-iron platters, the chicken, beef, and shrimp mixtures come with sides of warm tortillas, guacamole, salsa and beans . . . delicious! Mexican beers and sodas are the recommended beverages. Lunch and dinner daily. & (Downtown)

THE NEW YORKER
60 Market St.
Salt Lake City
801/363-0166
$$$

Ah, yes. Salt Lakers love their New Yorker, consistently naming it the top restaurant in town in almost every published survey. Its cut-glass doors enter onto a perfect, highly pampered world where cares are easily thrown away. The lights are low and twinkly and the waitstaff glides about the rooms. Formal dining (and often major power-brokering) is conducted upstairs in the rear; a more casual café near the door caters to the after-theater crowd. The menu leans toward the traditional: filets and steaks and seafood, all impeccably prepared and served. Lunch and dinner Mon–Sat. (Downtown)

OASIS CAFÉ
151 S. 500 East St.
Salt Lake City
801/322-0404
$$

Oasis is a full-service restaurant dedicated to calm and healthy survival in the late 20th century. The café shares space and a philosophy with a New Age bookstore, and the earth-toned digs pulse with a steadying beat just a bit slower than that of the rest of the world. The menu completely turns on its axis each equinox and solstice, with comfort food featured in the

winter and lighter entrées and sandwiches in the warm months. Seasonal vegetables always dominate. On a given day the disparate and hip crowd might dine on herbed focaccia sandwiches of herbs and cheese, a vegetable tofu stir-fry, or baby greens spiked with cilantro-lime. Breakfast is fabulous here, as are the vast selection of teas and freshly ground coffees. Breakfast, lunch, and dinner Mon–Sat, brunch Sun. ♿ (Downtown)

OH! BENTO
278 E. 900 South St.
Salt Lake City
801/363-5868
$

The Japanese version of fast food is much healthier and more elegant than its American counterpart. Bento translates, somewhat literally, into "box lunch," and the idea here is to serve fast, nutritious, and complete meals, packaged in compact, easy-to-carry-around boxes. Patrons order at a counter, and the food is delivered for either take-out or eat-in at the

Baci Trattoria, p. 51

Salt Lake Convention & Visitors Bureau

casual tables that dot the dining room. Most meals consist of grilled meat or vegetables on a bed of rice, with a couple of complementary side dishes. The decor is cheery, with a bright, Oriental color scheme. Lunch and dinner Mon–Fri. & (Downtown)

RUBY RIVER STEAKHOUSE
435 S. 700 East St.
Salt Lake City
801/359-3355
$$

Ruby River takes its responsibility as a Western steakhouse with utmost seriousness. Not only is most of the menu made up mostly of beef, but the decor is pure cowboy. Boots line the shelving, paintings of broncos dominate the walls, and it's okay to throw the appetizer peanut shells on the floor. As for the food, dieters had best move on. Almost everything that isn't grilled is breaded and deep-fried, including the traditional potato side dish. The steaks are excellent and the clientele loyal—most nights Ruby River's tables are full and there is a guaranteed wait on the weekends. Lunch and dinner Mon–Fri, dinner only Sat–Sun. & (Downtown)

SIZZLER
371 E. 400 South St.
Salt Lake City
801/532-1339
$

Patrons line up, grab a tray and cutlery, then give their order to the person working the cash register. Wise diners will skip the pre-set dinners (steak, shrimp, and chicken) and go for the all-you-can-eat buffet. "Buffet" should be plural, because there are about five different eating stations from which to fill a plate. Desserts, appetizers, pastas, soups, and salads all have their own areas.

Seniors, young families, and everyone in between loves "The Sizz" for its unfailing ability to satisfy even the heartiest appetites. There are seven locations in the Salt Lake Valley. Breakfast, lunch, and dinner daily. & (Downtown)

SNAPPY SERVICE
57 S. State St.
Salt Lake City
801/328-8503
$

Snappy's is the grandfather of all hamburger joints in town, having been in business continually since 1905. It is beloved for its true "lunch counter" ambience and admired for staving off any temptations at modernization—no caving in to trendy theme sandwiches or healthy fare. The owner (and only employee) flips burgers the old-fashioned way, one at a time, on his small, behind-the-counter grill. His cheese is at the ready, stacked tall in a pre-cut pile of orange. Hamburgers are served straight, with mustard and ketchup the only available condiments. Lunch Mon–Fri. & (Downtown)

SPENCER'S STEAKS AND CHOPS
DoubleTree Hotel
255 S. West Temple St.
Salt Lake City
801/238-4748
$$$

Spencer's is an old-time, big city–style, all-frills steakhouse. The red meat here is the best in town, aged and seasoned to perfection. Filet mignon, prime rib and other beef cuts are served on unadorned white plates, without even a garnish to detract from their perfection. Hamburgers are elevated to gourmet food—big and juicy and

Food for Thought

Tourists have been known to ask where "Mormon food" is served. Although there is no formal ethnic classification for this food group, Utahns are often noted for their highest–per capita Jell-O and ice cream consumption and are teased for their love of large portions. Restaurants that cater to these tendencies include all-you-can-eat buffets such as The Sizzler and The Pantry (located in Brigham Young's Lion House), which bases its recipes on wholesome pioneer fare.

made from prime beef. True meat lovers will want to try the steak soup. The decor perfectly matches the menu. Classy, private booths line the dining room, and the bar that serves as the lobby is elegant and refined. Lunch Mon–Fri, dinner only Sat–Sun. ♿ (Downtown)

URBAN BISTRO MARKET
215 E. 500 South St.
Salt Lake City
801/322-4101
$
If you follow the vegetable-colored walls back into the Urban Bistro's nether regions, you'll reach the open kitchen where chef/owner Ricc Esparza works his magic at the grill and hawks his favorite eclectic entrées. He favors nouvelle cuisine such as fontina quiche, radicchio pizza, and focaccia hamburgers. His sausage is homemade and excellent, filled with the freshest meat and vegetables of the season. Lunch Mon–Sat. ♿ (Downtown)

WASATCH PIZZA
280 E. 400 South St.
Salt Lake City
801/359-2300
$$
Wasatch specializes in the boutique pizza, leaving the traditional pies to the hundred or so other pizza parlors in the Salt Lake City area. There is a small area set aside for dining in; however, the huge bulk of Wasatch's business is carry-out and delivery. A first-timer will have difficulty choosing from the ingredient list. Sauces include pesto, Cajun, Dijonnaise, Mornay, and more. Toppings and cheese are too numerous to list, but there is help from a pre-chosen menu list that includes such selections as a Pfeifferhorn, a Mt. Wolverine, and a Cordon Bleu. Lunch and dinner daily. ♿ (Downtown)

XIAO LI
307 W. 200 South St.
Salt Lake City
801/328-8688
$$
The menu may be traditional Mandarin and Szechuan, but almost everything else about Xiao Li defies stereotype. Its home is a starkly mod-

ern, renovated warehouse space just west of downtown's business district. Its sleek interior spaces are minimally decorated and painted in luscious sunset colors. The table arrangements are formal, and a Chinese bent is revealed only after sitting down and scanning the menu. The 70 or so items are almost all very good, and some exciting entrées, such as ginger chicken and sha-cha beef, are included along with the standard moo-shus and curries. The Szechuan dumpling appetizer is highly recommended, but the lunch buffet is not. Lunch and dinner Mon–Fri, dinner only Sat–Sun. ♿ (Downtown)

SOUTHEASTERN VALLEY

BUSY BEE LUNCH
2115 S. State St.
Salt Lake City
801/466-0950
$

The Bee isn't much in the glammo department. It is a bar about as big as a living room, with painted cinderblock walls and lighting supplied by neon signs. Five TVs are always on, and the jukebox plays simultaneously. But the food here is dependably good, in a cholesterol-enriched sort of way. Take a tip from the regulars and order the garlic burger; for devotees of the genre this burger incites passion and calms cravings. Lunch and dinner daily. ♿ (Southeastern Valley)

CAFÉ MADRID
2080 E. 3900 South St.
Holladay
801/273-0837
$$

The union of a Utahn and a Spaniard has created one of the better ethnic restaurants in town. The couple has renovated a small mall space into an escape into the Spanish countryside. Whitewashed walls, planked floors, and spare table arrangements create a setting that's perfect for the deceptively simple menu. The food here is unadorned and basic, and at the same time rich and complex. Café regulars often make an entire meal of the tapas menu—appetizer-sized servings of disparate and beautifully presented dishes. Lunch and dinner Mon–Sat. ♿ (Southeastern Valley)

CHUCK 'N' FRED'S
2280 S. West Temple St.
Salt Lake City
801/467-7103
$

Chuck and Fred are so smitten with the sport of fishing that there is nary a square inch of their diner that does not celebrate the rod and reel. A fishing boat is mounted on the roof, emblazoned with the words "Try Us. You'll Get Hooked." A weekly updated fishing report is mounted on the wall. Wallpaper celebrates trout species of the world. A stack of Polaroids on each table shows a variety of strangers displaying dead fish for the camera. The menu does not carry on the fresh fish theme, however; the most popular meals are of the comfort variety—grilled hamburger steak, meat loaf, and the longtime house specialty, beef pot roast. Breakfast and lunch Mon–Fri. ♿ (Southeastern Valley)

CUISINE UNLIMITED
4041 S. 700 East St.
Murray
801/268-2332
$

Cuisine's raison d'etre is catering, but luckily they serve on-site diners as well. Patrons order custom meals from a long wall of glass cases that seem to feature whatever has been ordered for private parties that particular day, although a good variety of soups, sandwiches, and salads is always available. A lack of ambience is more than made up for by beautifully served food and fast, efficient service. The atmosphere is more like a hotel room than somebody's home—this is not a place where people hang out and drink coffee all afternoon. Breakfast and lunch Mon–Fri. & (Southeastern Valley)

GREEK MARKET AND DELI
3205 S. State St.
Salt Lake City
801/485-9365
$

The Greek Market's exterior is easy to spot: It's painted with huge dolmathes and dancing Greek people. Once inside, the balalaika music and blue-and-white color scheme leave no doubt as to the restaurant's ethnicity. The deli features a giant sample-of-everything platter called the "mezedakia plate." The market is a wonderful place to find unique foods, including dried legumes, chicory, and figs. A freezer chest holds octopus, tilapia, and milkfish; the refrigerator case has olives so acerbic that just their memory clenches the throat. The homemade pastries are fabulously gooey. Lunch Mon–Sat. & (Southeastern Valley)

HELEN'S RESTAURANT AND GARDEN CAFÉ
6055 S. 900 East St.
Murray
801/265-0205
$$

The reigning ethnic theme at Helen's is Eastern European, and food from that region is traditionally flavorful, spicy, and often rather heavy. Fabulous (albeit guilty) pleasures include Viennese pork cutlets, chicken paprikash served over spatzli, and Gypsy goulash. Lighter fare includes grilled chicken dishes and salads. The restaurant is located in an old, thick-walled house that sits well back from a busy street. The two rooms are filled with formally dressed tables. Helen herself is often on the premises, making sure the food and the setting are perfect for her guests. Lunch Mon–Sat, dinner daily. & (Southeastern Valley)

IL CAPRICCIO
2263 E. Murray-Holladay Rd.
Holladay
801/277-8080
$$$

Patrons are advised to slow down, relax, and savor this unique Italian food experience. The atmosphere is low key and perhaps a little worn. Fine-diners are more than willing to overlook any minor faults in the decor, however, in favor of the excellent menu. Il Capriccio's owner is from Tuscany, and his menu features the fresh vegetables and fish from that area. The food is rustic and authentic, made with simple, fresh ingredients. Specially imported cheeses, vinegars, and olive oils elevate even the most basic appetizers. Lunch and dinner Tue–Sun. & (Southeastern Valley)

JUICE ETC.
2041 S. 2100 East St.
Salt Lake City
801/466-5992
$

Loyal patrons insist that the wheatgrass drinks are fabulous, as well as the juices blended from 12

GREATER SALT LAKE CITY

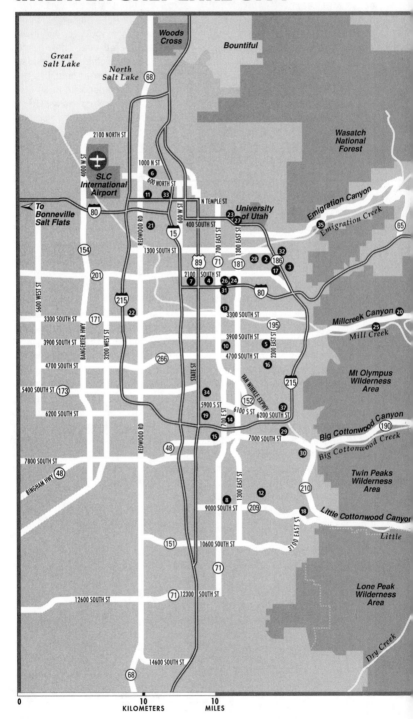

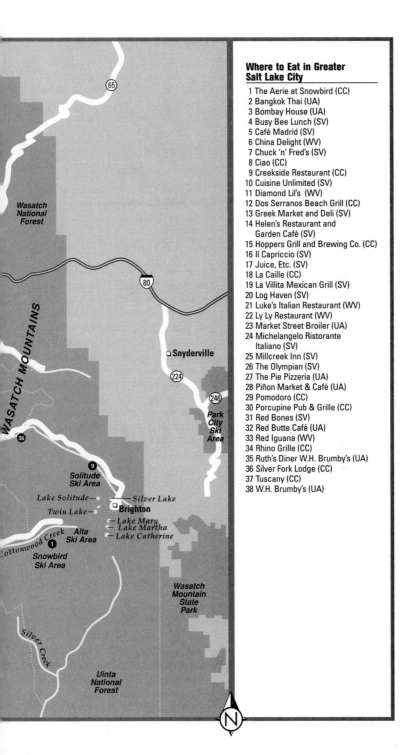

Where to Eat in Greater Salt Lake City

1 The Aerie at Snowbird (CC)
2 Bangkok Thai (UA)
3 Bombay House (UA)
4 Busy Bee Lunch (SV)
5 Café Madrid (SV)
6 China Delight (WV)
7 Chuck 'n' Fred's (SV)
8 Ciao (CC)
9 Creekside Restaurant (CC)
10 Cuisine Unlimited (SV)
11 Diamond Lil's (WV)
12 Dos Serranos Beach Grill (CC)
13 Greek Market and Deli (SV)
14 Helen's Restaurant and
   Garden Café (SV)
15 Hoppers Grill and Brewing Co. (CC)
16 Il Capriccio (SV)
17 Juice, Etc. (SV)
18 La Caille (CC)
19 La Villita Mexican Grill (SV)
20 Log Haven (SV)
21 Luke's Italian Restaurant (WV)
22 Ly Ly Restaurant (WV)
23 Market Street Broiler (UA)
24 Michelangelo Ristorante
   Italiano (SV)
25 Millcreek Inn (SV)
26 The Olympian (SV)
27 The Pie Pizzeria (UA)
28 Piñon Market & Café (UA)
29 Pomodoro (CC)
30 Porcupine Pub & Grille (CC)
31 Red Bones (SV)
32 Red Butte Café (UA)
33 Red Iguana (WV)
34 Rhino Grille (CC)
35 Ruth's Diner W.H. Brumby's (UA)
36 Silver Fork Lodge (CC)
37 Tuscany (CC)
38 W.H. Brumby's (UA)

separate vegetables. Less-serious health nuts love the fine array of fruit smoothies. There is a definite inclination toward the healthier aspects of life here, with a young, energetic staff, a clean and breezy atmosphere, and walls painted the colors of fruits and vegetables. Laggards are cheerfully tolerated, however, with a selection of sandwiches and salads. A nice patio is available for warm weather dining. Breakfast and lunch Mon–Sat. & (Southeastern Valley)

LA VILLITA MEXICAN GRILL
43 E. 5900 South St.
Murray
801/263-3479
$
Order at the counter, and then walk over to the fresh salsa bar to choose your condiments of choice. The food arrives fast and fresh (and filling!). The standard Mex food is all here, and pretty much everything is outstanding, especially the gorditas and the soft-shell tacos. The bill is most likely a lovely surprise—it's possible to feed the whole family and still have enough money to treat everyone to a movie. Lunch and dinner daily. & (Southeastern Valley)

LOG HAVEN
Millcreek Canyon
Holladay
801/272-8255
$$
Superlatives reign here. Log Haven is an exceptional restaurant in every way. The food tends toward nouvelle (sage pasta, mustard-crusted duck, and coriander-rubbed ahi, for instance). The table settings are formal and the staff is efficient. Best of all, though, is the setting. Log Haven is located four miles up Millcreek Canyon,

in the midst of pines and rivers, with a noisy waterfall just across the road. The building was built decades ago from local pine and stone, and a recent renovation has only added to its lodge-style appeal. A lovely patio catches the evening breeze in summer. This is a place to celebrate life's special events. Dinner daily. & (Southeastern Valley)

MICHELANGELO RISTORANTE ITALIANO
2152 S. Highland Dr.
Salt Lake City
801/466-0961
$$
Michelangelo's is upscale, below street level, and right on for lovers of primo Italian food. Guests enter and descend a row of stairs, where they are oftimes greeted by one or two of the proprietors—friendly, elegant people who are ready with plenty of food and wine advice. The tables are bright blue and the rest of the restaurant is stark white, which fits nicely with the Mediterranean/Sardinian menu. The owner says he imports much of his "real" food directly from Italy, and his cheeses, sauces, prosciutto, and pastas do indeed taste out of this world (or at least this country). Dinner Mon–Sat. (Southeastern Valley)

MILLCREEK INN
Millcreek Canyon
Holladay
801/278-7927
$$
Millcreek Inn is set in a lovely old house that a few decades ago was turned into a restaurant. Its burbling namesake next door lends a peaceful atmosphere, both on the large patio in summer and in the living room–style interior in winter. Mill

Creek takes a gentle turn just below the restaurant, and once you're through the door, the nearby city seems a hundred miles away. Silver and white linen decorate the tables, and meals are long and leisurely. The food—mostly fish, chicken, salads, and soups—is creatively prepared with herbs and sauces. Dinner Tue–Sun. ♿ (Southeastern Valley)

THE OLYMPIAN
2181 S. 700 East St.
Salt Lake City
801/487-1407
$
This throwback to the glory days of the diner is a big, busy, bustling place with waiters who carry six plates at once and patrons who are blissfully unaware of cholesterol dangers. The owners and many of the patrons are Greek, and feta and gyro dot the menu; however, the main theme is big. Huge platters, heaping servings, and slabs of meat rule the menu selections. Breakfast is famous and served all day— stuffed omelets, pork chops, steak and eggs, and a whole lot more. Breakfast, lunch, and dinner daily. ♿ (Southeastern Valley)

RED BONES
2207 S. 700 East St.
Salt Lake City
801/463-4800
$$
The deal here is ribs—baby-back, Memphis-style, and rib ends, all hand-rubbed with dry spices and then slow-cooked for at least a day. Secondary meats (also lovingly slow-cooked and excellent) are pulled pork and sliced brisket. The theme is not surprising; a vintage motorcycle is mounted on the wall, and bikers are allowed to park on the front sidewalk. What is different from most rib joints is the extensive "sides" menu, which includes the likes of Persian carrots, three-bean chili, and Greek potatoes. Lunch and dinner Mon–Sat. ♿ (Southeastern Valley)

Eating, Drinking, and Making Merry

Utah's liquor laws place restrictions on the time, place, and circumstances for ordering a drink in a restaurant. In order to serve cocktails or wine, a restaurant must have a special liquor license; most fine-dining establishments in the state have been allowed to obtain these permits. Alcoholic beverages may be served only to patrons who order a meal, and can be ordered from noon to midnight. If patrons have questions about a restaurant's ability to supply cocktails, it is best to call ahead and ask for specifics. The Utah Indoor Clean Air Act does not allow smoking in public buildings.

UNIVERSITY AREA

BANGKOK THAI
1400 S. Foothill Dr.
Salt Lake City
801/582-8424
$$

The Bangkok is a sea of calm—and an oasis of excellent food—in the middle of a busy shopping mall. The small dining room is crowded with white-linened tables and Thai artifacts. The lemongrass soup here, called po tak, will knock your socks off. The restaurant is known for its large vegetarian menu, which is specially priced on "Meatless Mondays," and its deliciously (and extremely) hot, spicy entrées. Patrons should be prepared to squeeze into a tightly packed table setup and to pay extra for rice. Lunch Mon–Fri, dinner only Sat–Sun. ⅙ (University Area)

BOMBAY HOUSE
1615 S. Foothill Dr.
Salt Lake City
801/581-0222
$$

The peaceful atmosphere of this Indian restaurant is established with a warm greeting at the front door, the sitar music playing in the background, and the soothing wall decorations. The waiters serve you in the purring dialect of their homeland. The food . . . oh, the food. If flowers and clouds could be eaten, this is what they would taste like. Amazing, subtle combinations that wind around the tastebuds and leave diners stricken with joy. The vindaloo and kurma items are bathed in heavenly mixtures, and the curries and tandoori are renowned. Naan is the preferred bread, and the yogurt-cucumber sauce is the favorite for dipping. Dinner Mon–Sat. ⅙ (University Area)

MARKET STREET BROILER
260 S. 1300 East St.
Salt Lake City
801/583-8808
$$

Patrons should prepare for aesthetic overload. This restaurant housed in a former fire station is filled with color and noise and all sort of people . . . and food, lots of food. A glassed counter holds the best and freshest selection of fresh fish in town. Metal shelving placed about is crammed with bright cans and jars of exotic spices and condiments. A huge, stool-lined counter surrounds an open kitchen where chefs perform theater. The upper level is filled with booths and tables. The menu features fresh fish and excellent salads. The clam chowder and shrimp salad combo is cheap and fast and very good. Lunch and dinner daily. ⅙ (University Area)

THE PIE PIZZERIA
1320 E. 200 South St.
Salt Lake City
801/582-0193
$$

This place a throwback to the cellar-style pizza joints of the 1960s, and indeed the Pie has attempted no major upgrades in the last three decades. No matter. The pizza is excellent, perhaps the best in town. Its location is a half-block from the University of Utah, which insures a crowd of college students will always be standing in line ahead of anyone walking in the door, but the wait (and the noise and the crowded conditions) are well worth it. Lunch and dinner daily. (University Area)

PIÑON MARKET & CAFÉ
2095 E. 1300 South St.
Salt Lake City

La Caille, p. 72

801/582-4539

$

Piñon is a neighborhood deli sought out by folks from both near and far. It offers a sandwich lineup of ham, turkey, and roast beef, but these old standards are given gourmet status with in-house roasting and imported cheese. Likewise, the salads and vegetarian specialties are somehow familiar, but are elevated to culinary masterpieces by mixing unusual combinations of nuts, vegetables, pasta, and spices. Breakfast includes muffins, scones, and a unique biscuit, egg, and cheese combo. The deli is located in a small business district, and is made distinct by a green awning and a small outdoor eating area. Breakfast and lunch Mon–Sat. &. (University Area)

RED BUTTE CAFÉ
1412 S. Foothill Dr.
Salt Lake City
801/581-9498
$

Red Butte, which takes its name from nearby Red Butte Canyon, de-

nies its shopping-mall location with lovely, upper-level views of the Wasatch Mountains. Decor is based on natural materials such as slate and granite, and the atmosphere is trendy and casual. In warm weather, the outdoor patio that wraps around the restaurant is the preferred place to dine. The nouvelle menu features an ever-changing list of fresh, homemade pastas, sandwiches, salads, and primo desserts. Lunch and dinner daily. &. (University Area)

RUTH'S DINER
2100 Emigration Canyon
Salt Lake City
801/582-5807
$$

Some locals remember when the legendary, chain-smoking, no-nonsense Ruth used to preside over the premises in person, but now only her photographs and keepsakes remain. Ruth's legacy is a 45-year-old diner that still retains its original railroad-car ambience. The beautiful surrounding Emigration Canyon, however, has matured into an upscale neighborhood that Ruth wouldn't recognize. This is a wonderful, albeit noisy and often too crowded, spot to enjoy Sunday brunch or a summer dinner. Breakfast, lunch, and dinner daily. ♿ (University Area)

W. H. BRUMBY'S
224 S. 1300 East St.
Salt Lake City
801/581-0888
$
Brumby's is a very civilized place in which to enjoy an espresso and a fresh fruit tart at the beginning of the day. Its proximity to the University of Utah campus ensures a young and academic crowd, who enjoy long coffee hang-outs in the afternoons. The setup is deli-style, with a large, glass-front counter filled with beautiful food, most especially outrageous desserts. Breakfast, lunch, and dinner daily. ♿ (University Area)

WESTERN VALLEY

CHINA DELIGHT
1447 W. 1000 North St.
Salt Lake City
801/364-8716
$
The proprietors are Chinese, the cooks are Chinese, and most of the patrons are Chinese and/or policemen—always a good sign. This gem of a restaurant occupies a tiny space in a tottery strip mall, but pay no mind to the funky location: The food here is excellent. There are nine fried rices from which to choose, five chow meins, and five lo meins. Add about 45 more items, and you have the complete menu. Each of the many entrées enjoys a distinct texture and taste, and the accompanying sauces are harmonious. Lunch and dinner Mon–Sat. ♿ (Western Valley)

DIAMOND LIL'S
1528 W. North Temple St.
Salt Lake City
801/533-0547
$$
Vegetarians had best stay away—Lil's is the steak capital of Salt Lake City, and a haven for the meat and potato lovers of the world. The restaurant is a maze of small rooms, each filled with plank tables and captain's chairs and imbued with the aroma of spicy grilled dinners. The decor is Old West and the menu is too. Lunch and dinner Mon–Fri, dinner only Sat. ♿ (Western Valley)

LUKE'S ITALIAN RESTAURANT
1374 W. Indiana Ave.
(850 South St.)
Salt Lake City
801/521-2322
$
Luke's has the handle on cheap, fast, and good on Salt Lake City's west side. The "Italian village" decor has not been updated in years, but patrons don't seem to care. This place is enormously popular for lunch, moving a hundred diners in and out of its doors during any given lunch hour. Speed is part of the appeal; it is possible to order, eat, and pay your check in 20 minutes. The food is another plus; the cooks are not on the cutting edge of innovation, but they turn out sturdy and reliable meals. Perhaps the most attractive aspect of Luke's is value. Most specials cost $3.99. Lunch and dinner Mon–Fri, dinner only Sat. ♿ (Western Valley)

LY LY RESTAURANT
1839 W. 3500 South St.
West Valley City

801/972-4177
$
It may look like just another Vietnamese restaurant squeezed into a low-rent strip mall, but Ly Ly rises above its surroundings with excellent food and service. The chef takes pride in his low-fat menu, but diners barely notice as they down the likes of curried chicken and charbroiled pork. Some patrons come just for the egg rolls—crispy chunks of perfection filled with pork, shrimp, and vegetables. Lunch and dinner Wed–Sun, lunch only Mon. ⅗ (Western Valley)

RED IGUANA
736 W. North Temple St.
Salt Lake City
801/322-1489
$
A famous country-western star named this as his favorite restaurant. Visiting pro sports players can be seen waiting for a table, and touring actors come here as well. These visitors learn what Salt Lakers already know: that the Red Iguana serves seriously good Mexican food in huge portions from its humble location just west of a freeway overpass. This is the Americanized, cheese-covered rendition of Mexican food, but with a welcome twist: The sauces, particularly the selection of moles, are excellent; the 100-year-old recipes require intense preparation. Lunch and dinner daily. ⅗ (Western Valley)

COTTONWOOD CANYONS AND ENVIRONS

THE AERIE AT SNOWBIRD
Cliff Lodge, Snowbird Resort
Little Cottonwood Canyon Rd.
801/521-6040

$$
The Aerie offers a bona fide fine-dining experience in the wilds of Little Cottonwood Canyon. Its perch on the 10th floor of the posh Cliff Lodge offers magnificent views outside (best at dusk, in both winter and summer), and the white-linen tables inside are both dashing and romantic. Fresh flowers and candles enliven the formal decor. The food is dressy as well: roasts and fowl and fish served with exotic salsas and vegetable purees, and wonderfully complicated desserts. The wine list is impressive. Dinner Mon–Sat, brunch Sun. ⅗ (Cottonwood Canyons and Environs)

CIAO
834 E. 9400 South St.
Sandy
801/571-8282
$
Ciao does a big dinner and weekend business, but you can enjoy the same great food in quieter surroundings weekdays at lunchtime. Other pluses are easy parking, a hovering waitstaff, and food that arrives promptly on the table if you're in a hurry. The cook really knows his herbs, and fresh basil and parsley make their way into most of the dishes. Cheeses are well-used here, and the made-fresh-daily soup is fabulous, as are salads and made-to-order pizzas. Lunch and dinner Mon–Sat. (Cottonwood Canyons and Environs)

CREEKSIDE RESTAURANT
Solitude Resort
Big Cottonwood Canyon Rd.
Solitude
801/534-1400
$$
Until a few years ago Solitude Ski

Resort was a funky, family resort, beloved by Salt Lakers for its affordable ski lift tickets. Recently, Solitude made some major capital improvements, and its food situation has changed from a mediocre cafeteria to one of the best restaurants around. Creekside's large rooms are made of stone and heavy beams, with large windows that look back up at the pine-lined ski areas. The menu consists of herb and fresh vegetable–laced pastas and salads, pizzas and meat entrées. A lovely patio gets cold after dark, even on the warmest summer days. Lunch and dinner Wed–Sat, brunch Sat–Sun. & (Cottonwood Canyons and Environs)

DOS SERRANOS BEACH GRILL
8657 S. Highland Dr.
Sandy
801/942-7988
$
The idea here seems to be to re-create the food and festivity of a Mexican beach resort. The decor is wild and colorful, the music is loud, and the waitstaff often dances the food to the table. The menu features mostly standard Mexican fare, albeit with a tropical accent. Rock shrimp burritos, shrimp rellenos, and California fajitas are among the choices. Daters and young families make up most of the clientele. Lunch and dinner daily. & (Cottonwood Canyons and Environs)

HOPPERS GRILL AND BREWING CO.

890 E. Fort Union Blvd.
Holladay
801/566-0424
$
The food is fine, but the main attraction here is the award-winning beers that are brewed on-site. The building is a nice advertisement for its specialty beverages, with larger exterior windows revealing the brewing apparatus inside. Beers range from pale ales to stouts, as well as seasonal specials, and a full wine list is available. The restaurant is family-friendly, and the clientele represents all ages. Younger patrons enjoy home-brewed sodas, including creme soda, root beer, and ginger ale. Pasta, burgers, salads, and boutique pizzas make up the menu. Lunch and dinner daily. & (Cottonwood Canyons and Environs)

LA CAILLE
9565 S. Wasatch Blvd.
Sandy
801/942-1751
$$$
La Caille is not just a mere meal: It's a full-sensory dining experience. Visitors travel from far away just to dine here, and many consider it the top restaurant in Utah. The main restaurant and several quaint outbuildings are set in the midst of acres of highly manicured grounds. Peacocks wander and chipmunks play in this re-creation of the French countryside, complete with châteaus and grape arbors. The

TRIVIA

According to the *Zagat Survey of Rocky Mountain Restaurants*, Utahns dine out 3.6 times a week.

setting is absolutely gorgeous, and the decor of the various dining rooms is stunning. The food is complicated, with most menu items having at least three foreign words in their description. Prices match the surrounding—impressive. Dinner daily, brunch Sun. ♿ (Cottonwood Canyons and Environs)

POMODORO
2440 E. Fort Union Blvd.
Holladay
801/944-1895
$$
The ambience of this small restaurant is pleasant enough to make diners forget its shopping-mall location, but food is the thing here: exquisitely delicious, mostly Italian-inspired creations that attract a loyal patronage from all over the Salt Lake Valley. Risotto, polenta, and pizette are perfectly cooked. The sauces may look familiar, but alfredo, marinara, and pesto take on new life with unusual herb flavorings. The wine list is award-winning. Patrons who love seriously rich and delicious food should be prepared to wait for a table, but will be rewarded with a wonderful food experience. Dinner Tue–Sun. ♿ (Cottonwood Canyons and Environs)

PORCUPINE PUB & GRILLE
3698 E. 7000 South St.
Holladay
801/942-5555
$
The Porcupine is found just below the roads to both Big and Little Cottonwood Canyons, and its small patio sports a great view of the valley below. A beautiful wood-and-slate interior and a waitstaff in shorts and hiking boots set the tone. This manages to be a great date spot and a family restaurant at the

same time. A long list of Utah's microbrewed beers is offered, along with a traditional assortment of appetizers. The menu is varied and mostly very good, with innovative pastas and sandwiches and dinner entrées featuring steak and seafood. Lunch and dinner daily. ♿ (Cottonwood Canyons and Environs)

RHINO GRILLE
155 E. 6100 South St.
Murray
801/262-6776
$$
Safari lovers might be disappointed, as the African theme pretty much ends at the front door. Teasers are the restaurant's logo, which is a sturdy rhino, and the building, which borrows elements from an arid savannah. But inside Africa disappears and a hip, young America emerges with a California-inspired menu and mostly domestic beers and coastal wines. Formerly a gym, the big, square spaces of the premises have been retained, creating a friendly seating arrangement. Lunch and dinner Mon–Sat. ♿ (Cottonwood Canyons and Environs)

SILVER FORK LODGE
Big Cottonwood Canyon Rd.
Sandy
801/649-9551
$$
Silver Fork has been a favorite with locals for over 50 years. Its superb location in the middle of Big Cottonwood Canyon and its laid-back atmosphere make it a perfect place to visit after a hike or ski expedition. Some of the exterior decorations, such as the wooden bear on the roof and the creaky, swinging entrance sign, have been part of the lodge since its beginnings in 1943. The

menu has something for everyone,
and an on-site smokehouse pro-
duces fab ribs. Breakfast features a
sourdough pancake recipe with bat-
ter that began its fermenting
process 50 years ago. Breakfast,
lunch, and dinner daily. &. (Cottonwood Canyons and Environs)

TUSCANY
2832 E. 6200 South St.
Holladay
801/277-9919
$$$
Tuscany is one of the few restau-
rants in Salt Lake City where you
can order a $150 bottle of cham-
pagne from the table. From its front
winding drive and valet service, to
its lord-of-the-manor candlelit
rooms, this place is formal and
fancy. An open kitchen reveals a
retinue of chefs busy preparing the
Italian-inspired menu, which fea-
tures complicated and artsy en-
trées. The wine and cocktail list is
impressive and extensive, and the
desserts are a must. A back patio is
the very best place in town to while
away a summer's evening. Dinner
daily. &. (Cottonwood Canyons and
Environs)

Utah Travel Council/Steve Greenwood —
Big Cottonwood Canyon

5

SIGHTS AND ATTRACTIONS

People visit Salt Lake City for so many reasons it is impossible to generalize about the city's appeal. Tourism marketing campaigns over the years, however, have tried. Thirty years ago posters proclaimed "Mormon Country" was a great place to visit, and pictorials featured Temple Square and other Latter Day Saint venues. Later, the city's recreation aspects were touted with the slogan "The Greatest Snow on Earth" splashed across pictures of powder skiers flying through white clouds of snow. "Shop the Mall That Has It All" is a typical enticing shoppers to Utah's biggest and best selection of boutiques and shopping centers, and "Where History Comes Alive" refers to Salt Lakers' passion for interpreting their past.

The performing arts, professional sports, and various museums have all been corralled by catchphrases, and a concerted effort in the promotion of Salt Lake City has led to a burgeoning tourism industry. But as any visitor knows, it is as often the intangible aspects of a city that form its character.

Visitors seem to like this city for the same reasons that residents do. Salt Lake City is pretty in both its layout and surroundings. The streets are wide and shady and remarkably clean. Recreation and solitude are just minutes away from the city center in the mountains and lakes. And people are nice here, noticeably so. The attractions listed below describe a wide selection of things to do and places to go. The reasons to visit, however, are often enhanced by the unexpected experiences that happen along the way.

TEMPLE SQUARE

It is said that a few days after he first entered the Salt Lake Valley, Brigham Young measured this 10-acre-square block by walking its perimeter and declared it to be the site of a future Mormon Temple.

Some 150 years later, the boundaries of the square remain, and the church's most famous temple building is found here. Although it is a sacred place for Mormons, visitors are welcome to stroll the beautiful gardens and to learn about the church. Temple Square is surrounded by a high stucco wall, and entrance gates are found on the south, west, and north sides of the block. The separate entities inside the square have varying hours and are listed separately below. Guided tours of the grounds and buildings begin at the flagpole, starting every few minutes. For more information, call 801/240-4869.

ASSEMBLY HALL

This granite, Gothic-style building serves a number of functions, including that of concert hall for the Temple Square Concert Series on Friday and Saturday nights at 7:30 throughout the year. Call 800/537-9703 for a schedule of performances. At this writing, the LDS Church is building a meeting hall on the block just north of Temple Square. The building is as yet unnamed, but one of its working titles is the "New Assembly Hall." One of the purposes of the building will be to seat the overflow crowd that comes to listen to the biannual Church Conference. The new building will seat 26,000, and completion date is scheduled for 1999. Free. ⅖ (Downtown)

GARDENS

Temple Square is famous for its expansive and highly manicured gardens. Designs feature native plants and pioneer-era arrangements. In summer, one-hour tours describe the gardens inside the square, as well as those of the church-owned buildings in the surrounding blocks. Beginning the Friday after Thanksgiving and continuing through the month of December, the gardens are decorated with hundreds of thousands of tiny lights that recreate the blooms of summer. A life-size, multimedia nativity scene is placed in front of the north visitor center, and nightly holiday concerts are held inside the tabernacle. An evening stroll through this winter wonderland is an integral part of Salt Lakers' holiday tradition. Daily 6–10. Tours given Apr 28–Oct 3 Mon–Sat at 10, 12, 2, and 4 (meet in southwest lobby of the Church Office Building), Tue–Thu nights at 7 (meet outside south doors of the Church Office Building), and Sun after the Mormon Tabernacle Choir concert, at about 10:15 (meet at east gates of Temple Square). Call 801/240-5916 for more information. Free. ⅖ (Downtown)

SEAGULL MONUMENT

Seagulls are revered in Mormon history for saving an early pioneer crop from a horde of grasshoppers. This monument celebrates their heroics with a 16-foot pillar topped

TRIVIA

The most popular tourist attraction in Utah is Temple Square, visited by an estimated 5 million people each year.

TEMPLE SQUARE

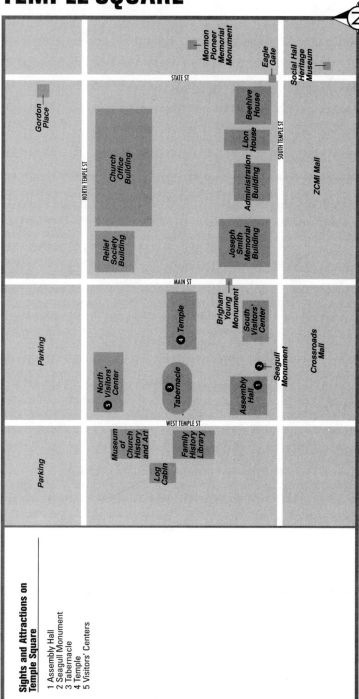

Sights and Attractions on Temple Square

1 Assembly Hall
2 Seagull Monument
3 Tabernacle
4 Temple
5 Visitors' Centers

TRIVIA

The Mormon Tabernacle Choir's weekly network radio show, *Music and the Spoken Word*, is broadcast live every Sunday morning from the Tabernacle on Temple Square. The program began in 1929 and has run continuously for 70 years. It is the oldest nationwide network broadcast in America, heard worldwide through 1,500 radio and television stations. The public is invited, free of charge, to the Tabernacle broadcasts.

with two gold-colored seagulls. The base of the pillar is engraved with pictures of pioneers, seagulls, and the saved crop of grain, and the monument is surrounded by a circular pool of water. Daily 7–10. Free. & (Downtown)

TABERNACLE

There are all sorts of reasons to visit this fascinating building, including its 12,000-pipe organ, its phenomenal acoustics (a dropped pin can be heard from the opposite end of the building), and its interior of pine painted to look like oak. But perhaps the best reason to come here is for the music that can be heard year-round. The world-famous Mormon Tabernacle Choir's Thursday 8 p.m. rehearsals are open to the public, as is the choir's weekly radio program, which is broadcast to a worldwide audience every Sunday morning. Visitors must be seated for the radio performance at 9:15 a.m. Organ recitals are given in summer Mon–Sat at 12 and 2, Sun at 2, and in winter Mon–Sat at 12, Sun at 2. The Mormon Youth Chorus and the Mormon Youth Symphony give concerts on Tuesday and Wednesday respectively at 8 p.m. Tabernacle opening hours vary according to concert times. Free. & (Downtown)

TEMPLE

The Mormon Temple is perhaps Salt Lake City's most famous architectural landmark. Its six magnificent spires form the backdrop for many of the tourism pictures that promote Salt Lake City. A statue of the Angel Moroni, an ancient prophet, sounds his golden horn from the topmost of these spires. Granite for the exterior was quarried in local canyons and ferried through canyon streams to this site. Construction began in 1853 and continued for 40 years. The final tally for the building was $3,500,000. Sacred ordinances of the Mormon Church are performed here, including marriages and baptisms, and only Mormon faithful are allowed inside. (Downtown)

VISITOR CENTERS

There are two visitor information buildings located on opposite sides of the square, and both are filled with volunteers, exhibits, films, and publications describing the philosophies and practices of the Mormon Church. The North Center is easily identified by its two-story exterior glass wall, through which an 11-foot statue of Jesus is seen. The South Center is just inside the south gate. Summer daily 8:30 a.m.–10 p.m., winter daily 9–9. Free. & (Downtown)

DOWNTOWN

ABRAVANEL HALL
123 W. South Temple St.
Salt Lake City
801/533-5626

At first glance the exterior may look modern and stark, but a second look shows that its four-story glass walls reflect the fountain just outside the front door as well as the distant mountains, and act as a frame for a lovely landscape. The interior is filled with multitudes of gold leaf and crystal chandeliers that befit a formal occasion. The concert hall is noted for its fine acoustics, which is fitting because the Utah Symphony performs its season of concerts here, and various other musical diversions take place as well. The hall is named after Salt Lake City's beloved former maestro and founder of the Utah Symphony, Maurice Abravanel, whose portrait hangs in the main lobby. Tours may be arranged by calling 801/323-6855. ふ (Downtown)

BEEHIVE HOUSE AND LION HOUSE
67 E. South Temple St.
Salt Lake City
801/240-2672

These adobe homes may seem out of place on downtown Salt Lake City's busiest intersection, but 150 years ago when Brigham Young built them for his large family, their grandeur dominated the landscape. The homes stand side by side and are connected by a small building that once was Young's office. The doorway of one is decorated by a lion, and a beehive sits on the roof of the other. The interior of the Beehive House has been carefully restored to look as it did when Young and his family lived here. It now serves as a museum where furnishings, books, toys, kitchen items, and clothing from that period can be seen. Tour guides describe not only the physical aspects of the home but also Young's fascinating work ethic, lifestyle, and philosophies. The Lion House is also restored in period decor and is reserved mostly for private parties. A public restaurant called the Lion House Pantry is found in the lower level of the home; it serves wonderful, albeit humble, dishes inspired by original Mormon pioneer recipes (see Chapter 4, Where to Eat). Tours of the Beehive House begin just inside the main entrance approximately every 10 minutes. Summer Mon–Fri 9:30–6:30, Sat 9:30–4:30, Sun 10–1; winter Mon–Sat 9:30-4:30, Sun 10–1; holidays 9:30–1. Free. (Downtown)

BRIGHAM YOUNG GRAVESITE
140 E. First Ave.
Salt Lake City

Some say that this small, nondescript green space is not a fitting tribute for the great Mormon leader. But it is a lovely place, a quiet spot for contemplation in the middle of the busy city. Young is buried here along with several of his wives and his oldest son, and their graves and markers remain simple and dignified. A separate monument is dedicated to William Clayton, author of the hymn "Come, Come Ye Saints," which the pioneers sang during their arduous trek across the plains, and which remains an often-sung and deeply felt song for today's Mormon congregations. Other stones in the yard are dedicated to various Mormon dignitaries. Daylight hours. Free. (Downtown)

CAPITOL BUILDING
Capitol Hill
400 N. State St.

Salt Lake City
801/538-1563

If Utah's imposing statehouse looks familiar, it is because it is modeled after the nation's capitol building in Washington, D.C. It sits atop one of the highest hills in the city and can be seen from all over town. The main rotunda is impressive in size and scope, with a ceiling that reaches 165 feet. To appreciate that height, visitors can find the seagulls painted in the central dome of the ceiling and guess their wingspan (it is six feet but looks to be about six inches). The large paintings that grace the far walls depict the Salt Lake Valley as it looked when the pioneers first arrived (east wall) and how the valley looked one year later planted with grain (west wall). The "gold room" has been the setting for official receptions of presidents and royalty; it can be viewed only from the roped doorway, since its intricate decorations and antique carpeting are too fragile for visitor traffic. Assorted Utah luminaries are depicted in statuary, including astronaut Don Lind, television inventor

Philo Farnsworth, and Mormon leader Brigham Young.

Many of Utah's elected officials have offices here, including the governor, who occupies the west end of the first floor. During January and early February the state legislature is in session, and visitors are welcome to watch the proceedings from upper-level galleries. A lower level has more exhibits, as well as a gift shop filled with Utah-shaped trinkets. Guided tours Mon–Fri 9–4. Self-guided tour brochures also available. Free. & (Downtown)

CATHEDRAL CHURCH OF ST. MARK
231 E. 100 South St.
Salt Lake City
801/322-3400

The Episcopal Cathedral is a lovely old sandstone building. When it was built in 1871, its architecture was meant to resemble the great cathedrals of England. Its buttresses, Gothic arches, stained-glass windows, and bell tower remain a grand tribute to high-church philosophies.

Beehive House, p. 79

Utah Travel Council/Salt Lake Convention & Visitors Bureau

Church volunteers run a food bank for the poor from the parish hall, and the lovely nave is a popular place for classical music concerts. Tours are available by contacting the above number Mon–Fri 10–5. Free. & (Downtown)

CATHEDRAL OF THE MADELEINE
331 E. South Temple St.
Salt Lake City
801/328-8941

Members of the Catholic faith were at one time a rarity in Utah, and their numbers did not become significant until the mining boom began in the late 1800s in nearby Park City. Several of those Catholic miners struck gold, and it was with their fortunes that this fabulous sandstone cathedral was built a century ago. It is worth a close look at the building to find the magical animals that are carved into the walls. The interior took over 20 years to complete and is perhaps most famous for its intricate stained-glass windows, which were specially commissioned from a royal glass cutter in Germany. Beautiful columns, carvings, and murals add to the exalted

atmosphere. The tomb of Bishop Scanlan, who oversaw construction of the cathedral, is beneath the altar. Forty-five–minute guided tours are given Fri 1 p.m. and Sun 12:30 p.m. Free. & (Downtown)

CHRISTMAS BOX ANGEL MONUMENT
Salt Lake City Cemetery
Fourth Ave. and "N" St.
801/532-6267

This monument springs from the pages of an enormously popular book titled *The Christmas Box*, written by Utahn Richard Paul Evans. The fictitious story tells of a mother who grieves the death of her child, and several key scenes take place at the base of an angel monument. The author received thousands of letters from parents who had lost children, so he had the monument built as a place where families could gather and begin what he calls "a healing process." Each year, on December 6, a public candlelight ceremony is held at the monument, and families are invited to leave a white flower at its base. Over a thousand people attend

Roots and Rock

Anyone interested in genealogy knows that the Mormon Church has the largest cache of family history records in the world. These records can be accessed at the Family History Library, just west of Temple Square. The church takes its stewardship of these documents very seriously; so seriously that duplicates of all the research materials are stored in solid granite vaults carved into the walls of Little Cottonwood Canyon. These vaults were built to be able to withstand all catastrophes, even a nuclear attack.

DOWNTOWN SALT LAKE CITY

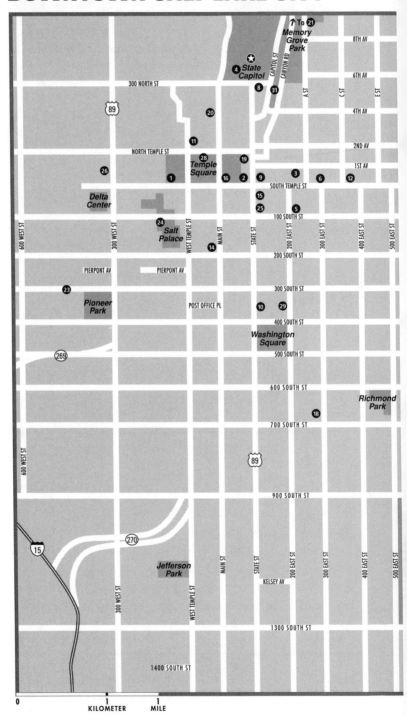

21 To Memory Grove Park

8TH AV

6TH AV

4 State Capitol

8

31

CAPITOL ST

CANYON RD

A ST

B ST

C ST

4TH AV

2ND AV

1ST AV

300 NORTH ST

89

20

11

NORTH TEMPLE ST

28 Temple Square

19

26

1

16 2

9

3

6

12

SOUTH TEMPLE ST

Delta Center

15

25

5

100 SOUTH ST

600 WEST ST

300 WEST ST

WEST TEMPLE ST

24 Salt Palace

MAIN ST

14

STATE ST

200 EAST ST

300 EAST ST

400 EAST ST

500 EAST ST

200 SOUTH ST

PIERPONT AV

PIERPONT AV

300 SOUTH ST

23

Pioneer Park

POST OFFICE PL

10

29

400 SOUTH ST

Washington Square

500 SOUTH ST

269

600 SOUTH ST

Richmond Park

18

700 SOUTH ST

89

900 SOUTH ST

600 WEST ST

270

15

Jefferson Park

300 WEST ST

WEST TEMPLE ST

MAIN ST

STATE ST

200 EAST ST

300 EAST ST

400 EAST ST

500 EAST ST

KELSEY AV

1300 SOUTH ST

1400 SOUTH ST

0   1 KILOMETER   1 MILE

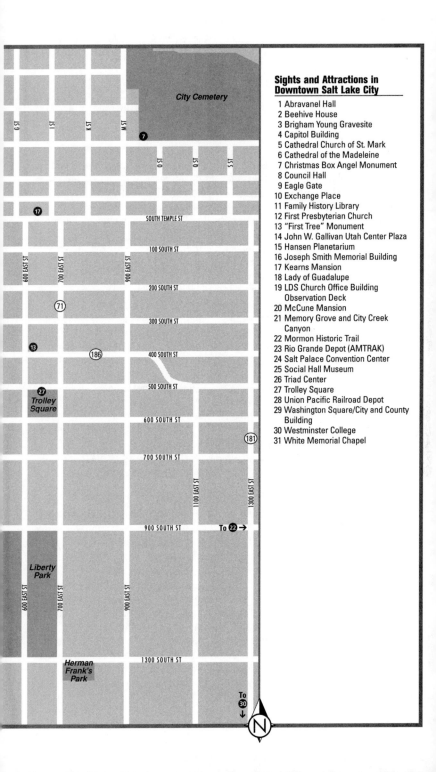

City Cemetery

9 ST
1 ST
K ST
M W

0 ST
0 ST
5 ST

❼

⓱

SOUTH TEMPLE ST

100 SOUTH ST

600 EAST ST
700 EAST ST
900 EAST ST

200 SOUTH ST

⑦¹

300 SOUTH ST

⓭

⑱⁶

400 SOUTH ST

500 SOUTH ST

㉗
Trolley
Square

600 SOUTH ST

⑱¹

700 SOUTH ST

1100 EAST ST
1300 EAST ST

Liberty
Park

900 SOUTH ST

To ㉒ →

600 EAST ST
700 EAST ST
900 EAST ST

1300 SOUTH ST

Herman
Frank's
Park

To
㉚
↓

N

Sights and Attractions in Downtown Salt Lake City

1 Abravanel Hall
2 Beehive House
3 Brigham Young Gravesite
4 Capitol Building
5 Cathedral Church of St. Mark
6 Cathedral of the Madeleine
7 Christmas Box Angel Monument
8 Council Hall
9 Eagle Gate
10 Exchange Place
11 Family History Library
12 First Presbyterian Church
13 "First Tree" Monument
14 John W. Gallivan Utah Center Plaza
15 Hansen Planetarium
16 Joseph Smith Memorial Building
17 Kearns Mansion
18 Lady of Guadalupe
19 LDS Church Office Building
  Observation Deck
20 McCune Mansion
21 Memory Grove and City Creek
  Canyon
22 Mormon Historic Trail
23 Rio Grande Depot (AMTRAK)
24 Salt Palace Convention Center
25 Social Hall Museum
26 Triad Center
27 Trolley Square
28 Union Pacific Railroad Depot
29 Washington Square/City and County
  Building
30 Westminster College
31 White Memorial Chapel

the annual ceremony, although the monument is also visited year-round, and flowers, notes, and candles continually crowd its base. Daylight hours. Free. ♿ (Downtown)

COUNCIL HALL
300 N. State St.
Salt Lake City
801/538-1900
Council Hall shares a similar history with its neighbor, the White Memorial Chapel (described below). Both buildings were old and in the way of downtown construction, but their architectural and historical significance saved them from demolition. Council Hall was built in 1864, and before statehood served as a territorial statehouse, later becoming the Salt Lake City Hall. In the early 1960s it was moved to make way for Utah's Federal Building. Its sandstone bricks were numbered and dismantled, and assembled in an exact reproduction in their new home on Capitol Hill. The building now serves as offices for Utah's Division of Travel Development, and a visitor center is located on the lower level. Summer Mon–Fri 9–6, Sat–Sun 10–5; winter Mon–Fri 8–5, Sat–Sun 10–5. Free. (Downtown)

EAGLE GATE
Corner of State and
South Temple Sts.
Salt Lake City
It is immediately noticeable that this is not a gate but in fact an arch that spans six lanes of traffic. A 6,000-pound bronze eagle perches at the top of the arch, keeping a stern watch on what once marked the entrance to Brigham Young's large estate. The arch and the eagle have been remodeled over the years to accommodate modern traffic, and are now much larger and more sturdy

than their predecessors. The original, carved wooden eagle now resides at the Pioneer Memorial Museum. Free. ♿ (Downtown)

EXCHANGE PLACE HISTORIC DISTRICT
350 South St.
Between Main and State Sts.
Salt Lake City
A hundred years ago the commercial interests of Mormons and non-Mormons were divided enough to warrant separate business districts. Market speculation was the domain of non-Mormons, and a wealthy stockbroker named Samuel Newhouse built the mirror-image buildings that mark the entrance to Exchange Place, as well as the historic Salt Lake Stock and Mining Exchange Building located to the east. Hotels, retail stores, and a park once lined the street, which has been protected by successive occupants and kept mostly in its original state. The buildings now house a popular restaurant called the Lazy Moon, as well as small shops and many offices. All hours. Free. ♿ (Downtown)

FAMILY HISTORY LIBRARY
35 N. West Temple St.
Salt Lake City
801/240-2331
The Family History Library is world-famous for its extraordinary cache of genealogical records. The Mormon Church owns the five-story building, but each year over 800,000 people of all faiths make pilgrimages here to research and record their roots. They hope to find the names and birthplaces, and perhaps even the diaries and personal records, of their deceased ancestors. Hundreds of employees and volunteers are needed to keep

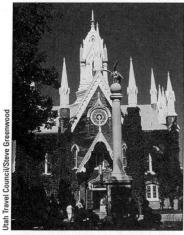

Assembly Hall on Temple Square, p. 76

track of the dense collection of microfilms, documents, and computerized data, which is constantly being updated from sources all over the world. A booklet and a short film educate visitors on how to begin, and a friendly staff answers questions about the more complex aspects of the process. The archives here are intended for the serious researcher; a more casual and much less complicated family search system is found nearby at the Joseph Smith Memorial Building (described below). Mon 7:30 a.m.–6 p.m., Tue–Sat 7:30 a.m.–10 p.m.; closed holidays. Free. ♿ (Downtown)

FIRST PRESBYTERIAN CHURCH
12 North and "C" Sts.
Salt Lake City
801/363-3889
This solemn and simply adorned church is a lovely place to consider the higher planes of existence. Its beamed, Tudor chapel is spare and elegant, and its two circular stained-glass windows are spectacular. The

windows, placed high in the east and west walls, are best seen at sunset, when their extravagant colors are shown to the best advantage. Church services are held Sunday morning at 9 and 11, and live concerts are performed occasionally. Tours on request, Mon–Fri 9–5. Free. ♿ (Downtown)

"FIRST TREE" MONUMENT
Median strip on 600 East St.
Between 300 and 400 South Sts.
Salt Lake City
The story goes that there was but one full-grown tree standing in the arid Salt Lake Valley when the Mormon pioneers arrived in 1847. The story continues that many years ago a marker was placed next to the tree, memorializing this feat of nature. Apparently, soon after the marker was placed, vandals cut the tree down. What can be verified is that a circular monument, imbedded with a fragment of a tree stump, now stands proudly in the middle of this busy street. All hours. Free. ♿ (Downtown)

JOHN W. GALLIVAN
UTAH CENTER PLAZA
36 E. 200 South St.
Salt Lake City
801/532-0459
Part park, part museum, the Gallivan Center likes to call itself "Salt Lake City's living room." The plaza takes up almost an entire city block and is filled with green spaces, oversized art, a winter skating rink/summer pond, a behemoth chessboard, and an amphitheater. Lots of fun activities take place here throughout the year, including free lunchtime concerts in summer, Wednesday and Thursday night festivals in July and August, and fireworks on New Year's Eve. Even when no official function is planned,

a walk through the Gallivan Center is a pleasant respite from the surrounding drone of city life. Year-round 7 a.m.–10 p.m. Free. & (Downtown)

HANSEN PLANETARIUM
15 S. State St.
Salt Lake City
801/538-2104
This historic building used to be the city's main library. Although its exterior remains staid and traditional, inside it is totally Space Age. Fun exhibits upstairs include a moon rock and a fascinating Foucault pendulum. The main attraction is the multimedia star shows, which are shown daily in the domed theater on the main floor. When the lights go out, guests are asked to sit back in their chairs and look up at perfect re-creations of the night sky. Laser rock and other high-tech spectacles are also shown. A nice gift shop sells astronomy-related items. Mon–Fri 9–9, Sat 9 a.m.–midnight. Star shows $4.50 adults, $3.50 children; laser shows before 9 p.m. $6 adults, $5 children; late-night laser shows $7.50. & (Downtown)

JOSEPH SMITH MEMORIAL BUILDING
15 E. South Temple St.
Salt Lake City
801/240-1266
For a century this building operated as the grand Hotel Utah and was a meeting place for the rich and famous. Since 1988 the building has served as office space for the Mormon Church, although its lovely lobby and lower levels remain open to the public. Of interest to visitors is an hour-long film shown in the theater, *Legacy*, which tells the story of the Mormon pioneers' trek across the western United States to

---

Where to Go for Great Views of Salt Lake City

*While Salt Lake City's skyline doesn't boast anything that can be termed a skyscraper, there are several buildings in town tall enough to offer sweeping views of the Salt Lake Valley. The **LDS Church Office Building**, at 50 East North Temple Street, offers the highest perch. Elevators take visitors to the 26th floor, where two viewing areas are located. On a clear day the Great Salt Lake can be seen, as well as all of the Salt Lake Valley and much of the Wasatch Range. The **Joseph Smith Memorial Building**, at 15 East South Temple Street, has valley views from its 10th-floor public areas. **Mulboon's** restaurant, on the 13th floor of the Cavanaugh Olympus Hotel at 161 W. 600 South St., is a great place to watch the sunset while eating dinner.*

---

the Salt Lake Valley. At the back of the lobby is the Family Search Center, where 200 computers are wired to a vast genealogical record system; most visitors are able, within minutes, to print out the names and birthdates of up to six prior generations of family members. Yet another tourist favorite is the 10th-floor viewing areas, with vistas from the east and west sides of the building. Two restaurants are also on this floor.

Building open summer Mon–Sat 8:30 a.m.–10 p.m., winter Mon–Sat 9–9. Viewing of the film is free, but tickets must be picked up in the back lobby or at either of the visitor centers at Temple Square. Visitors should get tickets as far in advance of the desired viewing time as possible, because seats fill up fast. Film times Mon–Sat at 10:30 a.m., and 12, 1:30, 3, 4:30, 6, and 7 p.m. ᪶ (Downtown)

KEARNS MANSION
603 E. South Temple St.
Salt Lake City
801/538-1005
This is the official residence of Utah's governor, and one of the most significant architectural landmarks in the city. It was built in 1902 by Thomas Kearns, who made his fortune in the nearby Park City mines and subsequently served as Utah's senator. Kearns' goal was to build the most elegant and opulent home in the West, and he spent (gasp!) a quarter-million dollars on its construction. The entrance opens to a winding staircase that reaches up three stories. Wild shades of natural woods and marbles create artwork of the floors, walls, and ceilings.The house was one of the first anywhere to boast an elevator, but is perhaps most famous for its huge ballroom, where many official receptions took place. In the 1930s Mrs. Kearns donated the house to the state of Utah. It was restored and remodeled in the 1970s and again, after a fire, in the 1990s. This latest remodeling incorporates fixtures, furniture, and art commissioned from Utah artists. Tours Apr–Nov Tue and Thu 2–4 (last tour at 3:30); enter through east gates. Free. ᪶ (Downtown)

LADY OF GUADALUPE
700 S. 300 East St.
Salt Lake City
Depending on your point of view, this site is either an accident of nature or a divinely inspired miracle. In the mid-1970s, in one of Salt Lake City's small pocket parks, someone noticed the Virgin Mary's likeness in the branch-removed orb of a mature tree. Word spread, and devotees began regular pilgrimages to the tree, bringing candles, flowers, and prayers. A wooden scaffolding now allows close-up views of the Virgin, whose likeness, even for the most cynical observer, is uncanny in its resemblance to accepted icons. The tree's location is easily noticed from the street, as it is always adorned with presents and offerings. All hours. Free. (Downtown)

LDS CHURCH OFFICE BUILDING OBSERVATION DECK
50 E. North Temple St.
Salt Lake City
801/240-2190
Hundreds of visitors every day give thanks to the Mormon Church for reserving space on the 26th floor of this building for public observation decks. The view of the valley in all directions is simply astounding. On clear days hundreds of square miles

of real estate can be seen, as birds and sometimes even airplanes, wing their way in the vast airspaces below. The observation area is accessed by taking an express elevator from the main lobby. Other worthwhile sights here are the lobby murals, which depict scenes from Mormon history, and the beautiful gardens south of the building, which frame the main entrance. Summer Mon–Sat 9–5, winter Mon–Fri 9–4:30. & (Downtown)

McCUNE MANSION
200 N. Main St.
Salt Lake City

This ornate mansion and its expansive grounds command the attention of everyone traveling on Main Street near the Capitol Building. It has been occupied by a number of families and businesses in its 100 years of existence. Its interior is currently closed to the public, but those fortunate enough to have been inside the former home of Alfred and Elizabeth McCune report a number of lovely architectural de-

The Temple, p. 78

Utah Travel Council/Frank Jensen

tails, including intricate flooring and hand-painted friezes. (Downtown)

MEMORY GROVE AND CITY CREEK CANYON
Canyon Rd. /135 E. North Temple St.
Salt Lake City

City Creek has carved a narrow jewel of a canyon through the foothills just east of Capitol Hill, which has been adopted with ferocity by hikers, joggers, and bicyclists. The twists and turns of the canyon's paved road, and a sharp dropoff into the fast flowing creek, prompted city officials to enact safety rules: Pedestrian traffic is always allowed, but cars and bicyclists must take turns on an every-other-day basis. The canyon is located directly above Memory Grove, a larger and more manicured canyon through which City Creek continues its run. Motorized traffic is severely limited in the Grove, which is dedicated to Utahns who have died while defending their country. Its proximity to busy State Street and Capitol Hill makes it a treasured green space in the center of the city. (See also Chapter 8, Parks, Gardens, and Recreations Areas.) City Creek Canyon open daily 8 a.m.–10 p.m. Memory Grove open daylight hours. Free. & (Downtown)

MORMON HISTORIC TRAIL
Begins at This Is the Place Heritage Park
801/533-3500

The much longer and more famous Mormon Pioneer Trail stretches from Illinois to the rim of the Salt Lake Valley, but this trail (actually four trails) picks up where that one leaves off, following the footsteps of the pioneers during the first days after they entered the valley. Historians have been able to trace, within a foot or two, the trails and camps and scout-

An Angelic Setting

The popular television show "Touched by an Angel" is filmed almost exclusively in and around Salt Lake City. Many residents are fond of watching the show to try to name the location sites. The Cathedral Church of St. Mark, the Capitol Building, and many residences were all temporarily spiffed up for their appearance on the small screen, but they remain recognizable to sharp-eyed Salt Lakers.

ing trips of the pioneers. The routes are now mostly overrun by concrete and asphalt, but it is a fascinating exercise to imagine how this valley must have appeared 150 years ago. These trails are not clearly marked from the ground; tracing their paths requires a map available by calling the number above. All hours. Free. (Downtown)

RIO GRANDE DEPOT (AMTRAK)
300 S. Rio Grande
Salt Lake City
801/533-3500
The Rio Grande Depot still retains all of the glamor from its glory days as a bustling transportation center. When standing in the cavernous, now-quiet lobby, it is easy to imagine that a century ago this place was filled with waiting passengers and noisy trains steaming just outside the door. The large arched windows remain, as well as the marble floors and gorgeous second-story balcony. When the importance of the railroads waned, the depot began a decline that was halted in the 1970s when the state of Utah bought the entire building

and grounds for $1. It was later remodeled into offices for the Division of State History, where the general public enjoys a bookstore and historic photo library. The Utah State Historical Society operates a museum in the lobby, and a popular Mexican restaurant, the Rio Grande Café, is located in the northern end of the building. (See also Chapter 6, Museums and Galleries.) Bookstore open Mon–Fri 10–5, Sat 11–3. Library open Mon–Fri 10–5, Sat 10–2. Museum open Mon–Fri 8–5, Sat 1–3. Free. & (Downtown)

SALT PALACE
CONVENTION CENTER
90 S. West Temple St.
Salt Lake City
801/534-4974
The Salt Palace's great girth anchors the west end of downtown's commercial district, and its eccentric glass tower is visible from many blocks away. Used as a meeting space for huge numbers of people, its hallways and rooms are crowded and busy most hours of the day. The 36,000-square-foot ballroom is the third largest in the western United

States: Salt Palace literature claims that 300 Mack trucks can fit in the ballroom at one time. The building also has hundreds of thousands of square feet of exhibit and meeting space. At this writing, plans are being made to expand the Salt Palace's meeting facilities to accommodate even larger convention groups. Its decoration is colorful and bold—the op art carpet, especially, has been the subject of controversy. The Salt Palace houses the offices of the Salt Lake Convention and Visitors Bureau, and an excellent visitor center and gift shop is located on the main floor. (See also Chapter 6, Museums and Galleries.) Visitor center open Mon–Fri 8–5, Sat–Sun 10–5. Free. & (Downtown)

SOCIAL HALL MUSEUM
39 S. State St.
Salt Lake City
801/321-8745
This museum is Greek-like in its homage to the ruins of a once-important edifice. Nothing remains of the original hall, which was built in the 1850s and served as Utah's first theater. The building was torn down in 1921, and its sandstone foundation was buried. A decade ago these remains were excavated. They are now encased in glass and can be viewed either from a street elevator/entrance or an underground passage accessed from the lower level of the ZCMI Center. Historical photos and exhibits line the walls, describing the original building and the important events that took place here. For more information, ask an attendant at ZCMI Mall's lower-level information desk. Mon–Sat 10–9. Free. & (Downtown)

TRIAD CENTER
DEVEREAUX HOUSE

300 W. South Temple St.
Salt Lake City
801/532-1350
The story of this square-block complex, found just north of the Delta Center, is both colorful and complicated. The Devereux is an elegant mansion built in the middle of the last century, and it is one of the oldest still-in-use buildings in the city. It was once the residence of a Salt Lake City mayor, and dignitaries including General William Tecumseh Sherman and President Ulysses S. Grant were entertained in its grand rooms. By the 1970s both the house and the surrounding neighborhood had fallen into decline. Preservationists enacted several fits and starts of renovation, but funding commitments were hampered by fire and egregious asbestos contamination. Just when it seemed the building was doomed, a wealthy Saudi Arabian family bought the block and surrounded the Devereaux with a sleek, cubic structure of bronze reflective glass called the Triad Center, which serves as a center of commerce. The mansion's location suddenly became desirable, and it is now beautifully restored as the Chart House/Devereaux Restaurant. An amphitheater and skating rink are also found on the grounds. Mon–Fri 8–6, Sat 8–1. & (Downtown)

TROLLEY SQUARE
500 S. 700 East St.
Salt Lake City
801/521-9877
Anyone interested in historic architecture, trolleys, or shopping will find this place fascinating. As the name implies, it is a square block that once served as the garage for Salt Lake City's trolley cars. An extraordinary and expensive renovation in the 1970s turned this tangle of

Memory Grove, p. 88

Quonset-shaped, red-brick buildings into an upscale shopping extravaganza. Care was taken to preserve the character of the "trolley barn." The original brick floors remain in place, although they have been glazed to protect their surface. The interior walls remain rough and unfinished, and dozens of original skylights provide natural light. Trolley Square's famous landmark is a huge outdoor water tower, which once held 50,000 gallons of water to be used in case of fire. Several old trolley cars are placed about the grounds, now pressed into service as shops and eateries. In summer an open-sided trolley replica called Old Salty ferries customers between the square and the downtown shopping district. (See also Chapter 9, Shopping.) Shops open Mon–Sat 10–9, Sun 12–5. Restaurants and movie theaters open daily 11–1. ♿ (Downtown)

UNION PACIFIC RAILROAD DEPOT
400 S. West Temple St.

Salt Lake City
This grand depot was once a major transportation center for Salt Lake City, when its block-long edifice marked the western end of town. It was built in 1909, and its beautiful facade is an interpretation of the French Renaissance style. The building is now owned by the state of Utah, and the state's large art collection is stored here. Renovation plans have been hampered by various problems, and currently only a small portion of the building is used as offices for State Museum Services. The Depot figures prominently in the city's future redevelopment plans, and someday the murals and stained-glass windows in its lobby may once again be accessible to the public. (Downtown)

WASHINGTON SQUARE/ CITY AND COUNTY BUILDING
State St. between 400 and 500 South Sts.
Salt Lake City
801/533-0858
One story claims that when the first

party of Mormon pioneers made their way into the valley, they established their first-night campsite here. The area became a public gathering place in the early history of Salt Lake City, and over the years was, by some accounts, used as a site for public markets, circuses, horse trading, and (it is rumored) a cops-and-robbers shootout. In the early 1890s an ambitious construction project was begun that culminated in the still-standing, castle-like edifice, which for its first two decades served as Utah's capitol building. It now houses the seat of Salt Lake City government. Guided tours include a visit to the clock tower and, for the adventurous, a harrowing walk on the roofline catwalk. Tours Tue at 12 and 1. Free. & (Downtown)

WESTMINSTER COLLEGE
1840 S. 1300 East St.
Salt Lake City
801/488-4280
This liberal arts college may be small, with only 27 acres and 2,100 students, but it has a large impact on the community. The public is invited to its regular schedule of lectures by renowned poets and scholars, its concert seasons span the year with a wide range of performers, and its theater season is impressive as well. A number of community courses are offered to non-matriculated students at night and on weekends. The campus has 15 major buildings, including a new library and School of Business. & (Downtown)

WHITE MEMORIAL CHAPEL
150 E. 300 North St.
Salt Lake Ctiy
801/538-3264
When this tiny Gothic Revival church became too small for its

downtown congregation, the Mormon Church dismantled it brick by brick and rebuilt it to its exact origins on Capitol Hill. It now belongs to the state of Utah, and is a popular place for weddings and other gatherings. Prior arrangements must be made to enter the building. & (Downtown)

SOUTHEASTERN VALLEY

SALT LAKE COMMUNITY COLLEGE
South City Campus
1575 S. State St.
Salt Lake City
801/957-3000
Formerly known as a "technical college," SLCC continues to aim its focus on the professional skills, including computer training, aviation mechanics, culinary arts, and much more. The school is Utah's fastest-growing college, with an enrollment of over 45,000 students. Its two main campuses add major buildings almost every year, and both boast state-of-the-art theaters. For information about the Redwood Campus, call 801/957-4111. (See also Chapter 11, Performing Arts.) & (Southeastern Valley)

WHEELER HISTORIC FARM
6351 S. 900 East St.
Holladay
801/264-2241
The Wheeler family lived here for eight decades, planting grain on their 75 acres and operating a successful dairy farm. Thirty years ago Salt Lake County made the wise decision to buy the farm and turn its home, grounds, and outbuildings into a working historic farm and public museum. Since then the city has grown up around the farm, and

its large expanses are now a historic oasis in suburbia. Tours of the Victorian farmhouse, horse-pulled tractor rides, and milking and egg collecting are daily events. (See also Chapter 7, Kids' Stuff.) Farm open Mon–Sat 9:30–5:30. $3.50 adults, $2.50 seniors, $2.50 children. ♿ (Southeastern Valley)

UNIVERSITY AREA

FORT DOUGLAS
500 S. Campus Dr.
Salt Lake City
801/588-5188
This collection of Victorian buildings and expansive lawns found on the east end of the University of Utah was once an active army base. President Abraham Lincoln sent Colonel Patrick Connor here in 1862 to keep on eye on the Mormon settlers, and to make sure that the U.S. mail was not disrupted by local zealots. Connor reportedly took his assignment seriously; enough so that relations between the Mormons and the soldiers were adversarial. In its early days the fort was comprised of thousands of acres, and the army's jurisdiction reached into the future states of Wyoming and Idaho.

Today Fort Douglas has shrunk to a few hundred acres and is owned by the University of Utah. Its cemetery is a fascinating place to visit; German prisoners of war are buried here, as is Colonel Connor and many of his soldiers. There are several other historic sites, as well as a small park and museum. Future plans include retrofitting of the lovely old administrative buildings and officers' homes as athletes' lodging for the Winter Olympic Games of 2002. A walking-tour brochure describing the history and construction of the fort is available at the museum. (See also Chapter 6, Museums and Galleries.) Museum open Tue–Sat 10–12 and 1–4. ♿ (University Area)

HOGLE ZOOLOGICAL GARDENS
2600 Sunnyside Ave.
Salt Lake City
801/582-1631
Salt Lake City is proud of its bona fide, 50-acre zoo, located in the foothills at the far eastern edge of town. Thousands of animals both exotic and familiar live here, many of them in re-created natural habitats. A number of community events and theme days entice the public to walk through its entrance gates to enjoy viewing the animals as well as participating in several hands-on exhibits. A miniature train ride winds through the park, and World of Flight bird shows are scheduled on Tuesday and Sunday. (See also Chapter 7, Kids' Stuff.) Open daily except Christmas and New Year's Day. $5 adults, $3 seniors and children. ♿ (University Area)

THIS IS THE PLACE
HERITAGE PARK
2601 Sunnyside Ave.
Salt Lake City
801/584-8391
One story goes that when Mormon Leader Brigham Young first espied the Salt Lake Valley, he said "This is the right place. Drive on." This park (see Chapter 8, Parks, Gardens, and Recreation Areas), encompasses Old Deseret Village, a fascinating re-creation of everyday life as it was lived in Salt Lake City from 1847 to 1869—the years between the first pioneer settlement and the arrival of the railroad. The idea here is for visitors not just to look at but to actually experience pioneer life. Guests are invited

GREATER SALT LAKE CITY

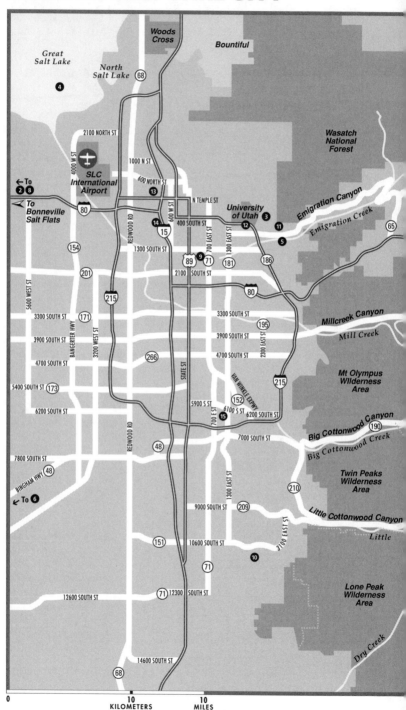

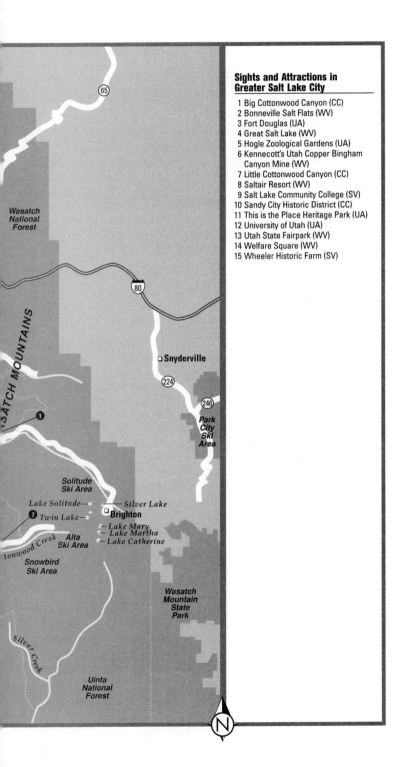

Sights and Attractions in Greater Salt Lake City

1 Big Cottonwood Canyon (CC)
2 Bonneville Salt Flats (WV)
3 Fort Douglas (UA)
4 Great Salt Lake (WV)
5 Hogle Zoological Gardens (UA)
6 Kennecott's Utah Copper Bingham
  Canyon Mine (WV)
7 Little Cottonwood Canyon (CC)
8 Saltair Resort (WV)
9 Salt Lake Community College (SV)
10 Sandy City Historic District (CC)
11 This is the Place Heritage Park (UA)
12 University of Utah (UA)
13 Utah State Fairpark (WV)
14 Welfare Square (WV)
15 Wheeler Historic Farm (SV)

Wasatch
National
Forest

Snyderville

Park
City
Ski
Area

WASATCH MOUNTAINS

Solitude
Ski Area

Lake Solitude
Silver Lake
Twin Lake
Brighton
Lake Mary
Lake Martha
Lake Catherine
Cottonwood Creek
Alta
Ski Area

Snowbird
Ski Area

Wasatch
Mountain
State
Park

Silver Creek

Uinta
National
Forest

*Kennecott's Utah Copper
Bingham Canyon Mine*

801/581-7200

Utah's largest university boasts some impressive stats: 150 years old, 27,000 students from all over the world, 120 undergraduate degree programs and 92 graduate programs, 3,702 faculty members, 280 buildings, 3 major libraries, and a 1,500-acre campus. Its sports teams rank nationally, and its football and basketball stadiums are world-class. The women's gymnastics team has won 10 national championships in the last 15 years. The university boasts a major research hospital, public radio and TV stations, and several theaters, including the professional Pioneer Memorial Theatre and the Marriott Center for Dance. The school is larger than many cities and is vital to Salt Lake City, both economically and culturally.

Research Park is a university-supported collection of about 50 businesses located next to the university campus. Many of these are high-tech, entrepreneurial pursuits, which share research, employees, and technology with the university. These businesses have propelled Utah to the forefront of the computer science, aerospace, and medical and engineering research industries of the United States. Various hours. ⅙ (University Area)

to walk through a "real" village with buildings, stables, pastures, and farms. Every detail, down to sidewalks, ditches, and fenceposts, is historically correct. Volunteers dress in period costume, performing chores and conducting business just as they would have 150 years ago, all the while explaining their activities to visitors. (See also Chapter 7, Kids' Stuff.)

The park also includes This Is the Place Monument, a tribute to the valley's earliest immigrants built in 1947 to commemorate the 100th anniversary of their arrival. A visitor center near the monument has exhibits and a gift shop. Monument and visitor center open year-round 7:30–sunset. Village open Memorial Day–Labor Day Wed–Sat 10–5. $5 adults, $3 seniors and children under 12. Guided tours Mon–Tue 10–5; $3 per person. Special rates and hours offered early spring and fall. ⅙ (University Area)

UNIVERSITY OF UTAH
University and 200 South Sts.
Salt Lake City

WESTERN VALLEY

BONNEVILLE SALT FLATS
Access road off I-80, Exit 4
Wendover
801/977-4300

To picture this place 110 miles west of Salt Lake City, imagine a beach that stretches for as far as the eye can see. But rather than sand, the flats

Kennecott's Utah Bingham Canyon Mine is reputed to be the largest and most productive open-pit copper mine in the world—one of the few manmade phenomena that astronauts can see from space. The mine employs thousands of Salt Lakers and brings millions of dollars to the economy.

are made of sparkling, crystallized salt, left behind several eons ago by a shrinking Great Salt Lake. This is one of nature's true wonders, and its barren, otherworldly beauty must be seen to be appreciated. Passenger cars are allowed to drive onto the Salt Flats; however, high water conditions must be considered, because some months of the year tires will sink in the salt. When conditions are right, the hardness of the salt crystals and the extreme horizontal aspects of the former lakebed have made it a mecca for race-car drivers. In August and September professional race events are held at the flats, and the public is invited to watch. (See also Chapter 10, Sports and Recreation.) All hours. Free. ॐ (Western Valley)

GREAT SALT LAKE
State Park access off I-80, Exit 104
Magna
801/250-1898

Its shimmering expanses of water have no business in the middle of a desert. Its saline depths have bewildered both ancient explorers and modern scientists. This is a lake that has killed off all fish life and allows only off-smelling brine shrimp and flies, along with the odd algae, to breathe in its soft gray water. This is a lake that creates its own weather, grabbing cumulus clouds by the neck and wringing from them stiff

winds and torrential rains. Swimmers bob endlessly, unable to sink in the salty water, and emerge covered with a white crust. This is a lake beloved by relatively few and ignored by most of its metropolitan neighbors.

It is a wonderful place, but perhaps not at first glance. An appreciation of this odd and lonely anomaly, a truly one-of-a-kind feature on the planet, is gained by a slow approach and a careful eye. Raftfuls of helpful literature describing the lake's geology and history are available in Salt Lake City bookstores, as well as the visitor centers located on the lake's south shore and Antelope Island. Great Salt Lake State Park has a 300-slip marina, picnic areas, and rest rooms. A concessionaire at nearby Saltair Resort offers snacks. May–Oct daily 8 a.m.–sunset, Nov–April daily 8–5. Free. - (Western Valley)

KENNECOTT'S UTAH COPPER BINGHAM CANYON MINE
Bingham Hwy. and State Rd. 111
Copperton

This is not an ordinary copper mine: It's the largest manmade excavation on earth! The open-pit mine, dug into the side of the Oquirrh Mountains, is a half-mile deep and 2.5 miles wide, and can be seen from 100 miles away. Six billion tons of rock and ore have been excavated from the site, producing more than 15 million tons of copper, as well as vast supplies of gold, silver, and molybdenum. Due to its girth and history, it's been designated a National Historic Landmark. A visitors center inside the mine has fascinating exhibits and films, and an observation deck allows viewing of the actual mining process. Mid-April–Oct daily 8–8. $3 per car. & (Western Valley)

SALTAIR RESORT
Access road off I-80, Exit 104
Magna
801/250-1308

Saltair's golden turrets rise high and bright above the surrounding desert—their exotic architecture as out of place as the inland sea that forms their backdrop. The current Saltair, 17 miles west of Salt Lake City, is a modernized replica of a pavilion and dance hall built here over 100 years ago. The original Saltair was accessed by trolley car and was a wildly popular place for socializing Salt Lakers in the 1800s. It was destroyed by fire in 1925, and subsequent attempts to regain its former glory have mostly failed. Saltair is a large, single building with a nice gift shop and a funky museum explaining the lifestyle and habits of the brine shrimp, an animal unique to the Great Salt Lake. A rocky trail from its back door leads to the shoreline of the Great Salt Lake. The resort shares an access road with the Great Salt Lake State Park, where camping and beach facilities are located. Summer Mon–Fri 9–6, Sat–Sun 10–7; winter hours vary. $2 per car. & (Western Valley)

UTAH STATE FAIRPARK
1000 W. North Temple St.
Salt Lake City
801/538-8440

The Utah State Fair is held in this large, multi-block area each September. For two weeks its exhibition buildings, animal barns, and expansive grounds come alive with carney acts, classic cars, vendor booths, local produce, quilts, wedding gowns, pigs, cattle, 4-H members, county fair queens . . . and much, much more. Each evening of the fair features a well-known musical act in the Grandstand. The other months of the year are relatively quiet at the Fairpark, but smaller exhibitions and concerts take place year-round, including cat shows, Western art shows, livestock sales, and pro-wrestling events. The coliseum building is a favorite venue for alternative music concerts. Regularly scheduled events include a swap meet at the Market Building Sat–Sun 8–3:30 and a fishing pond for kids Mon, Thu, Fri 4–dusk, Sat–Sun 10–dusk. Fairpark office open Mon–Fri 7–4. Fees vary with events. & (Western Valley)

WELFARE SQUARE
751 W. 700 South St.
Salt Lake City
801/240-7332

The Mormon Church looks after all of its members, supplying food and clothing to those who are unable to provide for themselves. An extensive welfare program is headquartered here, and the grounds include a canning plant, granaries, and storehouses. Cheese is made daily in the on-site dairy, and breadmaking begins each morning at 5. Tours are available by request from 10 to 3 on weekdays; large parties are asked to call ahead. Visitor center open Mon–Fri 10–4. Free. & (Western Valley)

COTTONWOOD CANYONS AND ENVIRONS

BIG COTTONWOOD CANYON
**Access road at 7200 South St.
and Wasatch Blvd.
Sandy**
Big Cottonwood is a glorious, steep-sided granite canyon just a short drive from the center of Salt Lake City. Its winding road is about 13 miles from its beginning to end, and roadside attractions provide not only a scenic drive, but also camping, fishing, and hiking activities. Solitude Resort is located near the top of the canyon, with year-round lodging and accommodations, and skiing and snowboarding in winter. Brighton Resort, another full-service ski and summer resort, marks the terminus of the canyon road. All hours. Free. (Cottonwood Canyons and Environs)

LITTLE COTTONWOOD CANYON
**Access road at 9400 South St.
and Wasatch Blvd.
Sandy**
Little Cottonwood is so named because its length and width are "littler" than its big neighbor to the north. Its steep walls and dramatic elevation rise cannot be belittled, however. From the canyon base of 5,000 feet, passenger cars rise over 3,000 feet over the 10-mile road to the canyon terminus. Near the top are Alta Resort, Utah's oldest ski resort, and Snowbird Resort, both full-service ski resorts famous for the quality of their powder snow. All hours. Free. (Cottonwood Canyons and Environs)

SANDY CITY HISTORIC DISTRICT AND MUSEUM
**8744 S. 150 East St.
Sandy
801/566-0878**
Sandy was first settled as a farming community in the 1860s. A decade later, the nearby discovery of precious minerals turned Sandy into a mining boomtown. Today this formerly quiet suburb of Salt Lake City has become one of the fastest-growing areas in the state. Sandy memorializes its colorful past in its historic district, a designated area of town where old buildings are protected from demolition and exterior renovation. The museum is in the center of Old Sandy, with exhibits both inside and outside. A pamphlet describing a self-guided walking tour of the historic district is available. Museum open Tue, Thu, Sat 1–5. Free. (Cottonwood Canyons and Environs)

6

MUSEUMS AND GALLERIES

Fine arts and cultural pursuits are serious endeavors in Salt Lake City, and support comes not only in the form of generous public subsidies, but also in personal contributions from the highest echelons of church and state. The Utah Arts Council was created in 1899, making Utah the first state with an official public arts entity. Ever since, socially prominent citizens have volunteered their time and money to run the larger museums and public galleries. Their dedication has kept these institutions afloat even through lean economic periods.

The independent galleries and museums are run with the same dedication and energy, but with a more eclectic and less formal flair. These smaller venues often showcase more unusual aesthetic perspectives than do their larger, more established counterparts. The latter are found in the heart of downtown, while the independents are often found further west, in what could be called Salt Lake City's avant-garde district. Though the art shown at the following places comes from a wide range of perspectives, some of them controversial, that very diversity contributes to a lively and healthy arts community.

FINE ART MUSEUMS AND PUBLIC GALLERIES

FINCH LANE GALLERY/ART BARN
Reservoir Park
1325 E. 100 South St.
Salt Lake City
801/596-5000
This renovated building, wedged between tennis courts and a large pub-lic park, has lost any similarity to an actual barn; however, it is still referred to as the Art Barn by many locals. It is operated by the Salt Lake City Arts Council, and a whole host of arty special events, readings, and classes take place here, along with the ever-changing exhibits that may be seen throughout the year. Finch Lane features lesser-known local

artists and prides itself on showing contemporary, provocative art. Mon–Fri 9:30–5, Sun 1–4. Free. &. (University Area)

GLENDINNING GALLERY
617 E. South Temple St.
Salt Lake City
801/236-7555

The Utah Arts Council was the first official arts institution in the country, and since the turn of the century it has collected the work of Utah artists. Its collection now numbers over 1,300 pieces, most of which must be stored out of public view. The Glendinning is a public facility and offers a chance for the arts council to host rotating exhibits from its permanent collection. Traveling exhibits sponsored by the state are also shown here, as well as historical and group shows. The gallery is located in the same Victorian mansion as the offices of the Utah Arts Council; it is named after James R. Glendinning, an early mayor of Salt Lake City. Mon–Fri 8–5. Free. &. (Downtown)

SALT LAKE ART CENTER
20 S. West Temple St.
Salt Lake City
801/328-4201

The Salt Lake Art Center is a much valued, publicly funded community resource where all manner of artistic endeavors are undertaken. The lovely lower-level gallery shows traveling exhibits of major contemporary art and does double duty as a popular setting for weddings, concerts, and performance art. The smaller exhibit rooms upstairs also host traveling shows, with an emphasis on non-mainstream art. Low-cost classes in photography, filmmaking, pottery, and other disciplines are offered, and a wonderful, most-always-open Kidspace is full of enticing (and free) creative projects for the under-10 set. The Salt Lake Film and Video Center is also found here, showing offbeat and often rewarding screenings of films made by local independent artists. Tue–Sat 10–5, Sun 1–5. Free, but donations encouraged. &. (Downtown)

UTAH MUSEUM OF FINE ARTS
University of Utah
101 Art and Architecture Center
Salt Lake City
801-581-7049

About 95,000 people walk through the doors of this publicly supported museum each year, noted as one of the major fine arts institutions in the West. The permanent collection numbers 10,000 works and spans the history of art. The museum's lofty goal is to represent the best of every principal style and period of art throughout civilization. A walk through the many smallish galleries

TRIVIA

Salt Lakers are committed art buyers, perhaps a reflection of the excellent health of Utah's economy. An informal survey taken by *The Enterprise* business newspaper shows sales at local art galleries have steadily increased over the past five years and that the buying trend is for larger and more expensive works of art.

Salt Lake Art Center, p. 101

offers a chronological view of history, representing cultures from all parts of the world. A large room on the museum's west side is reserved for traveling exhibits of local interest. The museum is scheduled to move to much larger and more elegant digs, which are in mid-construction as of this writing. The new building, located just off South Campus Drive, is scheduled to open to the public in spring of 2000. Mon–Fri 10–5, Sat–Sun 12–5; closed holidays. Free. & (University Area)

SCIENCE AND HISTORY MUSEUMS

PIONEER MEMORIAL MUSEUM
300 N. Main St.
Salt Lake City
801/538-1050
This museum is filled to the brim with Mormon pioneer artifacts. First-time visitors might need to take a deep breath when they first walk through the door, as the quantity and layout of the exhibits can be over-

whelming. The museum claims it displays the largest number of artifacts on a particular subject, and no one yet has taken exception. Extraordinary, eclectic, and happily organized collections of quilts, paintings, china, furniture, books, clothing, and much more are on display. The clock and doll exhibits are especially fine. An adjacent carriage house has all manner of transportation items, including the wagon in which Brigham Young was riding when he first entered the Salt Lake Valley. Guided tours of the museum are offered daily. Summer Mon–Sat 9–5, Sun 1–5; winter Mon–Sat 9–5. Free. & (Downtown)

UTAH MUSEUM OF
NATURAL HISTORY
Presidents Circle, University of Utah
200 S. University St.
Salt Lake City
801/581-6927
This museum is a favorite with children, who flock here to see mounted full skeletons of allo-saurus, stegosaurus, and camptosaurus—

dinosaurs that once roamed eastern Utah. A bunch of other really old things are on display, including hands-on (or more likely feet-on) dinosaur footprints, and a mammal exhibit featuring recreated woolly mammoths and cats of prey. A large rock exhibit includes a glow-in-the-dark collection and a simulated mine experience. Utah's earliest Native inhabitants are memorialized through exhibits interpreting their clothes, homes, and tools. Dioramas depict many of Utah's native plant and animal ecosystems. A fun bookstore is located on the main level. (See also Chapter 7, Kids' Stuff.) Mon–Sat 9:30–5:30, Sun 12–5; closed major holidays. $3 adults, $1.50 seniors, $1.50 children; admission may increase during premiere exhibits. ♿ (University Area)

UTAH STATE HISTORICAL SOCIETY MUSEUM
300 Rio Grande St.
Salt Lake City
801/533-3500

This museum is located in the cavernous lobby of what used to be the Rio Grande train depot; most of the rest of the building has been converted to offices for Utah's Division of History. The museum specializes in exhibits depicting Utah's past. A typical display might show mining and railroad equipment, or early medical offices and hospital rooms, or ancient Native tools and clothing. The exhibits are nice, but the wonderful on-site bookstore is the high point of the museum. A visit here is a must for any Utah history buff, who will find an excellent collection of books, as well as maps, posters, games, and trinkets that relate to Utah's past. A walk upstairs leads to a vast picture library, where reproductions of historical photos may be purchased. Mon–Fri 8–5, Sat 10–3. Free. ♿ (Downtown)

SPECIALTY MUSEUMS

CHASE HOME MUSEUM OF UTAH FOLK ART
Liberty Park
900 S. 700 East St.
Salt Lake City
801/533-5760

Isaac Chase built this now-historic home in 1853 and farmed the surrounding acres. By the end of the century the farm was turned into a public green space known as Liberty Park, and in 1984 the old home was remodeled by the Utah Arts Council.

T I P

On the third Friday night of each month, the Salt Lake Gallery Association hosts an informal tour of local galleries, called the "Gallery Stroll." Twenty-four participating galleries, most of which are in the downtown area, open their doors from 6 to 9 p.m. Stroll nights are often teamed with openings and special exhibits, and many galleries serve refreshments. For a list of galleries and a map, call any downtown fine-arts gallery.

Utah artisans designed and installed much of the interior infrastructure, and the result is one of Salt Lake City's most charming museums. Galleries house the state folk-art collection, which represents the work of Utah's various cultural communities. Quilts, saddles, and Native American beadwork are typical of the work displayed. The museum is scheduled for a major structural renovation, but barring construction, a Monday night series each August presents performance art on the museum grounds, featuring ethnic singing, dancing, and poetry. Memorial Day–Labor Day 12–5; weekends only during spring and fall; closed in winter. Free. (Downtown)

FORT DOUGLAS MILITARY MUSEUM
32 Potter St.
Salt Lake City
801/588-5188
Museum headquarters are located in a historic building, but the surrounding grounds of Fort Douglas make up most of the "exhibits." Fort Douglas was founded in 1862 by Abraham Lincoln to protect federal interests from independent-minded westerners. Many artifacts remain in their original placement, including cannons, officers' quarters, and a fascinating cemetery. The museum has permanent and changing exhibits, as well as a 1,500-volume library detailing the history of the armed forces in Salt Lake City. Guided tours of two century-old cemeteries, hand-built reservoirs, and Victorian-era barracks are available, although visitors are free to wander at their own pace. Lectures, films, and gallery talks are scheduled on a regular basis. (See also Chapter 5, Sights and Attractions.) Tue–Sat 10–4. Free. (University Area)

HELLENIC CULTURAL MUSEUM
279 S. 300 West St.
Salt Lake City
801/328-9681
Great numbers of Greek immigrants arrived in Utah during the mining booms of the late 1800s. Their early

Utah Museum of Fine Arts, p. 101

Salt Lake Convention & Visitors Bureau

years in Utah were filled mostly with struggle and sorrow, and many of the displays here reflect their hard times. Household items, toys, photos, and mining tools are shown, as are Greek artifacts. Wed 9–12. Free. (Downtown)

MUSEUM OF LDS CHURCH HISTORY AND ART
45 N. West Temple St.
Salt Lake City
801/240-3310
The LDS Church built this museum just west of Temple Square 15 years ago. Its four levels not only house the church's vast collection of art but also showcase current Mormon artists and their representations of 160 years of cultural history. One large gallery is reserved for classical paintings, another has separate displays holding portraits and possessions of each Mormon Church president. Dozens more exhibits display photographs, household items, tools, paintings, and sculpture from Mormon history. In the plaza outside the museum is a tiny log home in which a brave Mormon family spent the winter of 1847. Mon–Fri 9–9, Sat–Sun 10–7; closed major holidays. & (Downtown)

GALLERIES

A GALLERY/FRAMES INC.
4878 S. Highland Dr.
Holladay
801/277-8401
Fun and fab as well as fine art is sold at this gallery, which doubles as a custom frame shop. The walls and floor space are crowded with the original works of Utah's toniest artists, and a visit here is a lesson in

what's cool. Mon–Sat 10–6. Free. (Southeastern Valley)

APERTURE PHOTO GALLERY
307 W. 200 South St.
Salt Lake City
Photography, and only photography, is shown and sold here, but within that discipline an unlimited range of styles and techniques is on view. Abstract, collage, hand tints, cyanotypes, and silver gelatin images interpret just about every form that can be seen by the human eye. Studies of nature are featured, along with occasional still lifes and portraiture. Mon–Fri 9–5:30, Sat 2–5. Free. (Downtown)

ART ACCESS GALLERY
339 W. Pierpont Ave.
Salt Lake City
801/328-0703
This nonprofit gallery's mission is to provide a means for disabled or underserved artists to mainstream into the traditional arts community. Each year an array of artists apply to have their work shown here, and the result is a gallery filled with a mix of paintings, sculpture, and folk art. The works of respected professionals are placed next to unknown artists, creating "equal access" to commercial success. Although the quality of artwork remains consistently high, the pendulum of styles and media can swing wildly from exhibit to exhibit, making regular visits here an adventure. In late November and December the gallery mounts an excellent holiday show of smaller, lower-cost art. Mon–Fri 10–5. Free. & (Downtown)

CORDELL TAYLOR GALLERY
575 W. 200 South St.
Salt Lake City

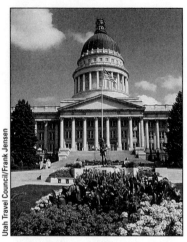

Utah State Capitol Grounds, p. 108

801/355-0333
The owner is a sculptor and his gallery doubles as his studio, which sometimes affords a view of works in progress. Mr. Taylor also shows the works of others, and acts as a sort of incubator for emerging artists. A visit to his gallery is sometimes amusing, sometimes startling, and always worthwhile. Mon–Fri 10–5. Free. (Downtown)

DOLORES CHASE GALLERY
260 S. 200 West St.
Salt Lake City
801/328-2787
Ms. Chase is one of the respected arbiters of the Salt Lake City arts scene, and her gallery, though small in size, has a reputation for showing artists with big reputations. Her changing exhibits often feature group shows, and regular visits afford an education in up-and-coming as well as established talent. The gallery's focus is contemporary art by Utah artists, and exhibits include lithographs, etchings, sculpture, and photography as well as paintings. Mon–Fri 10–5. Free. (Downtown)

GALLERY 56
DAVID ERICKSON FINE ART
260 S. 200 West St.
Salt Lake City
801/533-8245
Owner Dave Erickson has been called a human encyclopedia of Utah art, and the work shown in his gallery reflects his expertise. The acknowledged masters of early Mormon art are represented, as well as respected current artists. Much of the subject theme is landscapes of the state of Utah, and many of the images will look familiar to native Utahns. Mon–Fri 10–5. Free. (Downtown)

LEFT BANK GALLERY
242 S. 200 West St.
Salt Lake City
801/539-0343
The Left Bank is a brash, exciting place where mostly young and unknown artists are free to show whatever they want, without the formalities of a traditional gallery setting. The artists run this cooperative business, and the late hours reflect the need for most of them to keep day jobs. Their art shows a willingness to escape boundaries in both technique and subject matter, and the result can be a lot of fun. Wed–Sat 5–9. Free. (Downtown)

PHILLIPS GALLERY
444 E. 200 South St.
Salt Lake City
801/364-8284
For the past 30 years Bonnie and Denis Phillips have served as Salt Lake City's aesthetic conscience. Their gallery represents an assemblage of exceptional regional artists who represent all media of original

art. Many of the artists have been with the gallery for decades, and many have gone on to establish international reputations. Very expensive as well as affordable pieces, in styles ranging from high-minded to whimsical, are found on all three floors of the gallery. The below-ground level features sculpture and freestanding pieces; the main level hosts eight separate exhibits each year, mostly of single artists; and the upper floor's small rooms offer an eclectic selection. A sculpture court on the upper patio is a wonderful place to simply sit and breathe. Tue–Fri 10–6, Sat 10–4. Free. (Downtown)

ROBIN GREY GALLERY
ALPINE ART & FRAME
430 E. South Temple St.
Salt Lake City
801/355-1155
When Robin Grey took over Alpine Art a few years ago, it was well known as one of the best framing houses in town. He has continued that service, while making a success of the gallery portion of his business as well. Mr. Grey has said his goal is to become Salt Lake City's center for English art, and the gallery walls reflect that with pastoral scenes of the countryside and floral still-lifes. Mon–Fri 9–5. Free. (Downtown)

TIVOLI GALLERY
255 S. State St.
Salt Lake City
801/521-6288
Tivoli's exhibit rooms take up almost 20,000 square feet, and a gallery brochure describes it as "the largest fine arts gallery in the country." An afternoon can easily be whiled away here, strolling among the spacious displays. The art for sale is mostly of the traditional sort; realistic landscapes and sculpture depicting scenery and animals. Artists from all over the world are represented, as well as some of the better-known Utah artists. Tue–Fri 12–6. Free. (Downtown)

WILLIAMS FINE ART
60 E. South Temple St., Suite 150
Salt Lake City
801/534-0331
Clayton Williams specializes in representational, scenic landscapes. A secondary emphasis is on early Mormon art, again, mostly of pastoral scenes. Within the confines of this fairly narrow subject, however, he manages to display a treasure chest of colors and styles and textural qualities. Mon–Fri 12–6. Free. (Downtown)

PUBLIC ART

BRIGHAM YOUNG MONUMENT
Main and South Temple Sts.
Salt Lake City
There are monuments to the famous Mormon leader all over the town, but perhaps the most visible is this gigantic bronze placed in the middle of Main Street. At his feet are a Native American, a fur trapper, and a pioneer family, representing important settling influences in the Salt Lake Valley. The statue was unveiled in 1897 and was commissioned to celebrate Salt Lake City's first 50 years of permanent settlement. Detractors of the monument long complained that the posing of Young was too passive, and a few years ago a larger statue was placed inside the Capitol Building showing a vigorous Young in full stride. All hours. Free. ♿ (Downtown)

CAPITOL GROUNDS
Capitol Hill
400 N. State St.
Salt Lake City
801/538-1563

The spacious lawns and gardens surrounding Utah's capitol building are home to a number of historical monuments. A pink granite edifice east of the capitol commemorates the Mormon Battalion soldiers who were called to fight the Mexican–American War. Two Vietnam Memorials are west of the capitol, and a bronze replica of Chief Massasoit is on the capitol's front steps. A self-guide brochure of the capitol is available just inside the entrances, and tours of the building and grounds are conducted on the hour and half-hour. Mon–Fri 8–5. Free. & (Downtown)

GILGAL GARDENS
749 E. 500 South St.
Salt Lake City
801/359-8813

On first look, Gilgal sculpture garden might seem weird, but on second look it proves to be—well, weird. It's the former backyard of a passionate stonemason who felt compelled to construct his unique vision of religious stories. He's depicted Mormon Church founder Joseph Smith as a 25-ton sphinx, engraved a large granite hill with Old Testament scriptures, and created a sacrificial altar. Dominating the garden is a self-portrait of the stonemason wearing brick pants. To find the entrance, walk down a narrow driveway framed by two private residences. Sun daylight hours. Free. (Downtown)

SALT PALACE
CONVENTION CENTER
100 S. West Temple St.
Salt Lake City

When the Salt Palace was renovated and expanded in the early '90s, five commissioned works of art were included in the architectural plans. The juried pieces were chosen for their representation of Utah's unique environment. To view all of this art, visitors need to circumnavigate the behemoth Salt Palace but should first pick up a

---

Publicly Funded Art

The Scott M. Matheson Courthouse, Utah's largest courts complex, at 450 South State Street, represents an excellent example of publicly funded art. State law mandated that 1 percent of the cost of the $79 million building be set aside for on-site art, and the result is hand-painted ceilings, elaborate stencilings, etched skylights, paintings, and sculpture. Visitors lucky enough to enter the Supreme Court chambers will see a magnificent, two-story mural by V. Douglas Snow titled Capitol Reef, an abstract work depicting the sandstone cliffs of southern Utah.

---

descriptive brochure at the on-site visitors center. Three pieces are oversized sculptures outdoors, with the most noticeable being *Windmills*, which lines the front of the building. Inside, the *56 Views of Salt Lake City* mural illustrates landmarks in town, and the Salt Palace Wall transforms a passageway into a thousand-tiled wonder. For more information call the Utah Arts Council, 801/533-4039. Daily 7–9. Free. &
(Downtown)

THE TREE OF LIFE
I-80 100 miles west of the city

Bravo for the artiste who marches to a different drum. Karl Momen, a native Swede, visited Utah's vast, barren west desert in the 1970s and was inspired to create the *Tree of Life* (also known as the *Tree of Utah*). His gargantuan, twisted-metal vision can be seen for many miles in all directions, since the surrounding desert offers no trees or structures or any other sort of visual competition. The *Tree* keeps a lonely vigil just north of the freeway. Uneducated auto travelers are left to wonder just what the vertical mass, with its house-sized "berries," is all about. Momen hopes someday to add dozens more sculptures to the site, creating a "garden" for his "tree." All hours. Free. &
(Western Valley)

7

KIDS' STUFF

Utah's population is among the youngest in the nation, and the number of children per family is among the highest. These statistics add up to a whole lot of children looking for something to do. These kids are in luck! Salt Lake City is flanked by mountains to the east laced with canyons that provide fishing, hiking, camping, and general good times. The expanse west of town is laid bare by desert and saltwater—a geology that provides one-of-a-kind adventures. Rock hounding, sailing, and wildlife watching are among the possibilities. Both the mountains and the desert are located close enough to Salt Lake City's urban center that an afternoon wilderness getaway always within reach.

The life of the mind is encouraged in a variety of youthful settings. Nature museums, art centers, theater, and libraries are in rich supply, many offering multi-day camps and workshops. Sports centers swell with youngsters during the summer months, offering bowling, minigolf, batting cages, and the ever-popular laser tag. Shopping is a passionate pastime for older kids, and Salt Lake City's malls are fitted with a number of teen-trendy outlets.

Kids of all ages, from toddlers accompanied by parents to teens who pretend adults don't exist, can find experiences from the rugged to the readable within their own Salt Lake City neighborhoods.

ANIMALS AND THE GREAT OUTDOORS

BIG AND LITTLE COTTONWOOD CANYONS
**Access from 7200 South St. and Wasatch Blvd.
Sandy**

These two canyons are both major geologic phenomenons, with distinct scenery and geologic formations. It is probably remiss to list them under the same heading, however their physical proximity, as well as their scenic and recreational associations, have a singular appeal to children.

Both canyons have two ski resorts near their terminus: Brighton and Solitude in Big Cottonwood and Snowbird and Alta in Little Cottonwood. The resorts vary in terrain and elegance, yet all have excellent snow and special ski programs for kids. Cross-country ski facilities are especially child-friendly in Big Cottonwood Canyon, at the Solitude Nordic Center. In warm weather, both canyons also have plenty of fishing, camping, and picnic areas that are popular with small children.

Hiking can be treacherous in these steep, hard-rock canyons, however there are several easy hikes for kids. One of the most famous is the Donut Falls/Cardiff Fork hike in Big Cottonwood. The turnoff road is about nine miles up the canyon, and the actual hike is about one mile round-trip. The hike's end leads to—yes—a donut-shaped rock with water spewing from its donut hole. In Little Cottonwood a child-friendly hike is Cecret Lake in Albion Basin. The basin is world famous for its springtime array

Kids can learn to snowboard near Salt Lake City.

Utah Travel Council/Frank Jensen

of wildflowers, and its trailhe found at the very end of the up the road from Alta Resort. Parking is at the Albion Basin campground, and signs to Cecret Lake are clearly marked. The lake was named by a spelling-challenged miner, and its craggy mountain location is a beautiful—though often populated—end to this hike. (See also Chapter 5, Sights and Attractions, and Chapter 10, Sports and Recreation.) All hours. Rates vary for camping and skiing activities. (Cottonwood Canyons)

HOGLE ZOOLOGICAL GARDENS
2600 Sunnyside Ave.
Salt Lake City
801/582-1631
Over a thousand animals live inside this park-like preserve, segregated into zones replicating their natural habitats. Orangutans and gorillas are found in the Great Apes compound, butterflies are in the Tropical Garden, zebras are in the African Savannah, and so on. In Discovery Land, kids can burrow in a knoll or imitate lizards in a desert. A 30-minute free-flight bird show is scheduled regularly from May through September, and a child-sized train makes a loop around the zoo every so often. (See also Chapter 5, Sights and Attractions.) Summer daily 9–6, spring and fall daily 9–5, winter daily 9–4:30. $5 adults, $3 children. & (University Area)

LIBERTY PARK
500 E. 900 South St.
Salt Lake City
801/972-7800
This huge green space near the center of Salt Lake City is a dozen destinations in one and is a popular gathering spot for families year-round. In winter the gentle hills are

A survey by the U.S. Bureau of the Census shows that Utah takes first place in most of the "young population" categories. The state ranks first in the percentage of population under age 5 and in the percentage of population age 5 to 17. Not surprisingly, Utah has the youngest median age in the country—26.8 years old, compared to the national average of 34.6 years old.

perfect for sledding and cross-country skiing. Several large playgrounds are outfitted with swings and slides, and in warm weather a mini-amusement park sets up shop with a carousel, various kiddie rides, and a refreshment stand. The Children's Garden is of interest to older kids who enjoy the climbing/play areas and multistory slides. The large duck-filled pond is a nice place for a stroll, either on foot or via the paddleboats that are sometimes available for rent. A swimming pool here and tennis courts are open to the public. A truly unique fountain is found in mid-park; it re-creates the Wasatch Mountain waterways that feed into the Salt Lake Valley. The water runs down the "canyons," across a "valley," and then pools into the "great salt lake;" it is at the same time a geography lesson and a great place to cool off. (See also Chapter 8, Parks, Gardens, and Recreation Areas.) Daily 6–11. Tickets for amusement park rides about $1 each. ♿ (Downtown)

TRACY AVIARY
589 E. 1300 South St.
Salt Lake City
801/322-2473
The aviary is found inside the confines of the above-described Liberty Park, but its programs and exhibits deserve a listing of their own. Visitors might need to search for the entrance of this walled compound (on the west side of the park) and pay a small fee. But inside is a wonderful world of all things birdly. The rare and the common, the long-legged and non-winged, the exotic and the hairless can be seen by strolling the meandering pathways. Most birds are caged, and descriptions of their preferred habitats and patterns are posted. Wonderful bird shows are presented several times each day during the summer as aviary staff take turns showing off the power and finesse of their favorite birds, including eagles, hawks, and parrots. Most of the show birds came to the aviary either sick or injured, and though they are now healthy, they are not fit to return to the wild. Various other programs for kids are offered during the summer months. Summer daily 9–6, winter daily 9–4:30. $3 adults, $1 seniors, $1.50 children. ♿ (Downtown)

MUSEUMS AND LIBRARIES

BEEHIVE HOUSE
67 E. South Temple St.
Salt Lake City
801/240-2672
Many of Brigham Young's small chil-

Sugar and Spice and Everything Nice . . .

In the 1850s when Brigham Young and his large family lived in Salt Lake City, the duties and regimens for boys were very different from those of girls. These differences are reflected at the Beehive House, the home Young built in 1854. The boys rose early and left to work outdoors all day; thus, their rooms are fairly spartan. The girls' lives revolved around home life, and they spent much time indoors. Their rooms are much larger, sunnier, and more beautifully decorated than those of their brothers.

dren lived in this former home, now a museum that re-creates the life of early Mormon settlers in Salt Lake City. Modern-day children are provided a fascinating look into the past and an opportunity to contrast the affluence of today with the more difficult lot of the pioneers. The children's rooms here have been made to look just as they did in the 1850s, complete with original dolls, spinning tops, and other toys. Bedrooms show the carefully crafted furniture made especially for small people, and actual bedding and clothing are laid about. Young's children were schooled at home, and their books and desks remain in place. A mercantile, which was operated out of the Youngs' back door, sells horehound candy to youngsters, who tend to immediately appreciate the modern joy of refined sugar. Tours of the Beehive House begin just inside the main entrance approximately every 10 minutes. (See also Chapter 5, Sights and Attractions.) Summer Mon–Fri 9:30–6:30, Sat 9:30–4:30, Sun 10–1, winter Mon–Sat 9:30–4:30, Sun 10–1; holidays 9:30–1. Free. (Downtown)

CHILDREN'S MUSEUM OF UTAH
840 N. 300 West St.
Salt Lake City
801/328-3383
Over 80 exhibits are found within the expanses of this colorful and friendly museum, all of which disguise a learning experience inside a fun activity. Everything here is hands-on, including a grocery store, a wheelchair experience, and a basketball court with NBA aspirations. One of the newest exhibits is named after one of Utah's geologic wonders: Nine Mile Canyon creates a mini-version of the real thing with a military fort, flash floods, native animals, and a petroglyph wall. Birthday parties are popular and affordable here, and special programs such as clay sculpting, dance workshops, and "learning about your insides" are scheduled six days a week throughout the summer. ♿ Mon–Sat 9:30–5, Fri to 8. $3 adults and children. ♿ (Downtown)

HANSEN PLANETARIUM
15 S. State St.
Salt Lake City
801/538-2104

A generous donation by George T. Hansen bought a star projector for Salt Lake City, and by 1965 a first-rate planetarium was open to the public. Three floors of exhibits include a moon rock, heliostat, and dozens of interactive, spacey activities. Inside the domed planetarium, an ever-changing array of star shows explores the cosmos with light and sound and simulated space flight. Popular laser music concerts are offered most nights, including "Laser Aerosmith" and "Laser Zeppelin." The planetarium sponsors a series of star parties, where experts, with the aid of huge telescopes, help novices find the moon, planets, and neighboring galaxies. (See also Chapter 5, Sights and Attractions.) Mon–Fri 9 a.m.–9 p.m., Sat 9 a.m.–midnight. Star shows $4.50 adults, $3.50 seniors and children; laser concerts before 9 p.m. $6 adults, $5 seniors and children; late-night laser concerts $7.50. ঔ (Downtown)

OLD DESERET VILLAGE
This Is the Place Heritage Park

2601 Sunnyside Ave.
Salt Lake City
801/584-8391
Old Deseret Village is a carefully researched and implemented re-creation of pioneer life in the Salt Lake Valley from 1847 to 1869, the years when the greatest numbers of Mormon pioneers emigrated here. Homes, stores, farms, schools, and churches are laid out in the style of a village. Much pioneer-era fun can be had at the village. Ride a wagon, see adobe bricks being made with mud and bare feet, witness Civil War battles reenacted, and dance in the social hall. Guides dressed in period costumes lend an authenticity to the activities and tell stories of pioneer days.

A restaurant, ice-cream parlor, and bookstore conduct 1990s-style commerce, and an outfitter offers custom wagon and sleigh rides and chuckwagon dinners. Special events are scheduled throughout the year, including sheep shearing, adobe brickmaking, quilting, planting, and harvesting. Pioneer Christ-

Days of '47 Parade, one of many kid-oriented celebrations in Salt Lake City

Utah Travel Council/Frank Jensen

mas Tours feature the sale of old-fashioned crafts. (See also Chapter 5, Sights and Attractions.) Memorial Day–Labor Day Wed–Sat 10–5; $5 adults, $3 seniors and children under 12. Guided tours Mon–Tue 10–5; $3 per person. Special rates and hours offered early spring and fall. & (University Area)

SALT LAKE ART CENTER'S KIDSPACE
20 S. West Temple St.
Salt Lake City
801/328-4201
The Salt Lake Art Center is Salt Lake City's primary public art gallery, and one of its missions is to educate and encourage the next generation of art lovers. To this end Kidspace was founded, with the goal of providing hands-on arts and crafts activities that expand the perception and knowledge of the adult exhibits located elsewhere in the gallery. Separate workstations allow children to individualize their creations, and staff are available with support and supervision. Adults are asked to remain with children, and Kidspace welcomes those over five years of age. Wed–Fri 1–4, Sat 10–4, Sun 1–4. Suggested donation $2 adults, $1 children. & (Downtown)

SALT LAKE CITY LIBRARIES
209 E. 500 South St. (main branch)
Salt Lake City
801/524-8200
Salt Lake City's public library system has six locations. All are found within residential neighborhoods, except for the main branch, which is in the city/county complex downtown. To apply for a library card, simply sign a membership card (parents, rather than children, are encouraged to apply). The libraries all have exten-sive selections of children's books, tapes, and videos, and story times and other activities are scheduled throughout the year. Hours vary. Free. & (Downtown)

UTAH MUSEUM OF NATURAL HISTORY
Presidents Circle, University of Utah
200 S. University St.
Salt Lake City
801/581-6927
A dinosaur talks to children who throw quarters into its gaping jaws. Birthstones are explained, fluorescent rocks shine, and other minerals light up at the touch of a button. Woolly mammoths live upstairs, as do two full-sized allosauruses and lots of dinosaur skulls and footprints. Native American clothes and tools are housed in glass cases, and coyotes, mule deer, and cougars are displayed in their natural habitats. On some days kids can grind corn between rocks or grow mold in a Petri dish. A yearlong series of classes for kids interprets nature in myriad ways. (See also Chapter 6, Museums and Galleries.) Mon–Sat 9:30–5:30, Sun 12–5. $3 adults, $1.50 seniors and children. (University Area)

WHEELER HISTORIC FARM
6351 S. 900 East St.
Murray
801/264-2212
The Wheelers lived here during Victorian times and farmed the surrounding acres. Their way of life is re-created daily for the benefit of visitors. See farm animals, butter churning, gardening, and more. In warm weather, tours of the farmhouse and wagon rides are given every half hour, and in late afternoon children are invited to participate in milking cows and gathering

Wheeler Historic Farm, p. 115

Utah Travel Council/Frank Jensen

eggs. In October the woods surrounding the farm become haunted, and a popular (and scary) tour of the grounds is offered. During the winter holidays the same acreage is transformed into a fairyland with hundreds of thousands of tiny lights. Country dancing is popular for older kids on weekend nights. (See also Chapter 5, Sights and Attractions.) Mon–Sat 9:30–5:30. $3.50 adults, $2.50 seniors and children. & (Cottonwood Canyons and Environs)

THEATER

CHILDREN'S DANCE THEATRE
University of Utah
Salt Lake City
801/581-7374
Lauded as the only professional all-children's dance troupe in the western United States, Children's Dance Theatre has provided modern dance performance experience for Utah children for over 50 years. Children ages eight through 18 are chosen, through audition, to participate in the

program, and each spring a full-scale performance is mounted, complete with original choreography by the children and their teachers. The dance's storyline is generally taken from a book or fable with special meaning for children. The company performs in Utah schools throughout the year, and once a year selected students travel out of the country to dance, acting as Utah cultural ambassadors. Ticket prices vary. & (University Area)

CITY REP'S FAMILY THEATER
638 S. State St.
Salt Lake City
801/532-6000
Children love these professional-style performances of their very favorite plays, such as Jack in the Beanstalk, and Princess and the Pea. Everything centers around kids in this live theater facility. There are matinee and early-evening performances of the solid, child-centered rotation of plays. City Rep hosts a theater school, auditions local kids for all of its plays, and is a favorite destination for grade

school field trips. Evening performances and Sat matinees. Tickets about $7. (Downtown)

DESERT STAR PLAYHOUSE
4861 S. State St.
Murray
801/266-7600

Melodrama is the primary activity here, and patrons are encouraged to boo and cheer, and laugh and cry at appropriate times during the performance. Spoofs are popular, and it seems there is nothing too important to be laughed at, including Dracula, *Star Trek*, and *Phantom of the Opera*. Patrons can purchase pizza and soda for in-performance dining, and popcorn is free. For some performances, matinee and late-night showings are added to the roster. Mon, Thu–Sat 7 p.m.–10 p.m. $10 adults, $6 children. ♿ (Southeastern Valley)

STORES KIDS LOVE

THE CHILDREN'S HOUR BOOK & TOY STORE
928 E. 900 South St.
Salt Lake City
801/359-4150

Make-believe is the primary subject matter here, and the clients prefer their reading material in the form of a bedtime story. This small, cozy store is filled with beautiful books, including the best of the new authors and illustrators as well as re-

workings of the classics. Gifts, jewelry, clothing, and stuffed animals are also sold here. (Downtown)

FLYING COLORS
931 E. 900 South St.
Salt Lake City
801/532-2529

Anyone can create a masterpiece at Flying Colors. This is a store crammed with unfired, unglazed ceramics just waiting to be turned into unique treasures. Children can choose from a number of undecorated ceramic items, including bowls, plates, clocks, and animal figures. Next, they can choose from a wide palette of paint hues. Then the fun begins as the ceramics come alive with designs and color. Finished items are left to be fired by professionals, and a few days later can be picked up and used at home. ♿ (Downtown)

HIJINKS
Trolley Square
700 E. 500 South St.
Salt Lake City
801/531-7434

Kite fanatics are in heaven here, as almost anything that will fly unaided through the air is available for sale. There are also gadgets of all kinds—puzzles, yo-yos, magic cards, model planes, and dozens more mind-bending objects which blend science, math and creativity. Kids are encouraged to test out the

TRIVIA

Lagoon Amusement Park is one of Utah's top 10 most-visited tourist attractions, with over 1.5 million visitors each year.

equipment, and the store is usually a beehive of small people happily engaged in intellectual pastimes. ⚬ (Downtown)

STRING BEADS
2223 S. Highland Dr.
Salt Lake City
801/487-1110
This is a store for all ages, but children are catered to with special birthday-party packages and occasional low-cost, for-kids-only weekend workshops. Young girls especially love the excellent variety and selection of beads displayed in myriad small boxes and arranged in rainbow-like waves of color. A friendly staff seems to always have the time and patience to help a child complete a necklace or other ornament. A second location is at 7186 South Union Park. ⚬ (Southeastern Valley)

FUN CENTERS

LASER QUEST
7202 S. 900 East St.
Holladay
801/567-1540
Even the smallest children seem to enjoy putting on a special glow-in-the-dark vest, grabbing a laser gun, and setting out on a quest for other humans. This contest is either a modern upgrade from the game of tag or a societal comment on television violence, depending upon one's point of view. Nobody gets hurt, however, "hits" result in a mild vibration in the vest. Players are divided into equal-stature teams for each 15-minute game. Mon–Fri 2–10, Sat 12–12, Sun 2–10. $6 per person, per game. (Southeastern Valley)

Eccles Dinosaur Park, p.119

Utah Travel Council

RAGING WATERS
1200 W. 1700 South St.
Salt Lake City
801/972-3300
Raging Waters calls itself "Utah's Beach," and with good reason. There are dozens of ways to get wet here, and the acres of surrounding greenspace offer a chance to picnic, sunbathe, and people-watch. The terrifying-for-some multistory slides are the main attractions. There are also water activities for the less adventurous, including a huge pool that simulates wave action and a gentle water playground set aside for little kids. May–Sept daily 10:30–7. $13.95 adults, $9.95 children. ⚬ (Western Valley)

ROCKREATION SPORT CLIMBING CENTER
2074 E. 3900 South St.
Holladay
801/278-7473
The walls are faux, undulating sandstone fitted with all manner of plastic grips and impossible toe-

holds. The floor is a soft bed of black rubber shoe soles. The activity is rock climbing, for both novices and experts, and everybody has fun under the supervision of trained professionals. Birthday parties and large groups are accommodated with special rates. Mon–Thu 12–10, Fri–Sat 10–8, Sun 12–6. Day passes $14 adults, $9 children; rental equipment extra. (Southeastern Valley)

UTAH FUN DOME
4998 S. 360 West St.
Murray
801/263-2987
The Fun Dome is always full of lights, color, activity . . . and kids, lots of kids. There are acres and acres of indoor fun here, with an unending list of things to do. Thirty bowling lanes go mod with neon colors and rock music. A huge skating facility features disco ball lights and theme go-rounds. Laser tag, a gravitron, hundreds of video games, 3-D movies, a double-decker carousel,

Rockreation Sport Climbing Center

© James W. Ray

bumper cars, go-carts, and an indoor roller coaster are just the beginning of the activities list. Birthday parties are extremely popular here, and special packages and group rates are available. Mon–Thu 12–11, Fri 12 p.m.–1 a.m., Sat 11 a.m.–1 a.m. Each activity is separately priced, with a $5 per ticket average for skating, mini-golf, and laser tag.♿ (Southeastern Valley)

WITHIN A SHORT DRIVE

ECCLES DINOSAUR PARK
1544 E. Park Blvd.
Ogden
801/393-3466
Over 100 dinosaurs, flying reptiles, and other prehistoric creatures are hidden amongst the winding paths and foliage of this fun outdoor theme park. Sounds emanate from hidden speakers, adding a realistic touch to this current home of fierce creatures who stalked and hunted a hundred million years ago, and some are portrayed in the act of devouring their prey. A "Jurassic Fantasy" playground features dino slides and swings, and a learning center has daily arts, crafts, and game activities. A gift store and restaurant are found near the entrance. Apr–Oct Mon–Sat 10–8, Sun 12–6. $3.50 adults, $2.50 seniors, $1 children. ♿ (45 minutes north of Salt Lake City)

LAGOON AMUSEMENT PARK
375 N. Lagoon Lane
Farmington
801/451-8000
For most Salt Lake City children, it wouldn't be summer without a trip to Lagoon. This is the premiere amusement park in the Intermountain West,

and one of Utah's top tourist attractions, with over a million visitors each year. Lagoon has over 125 attractions, including the hair-raising Colossus and Wild Mouse roller coasters, and a white-water tubing experience called Rattlesnake Rapids. An entire section of the park is given over to very small people, with slow and gentle rides. Another park area , Pioneer Village, re-creates a Wild West town, complete with gunfights and other regularly scheduled cowboy shenanigans. Lagoon A Beach Waterpark has a dozen thrilling waterways. Entertainers wander the midway, and melodramas are featured most summer nights. A full-service campground and RV park are on-site. June–Aug Mon–Thu 11–11, Fri 11 a.m.–midnight, Sat 10 a.m.–midnight, Sun 11–10:30. May and Sept weekends only. Day pass $25.95. &
(20 minutes north of Salt Lake City)

8

PARKS, GARDENS, AND RECREATION AREAS

One reason the Mormon pioneers loved the mountains that surround the Salt Lake Valley is that their steep, rugged peaks kept this a private place, discouraging casual visits from the rest of the world. A century later, those same mountains are still appreciated for their solitude and privacy, but now they offer shelter from the hectic pace inside the valley below. The major canyons rising from Salt Lake City into the Wasatch Range provide a wealth of recreational opportunities for Salt Lakers year-round. Some of the best hiking, fishing, camping, bicycling, and skiing in the world are only a few minutes drive from the center of town.

The large green spaces inside the city proper, however, can be counted on one hand. The existing parks were planned earlier in the century, and the fast and unprecedented growth of Salt Lake City in the last few decades left planners at a loss for new park space. A plan was developed for "pocket parks"—a series of small spaces in the middle of residential neighborhoods where people can enjoy the outdoors close to home. These parks are now located all over the city, often on corner lots, and are usually outfitted with playground equipment and tree-shaded benches.

BIG COTTONWOOD CANYON
7200 South St. and Wasatch Blvd.
Holladay
801/943-1794
If ancient gods created the world, they were showing off when they made Big Cottonwood. The terrain here is tough and steep and its canyon floor is traced by a river that can't make up its mind which way to go. Views upward show sheer granite cliffs one moment,

then a turn in the road reveals gentle, high-mountain meadows. At the top of the canyon are two ski resorts, Brighton and Solitude, both of which offer food and lodging services year-round. Hiking, biking, and rock climbing are practiced daily here. No dogs are allowed in this watershed area. Year-round. Free. (Cottonwood Canyons and Environs)

**BRIGHAM YOUNG
HISTORIC PARK
State St. and Second Ave.
Salt Lake City**
This park is dedicated to Salt Lake City's pioneer heritage and has a number of unusual attractions. A statue of a mother tending a crop of vegetables and flowers sits along the banks of an irrigation ditch. A paddlewheel turns under the weight of a stream, and large sandstone rocks create barriers to a cool green space below. Free one-hour concerts sponsored by the Mormon Church are held here Tue and Fri nights in July and Aug. Year-round. Free. & (Downtown)

**CITY CREEK CANYON
Bonneville Blvd.
Salt Lake City**
City Creek is a much-appreciated treasure—a natural area above the state capitol building just a few minutes from the center of downtown Salt Lake City. The canyon is one of the major incisions in the Wasatch Range leading into the Salt Lake Valley, and its original "scissors," City Creek, continues to roar down the canyon almost year-round. Other highlights are a fairly apparent display of wildlife and plenty of vegetation. The canyon is accessible to hikers every day, and to motorists and cyclists on an every-other-day rotation. (See also Chapter 5, Sights and Attractions.) Daily 8 a.m.–10 p.m. Free. & (Downtown)

Keeping Canyon Waters Clean

Several of the Wasatch Front canyons east of Salt Lake City have major stream flows that supply drinking water to the valley below. These watershed canyons have special use restrictions to protect the cleanliness and access of the water supply. Big Cottonwood, Little Cottonwood, and upper City Creek Canyons are off limits to dogs and horses, and lower City Creek Canyon restricts car traffic. Swimming is not allowed in any of the canyon streams, and campers must stay at least 200 feet away from a water source. Visitors should use the toilet facilities located at most major trailheads, and, of course, carry out all litter.

CITY CREEK PARK
State St. and Second Ave.
Salt Lake City
801/972-7800

For decades City Creek was totally enclosed once it left its canyon home. City Creek Park changed all that when it was built a few years ago, showcasing the waterway that once flowed across Salt Lake City's primary business district. The creek runs though a series of cement diversions, and seating areas and walkways are positioned to catch the best views of the water and mountains to the east. Year-round. Free. ♿ (Downtown)

City Creek Park

DIMPLE DELL REGIONAL PARK
10400 S. 1300 East St.
Sandy
801/493-5473

Dimple Dell is found near the base of Little Cottonwood Canyon, and its views of the splendid Wasatch Front are unparalleled. The wide green spaces are used for league games and practice, and the picnic areas here are popular for family reunions. In winter the sloping hills are perfect for sledding and cross-country skiing. Year-round. Free. ♿ (Cottonwood Canyons and Environs)

EMIGRATION CANYON
Sunnyside Ave. (850 South) and
3000 East St.
Salt Lake City

Emigration is one of the major canyons that cuts through the Wasatch Mountains and pushes into the Salt Lake Valley. It is famous as the route taken by the Mormon pioneers when they made their final descent into the Salt Lake Valley. Its walls are mostly taken up with private housing; however, the following recreation areas are lo-

cated just above and below the canyon proper:

This Is the Place Heritage Park is just north of the base of the canyon. It commemorates the pioneers and other early Salt Lake Valley inhabitants and is named after Mormon Leader Brigham Young's words when he first saw his new home: "This is the right place. Drive on." (See also Chapter 5, Sights and Attractions.)

The Shoreline Trail is a hiking and biking trail that follows the shoreline of ancient Lake Bonneville; fossilized remnants of the shoreline can occasionally be seen from the trail. One of its access areas, just east of the Heritage Park, is reached directly from Sunnyside Avenue.

A favorite spot for Frisbee throwers and picnickers, Rotary Glen is a large grassy space just to the south of the canyon's base. The covered pavilion at Rotary is available by reservation only, 801/972-7800. The cost is $30.

Donner Park is a bit further south from Rotary Glen, in the middle of a residential area. Its manicured grounds hold playground equipment and playing fields, and it affords a wonderful city view.

Little Mountain is found by traveling all the way up Emigration Canyon. Its large parking lot is the first open space after a series of U-turns that mark the top of the canyon. This area is popular with bicyclists in summer, sledders and tubers in winter.

All areas open year-round. Free. (University Area)

FAIRMONT PARK
2245 S. McClelland St.
Salt Lake City
801/972-7800
Visitors can usually tell when they are nearing Fairmont by the number of ducks waddling through the surrounding streets. A lovely stream runs through the park (home of the wandering ducks) and picnic tables line its bank. Fairmont has one of the few large public pools in a city park, as well as acres of green space, often filled with soccer players and pickup games of ball. Year-round. Free. (Southeastern Valley)

Millcreek Canyon, p. 126

Utah Travel Council/Frank Jensen

GLACIO PARK
9400 South St. and Wasatch Blvd.
Sandy
Residents ought to thank the visionary who set aside this small plot of land to be protected from the housing developments that today crowd ever closer. At the base of Little Cottonwood, Glacio is a nature trail with signs along the way that explain the geology and fauna of the Wasatch Mountains and the Cottonwood Canyons in particular. Walking its trails, visitors will find it almost possible to believe that major roadways are not just a few feet away. ఉ (Cottonwood Canyons and Environs)

GREAT SALT LAKE STATE PARK
Access road off I-80, Exit 104
Magna
801/250-1898
Some years the park offers camping, but currently its primary activities are beachcombing, swimming, picnicking, and watching the myriad species of birds that stop at the lake for food and rest. Sailing is enormously popular on the lake that never freezes (its salt content is too high), and a boat ramp and 300-slip marina is open year-round. Drinking water and restrooms are provided. The park is 17 miles west of Salt Lake City. Year-round. Free. ఉ (Western Valley)

INTERNATIONAL PEACE
GARDENS
Jordan Park
1000 S. 900 West St.
Salt Lake City
801/972-7800
Ethnic pride takes on a new dimension here. Several dozen individual gardens are laid about, each representing the homeland of a group of Utah immigrants. A stroll through the grounds shows a Dutch garden with

The equivalent of a bird's-eye view of the Wasatch Mountains is found in the middle of Liberty Park. A unique water sculpture mimics, in miniature dimensions, the topography of the mountains and the canyons, and water runs a course identical to the real canyon streams. A flat cement space at the base of the sculpture is meant to symbolize the Salt Lake Valley, and a pool beyond, which is the final resting place for the stream water, is meant to be the Great Salt Lake.

a windmill, a Japanese garden with a footbridge, a Norwegian garden with a mermaid . . . and the list goes on. Volunteers tend the gardens, and it appears that they take pride in this horticultural expression of their nationality. Seasonal hours. Free. ♿ (Western Valley)

JORDAN RIVER STATE PARK
1084 N. Redwood Rd.
Salt Lake City
801/533-4496

This nontraditional park is a wonderful resource for Salt Lakers, who have the opportunity to follow the narrow, windy shoreline of the Jordan River for almost five miles, heading in both south and north directions from 1000 North and 1700 West. Its primary amenity is the asphalt path which runs along the river, used by joggers, bicyclists, and skaters. Put-in and take-out points for canoe trips and floaters are usually equipped with restrooms and picnic tables and are found at 1700 South, 800 South, and Cottonwood Park. The park also has a golf course and a model airplane facility. Year-round. No charge, except for the model airplane facility, which is $4 for a day permit. ♿ (Western Valley)

LIBERTY PARK
1100 S. 600 East St.
Salt Lake City
801/972-7800

Liberty is Salt Lake City's central park, an entire block of green space near the center of the city, given over to public recreation. A full-sized public pool is here, as well as tennis courts, playgrounds, picnic areas, a children's park, amusement rides, a first-class aviary, and a large duck pond. The park is a popular place for festivals and concerts in warm weather, and its gentle hills are perfect for sledding in winter. Year-round. Free (amusement rides and aviary charge a nominal fee). ♿ (Downtown)

LITTLE COTTONWOOD CANYON
9400 South St. and Wasatch Blvd.
Sandy
801/943-1794

This ten-mile natural wonder is extremely narrow at its base, and its run is fairly straight, thanks to a fast-moving, ancient glacier. Peaks rise sharply on either side of the paved road, rising to over 11,000 feet in several places. Hiking is extremely popular in the canyon, and there are many excellent trails. Two major ski resorts, Alta and Snowbird, are found at the top of the canyon. Both offer food service and various entertainments during all seasons of the year. The fields of wildflowers in spring and summer and the mountainside fall leaf colors are simply stunning. Visitors who wish to remain in their cars are rewarded with spectacular views, and this road has been named as one of Utah's official scenic byways. Year-round. Free. (Cottonwood Canyons and Environs)

MEMORY GROVE
Canyon Rd. and Second Ave.
Salt Lake City
801/972-7800
This lovely park is hidden in the midst of the downtown area, and hundreds of motorists pass its perimeter each day, many probably never guessing that a refuge of solitude and nature are nearby. The grove is beautifully manicured with trails, stairs, and walkways, and City Creek runs in controlled order through its central green space. Monuments to Utah's war dead are located in select areas, lending a solemn and formal atmosphere. Cars are not allowed into the grove. Year-round. Free. & (Downtown)

MILLCREEK CANYON
3600 South St. at I-215
Holladay
801/943-1794
Millcreek is one of the major canyons in the Wasatch Mountain Range that terminate in the Salt Lake Valley (four others are described in this chapter). Its uproad is literally minutes away from a populated area; just a half-mile farther along, the urban sprawl below is hidden from view. The Boy Scouts have established large private campgrounds in the area, and there are two very nice restaurants here, but the rest of the space is open to the public. A number of hiking trails branch off from the main road; many are groomed and some are appropriate for beginners. There are some restrictions placed on bicycle use. Fall leaf color is especially beautiful in this canyon. In winter the upper paved road becomes a popular cross-country ski trail. Year-round. $3 per car. (Southeastern Valley)

MOUNT OLYMPUS
WILDERNESS AREA
Wasatch Blvd., just north of
Tolcats Canyon
Holladay
801/943-1794
Mount Olympus rises high on the eastern edge of Salt Lake City. Its peaks are often shrouded in clouds, and its name is taken from the

T I P

Hikers and campers are advised to always check with administering agencies before heading out on public lands. Trails may look deceptively easy at the beginning, but rugged terrain and difficult conditions hidden ahead can leave a hiker stranded. There are several excellent outdoor guides to the Wasatch Front area in local bookstores. Their use is highly recommended.

International Peace Gardens, p. 124

legendary mountain where gods and goddesses hid themselves from their subjects below. The Wilderness Area was established by Congress in 1984, and it is much bigger than the actual mountain. Its 16,000 acres reach to Millcreek Canyon on the north and Big Cottonwood Canyon on the south. Camping and hiking are especially valued here, as there are so many other use restrictions on this fragile ecosystem. No motor vehicles, hang gliders, or bicyclists are allowed. Part of the area is watershed, and camping and pet restrictions apply. There are many hiking trails in the area; some are easy and most are hard. Guidebooks are recommended, and are sold at most sporting-goods stores in the area. Year-round. (Southeastern Valley)

PIONEER PARK
300 S. 300 West St.
Salt Lake City
801/972-7800
In pioneer times this large expanse of green was the scene of socials and concerts. Today, however, it is mostly a place to avoid, especially after dark, with an ever-present crowd of inhabitants engaging in what might be illegal activities. Perhaps Pioneer's location just east of the railroad tracks is responsible for its demise. In the last few years a number of stylish retail shops and hotels have located on the perimeter of the park, and their presence might bring about a safer atmosphere. The park does shine on Saturday mornings in the fall, when the best farmer's market in the city sets up shop, selling all manner of produce, cut flowers, and small gift items. Free. ♿ (Downtown)

RED BUTTE GARDEN AND ARBORETUM
University of Utah
300 Wakara Way
Salt Lake City
801/581-5322
This is a wonderful place to get lost amid 16 acres of manicured gardens and paths and a surrounding 150 acres of natural area. The sculptured flower beds are laid out in themed gardens, including a Japanese

gazebo, a water-lily garden, an oak tunnel, and a large field of wildflowers. Four miles of groomed trails lead visitors through the grounds, and a visitors center and gift shop is found near the parking lot. May–Sept daily 9–8, Oct–Apr Tue–Sun 10–5. $3 adults, $2 seniors and children, free to all Mon. ♿ (University Area)

SUGARHOUSE PARK
1300 E. 2100 South St.
Salt Lake City
801/972-7800

A hundred years ago this area was on the far reaches of town, and officials chose these gentle rolling hills as the site for Salt Lake City's prison. It served that purpose until well into this century, but the prison was finally torn down to make room for a much-used park and recreation area. Sugarhouse has several large playgrounds, open spaces that are often filled with soccer and volleyball teams, a pond filled with ducks, and acres of hills that are perfect for massive games of tag. In winter, the park's steepest hills are hugely popular as sledding hills. Year-round. Free. ♿ (Southeastern Valley)

TWIN PEAKS WILDERNESS AREA
Holladay
801/943-1794

This is seriously rugged country, marked by high peaks and narrow canyons. It is bounded on either side by Big and Little Cottonwood Canyons. For 15 years it has been protected by Congress from heavy use and all forms of development, and its pristine qualities remain intact. All sorts of land use restrictions apply, including no motor vehicles, bicyclists, or pets; however, hiking and camping are unequaled. There are virtually no easy hiking trails here, and most are difficult, especially when the terrain becomes rough at higher elevations. Year-round. (Cottonwood Canyons and Environs)

9

SHOPPING

Salt Lake City is an island of urbanity floating in a sea of rural life. Surrounded by ranches and farms, wilderness areas and desert expanses, Salt Lake City is the only shopping mecca serving a huge but sparsely populated area. This happy circumstance has given the city the shopping advantages of much bigger metropolitan areas. People from all over the West come to shop for things that cannot be found between Denver and Las Vegas.

The rural surroundings and cowboy influence in Utah enriches Salt Lake City shopping in other ways. Shopping for native stones, such as topaz and turquoise, is rewarding at a number of small jewelry shops in town, as is the large number and high quality of wrought silver items handmade by Native American craftspeople. Western wear is another unique feature of shopping in Utah. For patrons who want the "real stuff" as well as those who are looking for a fashionable pair of cowboy boots, there are a number of choices to be found.

SHOPPING DISTRICTS

Ninth and Ninth

This funky array of shops is somewhat comparable to Manhattan's SoHo district—only much, much smaller and not nearly as hip. The dozen or so shops that spread out from the intersection at 900 East and 900 South reflect a concentration of diversity not found elsewhere in Salt Lake City. There are a couple of good coffeehouses, an art cinema, and a good bakery, as well as an eclectic mix of independent ventures run by owners with a variety of interests.

CAHOOTS CARDS AND GIFTS
878 E. 900 South St.
Salt Lake City
801/538-0606
The store is aptly named. Look for gag and other funny items. The store is filled to the brim with small items—toys, household decorations, pictures, and lots and lots of cards. Check any prudish tendencies at the door; much of the stock is racy, some graphically so. (Downtown)

CHAMELEON ARTWEAR
875 E. 900 South St.
Salt Lake City
801/363-6463
A casual onlooker might call this a hippie store, but closer inspection shows Chameleon to have some sophisticated merchandise among its tie-dyed clothing. Shoppers are treated to a wonderful, slowed-down, incense-scented experience. Shop for loose, comfortable clothing, jewelry set with semiprecious stones, gifts, and knickknacks. (Downtown)

CUMMINGS STUDIO CHOCOLATES
679 E. 900 South St.
Salt Lake City
801/328-4858
First-time patrons have a hard time believing that so many different types of gourmet chocolates and candies exist on the planet, let alone in one small store. The long glass counters hold a hundred small islands of confections—light and dark, filled and rolled and covered with every imaginable sweet thing. Cummings is famous for the freshness and quality of its sweets, which are all handmade in small batches. (Don't miss the chocolate-covered strawberries and raspberries!) (Downtown)

RANDY'S RECORD SHOP
157 E. 900 South St.
801/532-4413
Randy is one of the last of the breed of true music lovers who run small, independent shops. His passion is clearly evident to anyone who walks through the door—vinyl, and lots of it. Used records are carefully crammed into bins that cover and surround the floor space. Randy is often found talking with fellow vinyl-heads about their latest rare acquisitions. He also has a smattering of tapes and new CDs and one of the best used CD collections in town. (Downtown)

SCENTSATIONS LOTIONS AND OILS
865 E. 900 South St.

TRIVIA

A sure way to discover how long a Salt Laker has lived in town is to mention some of the retail shops that were household names a mere generation ago. Makoff's, Castleton's, and Auerbach's were all locally owned, upper-end clothing and department stores named after their founding families. They have all gone the way of the dinosaur, closing their doors after being unable to compete with powerful national chains.

Salt Lake City
801/364-0168
This bright and cheerful shop makes its own massage oils, bubble bath, bath salts, soaps, body creams, and facial products. Patrons choose an item and then add one or a combination of scents if desired. An extensive array of other products can be found here as well, including relaxation and meditation enhancers, exfoliators, and special children's products. Gift items are beautifully wrapped for no additional charge. (Downtown)

TAI DO MARKET
422 E. 900 South St.
Salt Lake City
801/363-5474
Tai Do is an authentic Chinese market patronized by a mostly Chinese clientele. Gourmands of all ethnic persuasions, however, will find new and exciting food products here, and the casual window-shopper will find a visual feast. The rice aisle has seemingly a hundred different choices, as do the aisles for soy sauce and sesame oil. Hard-to-find fresh herbs and vegetables are here, as well as unusual types of fresh fish. (Downtown)

WESTERN RIVERS FLYFISHER
1071 E. 900 South St.
Salt Lake City
801/521-6424
Most weekend days a cadre of fly fishers can be seen on the front lawn, receiving instruction and practicing casting techniques. Inside awaits all manner of fly-fishing gear, accessories, recreational clothing, and a small bookstore. Fly fishers love this store, of course, but their relatives and friends also appreciate it as the perfect place to buy a gift. Equipment for both stream and saltwater is sold,

and a year-round guide service is offered. (Downtown)

Business District

Salt Lake City's central business district is a mall shopper's dream. Two huge malls, ZCMI and Crossroads, face off at the corner of South Temple and Main Streets, both filled with major department stores and specialty boutiques that can corral patrons for days. Downtown's non-mall shops are mostly locally owned and independently operated, and offer a carefully chosen and unique array of merchandise for the discriminating shopper.

BENNION JEWELERS
59 S. Main St.
Salt Lake City
801/364-3667
Lovely, lovely jewelry is found here, and everything is personally hand-picked by a member of the Bennion family. The settings tend toward the tasteful and refined, and the stones toward the big carats. Pearls are a specialty, from the palest to the delicately pastel, many in unusual settings. Semiprecious stones are sold as well, wound with gold and silver into beautiful styles. Service is reliably excellent. (Downtown)

BENTLEY SQUARE
ZCMI Mall, lower level
36 S. State St.
Salt Lake City
801/359-7006
The store is literally a square that has been divided into 160 separate cubicles, each operated by a separate artisan who sells his or her own handicrafts. Stroll up and down the narrow aisles to peruse thousands of items, including dolls, jewelry,

T-shirts, candles, jarred food, dried flowers, holiday ornaments, baby blankets, and much, much more. Bentley Square calls itself a craft boutique, but the first-time visitor might call it a craft extravaganza. A second location is in Kearns (801/966-6919). (Downtown)

BROWN-EYED SUSAN
425 E. 100 South St.
Salt Lake City
801/355-8650
Housed in a stately old mansion, Brown-Eyed Susan sells the loveliest clothing imaginable, mostly in children's sizes. The real Susan carefully chooses all of the items in her store, and many of the clothes, shoes, hats, and coats are imported from Europe. Prices reflect the quality and style found here. Regular patrons don't mind paying $85 for a tiny, flannel-lined coat, $300 for a fabulous, mini-sized, crushed velvet party dress, or $75 for lovely leather slip-ons. The basement level is reserved for sale items, and sometimes real bargains can be found. These truly beautiful items manage to make any child look positively angelic. (Downtown)

EC-LEC-TIC
380 W. Pierpont Ave.
Salt Lake City
801/322-4804
The owner of ec-lec-tic is a whiz on the estate-sale circuit, and her shop is filled with a little bit of everything. Fab antiques and secondhand objects both large and small fill the large, multi-roomed store, including paintings, wonderful furniture, vintage clothing, jewelry, and housewares. A café that sells sandwiches and coffee is in the northwest corner of the store. (Downtown)

ELEMENTE
363 W. Pierpont Ave.
Salt Lake City
801/355-7400
Yahoo, Elemente! This is one of the biggest and best consignment stores in town, specializing in furniture suites, paintings, outdoor furniture and anything else that catches the owners' eye. It could be said that the primary style is '50s kitsch, but many objects defy classification. The stock is always changing; a look around the cavernous interior is bound to yield something new. A basement holds the junkier items that can be had at super-bargain prices. (Downtown)

MORMON HANDICRAFT
ZCMI Mall
36 S. State St.
Salt Lake City
801/355-2141
Mormon Handicraft is a destination unto itself for many visitors. The quilts, linens, toys, and gifts sold here are all lovingly hand-stitched,

Trolley Square is home to several interesting shops (p. 141).

Utah Travel Council/Frank Jensen

and no two of the 9,000 items in stock are alike. The store was founded in the Depression era, and its purpose has remained the same for 60 years: to create a means for Mormon church members to supplement their income, and also to preserve the traditional pioneer crafts. Store highlights include wonderful women's and girls' nightgowns and one of the best bolt-fabric selections in town. The handmade lace and homemade quilts are exquisite. Weekly quilting classes are offered. (Downtown)

O.C. TANNER
20 E. South Temple St.
Salt Lake City
801/532-3222
Just the sight of an O.C. Tanner gift box can send many women reeling with joy. They know that what is inside will be unique and gorgeous (and probably expensive). O.C.'s is one of the classier jewelry shops in town, with an opulent selection of the usual finery, including to-die-for diamond rings. A section of the store is set aside for gifts, silver, and china. At holiday time the street-level windows are famous for their theme displays. (Downtown)

U.S. OLYMPIC SPIRIT STORE
Crossroads Mall
50 S. Main St.
Salt Lake City
801/364-9994
Salt Lake City will host the Olympic Winter Games of 2002, and locals can already buy officially licensed Olympic merchandise. The five-ringed logo adorns T-shirts, hats, jackets, mugs, and much, much more. Every purchase goes to support the Games and the Olympic athletes. Other locations are at Trolley Square

(801/595-8045) and Park City (435/655-7597). (Downtown)

Sugarhouse

Located just south of downtown, tiny Sugarhouse has become one of the most interesting areas in town, with a mix of big stores (a four-story Barnes and Noble) and little (tattoos and antiques). Through several large renovations, it has managed to keep its lovely streetscape, and window-shopping is still an enjoyable activity. There is also a city library here, as well as several excellent restaurants.

BLUE BOUTIQUE
1080 E. 2100 South St.
Salt Lake City
801/485-2072
The large street-facing windows make a bold display of the Blue Boutique's wares—racy, lacy lingerie for women. The colors, styles—and uses—vary widely, but the merchandise has a common theme of sensuality. And believe it or not, once inside, even timid patrons have a blast picking out an "outfit." (Southeastern Valley)

CACTUS AND TROPICALS
2715 S. 2000 East St.
Salt Lake City
801/485-2542
This is a wonderful place for a plant lover to get lost. Wild, exotic species are everywhere, flowering indiscriminately and uncoiling otherworldly displays of flora. Unusual pots and garden ornaments are here, as well as practical tools and plant enhancers. (Southeastern Valley)

LIBERTY HEIGHTS FRESH
1100 E. 1300 South St.
Salt Lake City

801/583-7374

Liberty Heights' small building fits right in with its residential neighbors, and stands out only because of the ever-changing displays of colorful produce and flowers that spill out of its garage doors each day. The emphasis here is on fresh, organic foods, produced on small farms or made by hand in kitchens and bakeries. The canned and jarred foods are lovely, and feature mostly gourmet oils, vinegars, pastas, and condiments. (Downtown)

UINTA GOLF
560 E. 2100 South St.
Salt Lake City
801/487-8233

Golf is the only language spoken here. A huge selection (company literature says the largest in the country) of brand items is offered, generally at discount prices. All of the expected golf paraphernalia may be purchased, as well as unusual accessory gifts that will mystify even avid golfers. Demo clubs are available for rent. (Southeastern Valley)

WOOLY WEST
1417 S. 1100 East St.
Salt Lake City
801/487-9378

This shop is dedicated to the serious knitter, and usually a few of them are hanging around, practicing their craft and discussing the finer points of perl. The yarn that lines every conceivable wall space constitutes a work of art—gradations of colors that build and crescendo into stunning palettes. The variety of textures is amazing as well. Classes are taught by experts and are available most of the year. (Downtown)

Holladay

The Holladay area was once Salt Lake City's rural suburb, but no longer. Its fields and farms are now covered with homes and small businesses. There is no central shopping district (other than the Cottonwood Mall), and the spread-out retail scene requires some initiative. But the adventurous and determined shopper will find a number of gems hidden in the business areas of this part of town.

BELLE MAISON
4884 S. Highland Dr.
Holladay
801/272-8003

Belle Maison is about pampering oneself, from the heavenly lotions and scented soaps, to the beautifully packaged foods, to the English and French antiques. Wise patrons will succumb and purchase something from this luxurious store located in a lovely former house. (Southeastern Valley)

REI
3285 E. 3300 South St.
Holladay
801/486-2100

REI, near the base of three major Wasatch Front recreation areas, does a booming business providing high-quality equipment to sports enthusiasts. A two-story rock climbing wall is just inside the front door, and just beyond it are cases and racks of rock climbing equipment. Ski gear and clothing take up a lot lof space, and a special room has recently been built to house bicycle sales and maintenance. The rest of the sports are represented as well. (Southeastern Valley)

Downtown Antiques

The Salt Lake Valley has half a dozen pockets of antique stores. An excellent example of this kind of clustering is found near the downtown business district, in the 300 South and 300 East area. Located among hippie clothing stores and small law offices, these generally small antique stores are usually crammed to the gills with fab stuff. **Anthony's Antiques**, *801/328-2231, is the Papa Bear of the group, with a huge space made up of small rooms filled with French furniture and impressive paintings.* **Salt Lake Antiques**, *801/322-1273, also deals in large furniture items, albeit with a more eclectic selection.* **Thomson and Burrows**, *801/521-0650, features small, carefully chosen pieces, such as perfect lamps and heavy silver.* **Carmen Miranda's**, *801/359-7741, is just plain fun, with a kitschy selection of jewelry and home decor.* **Antoinette's**, *801/359-2192, has exquisite estate rings favored by nontraditional brides.* **Briar Patch Antiques**, *801/322-5234, is a wonderful bramble of china and glassware and jewels, and upstairs, at* **Arsenic and Old Lace** *(same number), is an equally wonderful selection of linens and lace.* **Copper Cowboy**, *801/328-4401, sells almost anything of the Old West, and* **Olympus Cove Antiques**, *801/532-1070, offers full and partial sets of china.*

RICHELLE'S AND DUSTIN'S DESIGNER CLOTHING AND SHOES
4699 S. Highland Dr.
Holladay
801/272-3111
Richelle not only manages to fit a large women's-wear section in her building, she has also made room for a men's section and a full-service spa. For women, the shoes are the thing here—beautiful, unusual, and dressy styles that are surprisingly reasonably priced. The clothing for both men and women is sophisticated, in a bold and colorful way. (Southeastern Valley)

STATEMENT BOUTIQUE
3981 S. 700 East St.
Holladay
801/268-2639
The statement made here is young and fun and chic. The small store is a full-sensory delight of color and

texture and exquisite perfumes. Patrons should plan to stay a while, because the store is as much art gallery as clothing store, and the merchandise should be viewed with a thoughtful eye. Men's and women's clothes are sold, as well as jewelry and collectibles. (Southeastern Valley)

OTHER NOTABLE STORES

A A CALLISTER CORP
3615 S. Redwood Rd.
West Valley City
801/973-7058
Giddyup. Cowboys and cowgirls shop here, for clothing as well as all sorts of horse equipment and tack that would puzzle most city folk. This store is authentic—no imitations here. The hundreds of boots, hats, shirts, and suits are all high-quality merchandise. Service is excellent. (Western Valley)

CHALK GARDEN
Trolley Square

ZCMI Center Mall, p. 141

700 E. 600 South St.
Salt Lake City
801-521-0885
First there is the antique and estate jewelry—five cases full of gorgeous jewels; some eccentric, some encrusted, and all gorgeous. The brooches and rings are mostly old, while the earrings are mostly new. The selection is constantly changing, and some jewelry lovers make it a point to visit once a week. Then there are the clothes—small rounders and short shelves placed all about, arranged by color and style, and filled with delectable designer outfits. Most of the merchandise here is pricey, but budget shoppers can usually find a beautiful item or two to take home. (Downtown)

DESERET INDUSTRIES
743 W. 700 South St.
Salt Lake City
801/579-1200
Sixty years ago the Mormon Church created the Deseret Industries thrift stores and began accepting castoffs and donated items, which workers refurbished and sold at discount prices to the public. Today there are more than 46 stores spread throughout the western U.S., selling used . . . everything. A walk through the jumbled aisles at any "D.I." is an adventure in both retail and archeology, sometimes revealing fabulous goods and sometimes not. The Mormon Church hires many physically challenged workers to sort and process the donated items—a large percentage of these workers are able to learn the necessary skills to find other jobs. (Western Valley)

EVOLUTION SKI COMPANY
1435 S. State St.

Salt Lake City
801/972-1144

This small, gutsy company has made a national name for itself producing custom skis by hand, one pair at a time. Not only is the finished product a great ski, but customers who so desire can designate their own ski graphics, which appear on the top side of the finished product. Company logos as well as personal artwork can be incorporated into the ski design, producing a truly one-of-a-kind set of skies. Factory tours are available. (Western Valley)

MISCHIEVOUS
559 S. 300 West St.
Salt Lake City
801/530-3100

Mischievous' ads promise to put some "spark back into life," and the store offers to light that spark with lotions and massage oils, adult toys, leather wear, men's and women's lingerie, and more. The merchandise may be too provocative for some, but for others a visit here is a fun and off-the-wall experience. The cards, gifts, and T-shirts hover between tasteful and not-so-tasteful. (Downtown)

Q STREET FINE CRAFTS
Second Ave. and "N" St.
Salt Lake City
801/359-1899

The owner has assembled a stable of artists and artisans who create wonderful things expressly to be sold at this shop. There is no real categorization for the stock, other than that it is one-of-a-kind and artsy. Hand-blown crystal, watercolors, exquisite jewelry, photographs, household items, and welded iron furniture might be found one day,

and a new bunch of things will be here the next. (Downtown)

QUILTED BEAR
145 W. 7200 South St.
Midvale
801/566-9382

Crafting is a major sport in Utah, and devotees of the art take both its practice and purchasing very seriously. The Quilted Bear provides a haven for the crafters, selling literally thousands of handmade items from its cavernous interior. For-sale items are chosen through a jury system, and local artists are invited to submit their wares. Merchandise ranges from the practical to the decorative (and include everything imaginable that can be made with two hands). The Hungry Bear restaurant is found within the store. Additional Quilted Bear locations are in Provo, Ogden, Boise, and Las Vegas. (Cottonwood Canyons and Environs)

ROCKPICK LEGEND CO.
1955 N. Redwood Rd.
Salt Lake City
801/355-7952

Rockpick is a good, old-fashioned rock shop found right in the middle of suburban sprawl. Its selection of fossils, beads, gifts—and, yes, rocks—makes for a fun and educational shopping experience. There are plenty of affordable rock-like things to purchase, as well as some rare minerals and gems. (Western Valley)

T P GALLERY
252 S. Main St.
Salt Lake City
801/364-2961

High-quality, authentic Native American jewelry and Southwest-inspired art is sold here. Many of the pieces are brought directly from the tribal areas, chosen for the superiority of their craftsmanship. T P is indeed a gallery—a fun place not only to buy but to just look at hundreds of beautiful things. (Downtown)

UTAH WOOLEN MILLS
59 W. South Temple St.
Salt Lake City
801/364-1851
Utah Woolen Mills is somewhat of a legend in town. Five generations of a family have owned the store for almost 100 years, and during that time its men's and women's clothing selections have not succumbed to fads, never wavering from classical, tailored, and traditional styles. Most clothes fall into the dressed-up category, and women's fashions include Scandinavian-made clothing. A full-time tailor creates custom suits and shirts. (Downtown)

ZACHARY'S GARDEN
1321 S. 2100 East St.
Salt Lake City
801/581-1189
When visitors enter Zachary's through a gated courtyard filled with all manner of exotic flowering plants, shrubs, and trees, they'll immediately understand its purpose as a serious garden store. Inside, garden tools and furniture are on display, as well as a large selection of items having nothing to do with the out-of-doors. Soaps and bath accessories, candles, lamps, and more are are sold among the horticultural displays. (University Area)

NOTABLE BOOKSTORES

BIBLIOTECT
329 W. Pierpont Ave.

Salt Lake City
801/236-1010
This small bookstore is a treat to visit, both because of its interesting architectural space and its informal arrangement of books, paintings, and objets d'art. The literary emphasis leans to the utilitarian and includes fine art, architecture, interior design, graphic design, landscape design, home improvement, and gardening. Both new and rare art books are sold. (Downtown)

DESERET BOOK
ZCMI Mall
36 S. State St.
Salt Lake City
801/328-8191
Deseret Book is owned by the Mormon Church, and its clear purpose is to enhance both the intellectual and spiritual needs of its members. The store first operated in 1900, selling manuals for teachers of Sunday school. Today its operations comprise an entire industry, with a publishing division, a wholesale distributor, and 33 retail book-

Crossroads Mall, p. 140

Salt Lake Convention & Visitors Bureau/Steve Greenwood

Mormon Leader Brigham Young founded Zion's Cooperative Mercantile Institution in 1868, creating the first department store in the country. Young made the first purchase at ZCMI, reportedly spending $1,000. The store was a true co-op, for many years sharing profits among its members.

stores in Utah and surrounding states. The flagship store sells religious books as well as fiction, children's books, cookbooks, cassettes, CDs, videos, and greeting cards. (Downtown)

GOLDEN BRAID BOOKS
151 S. 500 East St.
Salt Lake City
801/322-1162

This is perhaps the most beautiful bookstore in town, built with exquisite natural materials and filled with sunlight for most of the day. It shares both space and philosophy with a health-food restaurant. New Age, alternative healing, and self-help books take up a lot of the shelf space. Besides the literature, there are hundreds of beautiful things to look at: incense burners, amulets, jewelry, and more. (Downtown)

KING'S ENGLISH BOOKSHOP
1511 S. 1500 East St.
Salt Lake City
801/484-9100

Book lovers are in heaven in this many-roomed, cubbyholed, up-and-down stairs arrangement of a thousand bookshelves, which has been on the same site for 20 years. The merchandise is gloriously laid about, crammed here and everywhere, mostly in a methodical order, but sometimes not. The children's and mystery selections are extensive,

and the paperback fiction section is an intellect's delight. The store is locally owned and independent. (Downtown)

SAM WELLER BOOKS
254 S. Main St.
Salt Lake City
801/328-2586

It is not an exaggeration to call Sam Weller's an institution in Salt Lake City. All lovers of books have at least graced the doorway, and patrons who seek hard-to-find and out-of-print books are generally satisfied here. The store, which covers three floors and 30,000 square feet, has perhaps the premiere collection of Western Americana in the country. Sam and his wife, Lila, remain at the helm of the store, although their son Tony has taken over much of the day-to-day operations. A second location is in Sandy at 8191 S. 700 East St. (801/566-0219). (Downtown)

DEPARTMENT STORES

DILLARD'S
Fashion Place Mall
6191 S. State St.
Murray
801/266-2006

The Dillard retail chain spread its wings to the Salt Lake Valley several years ago, anchoring the upscale Fashion Place Mall. It has become a favorite with locals for its selection of clothing and housewares. Brides are especially enthralled with the china, crystal, and silver here, and it has become one of the primary bridal registries in town. A second Dillard's store is found in the South Towne Mall in Sandy, 801/553-8800. (Cottonwood Canyons and Environs)

MERVYN'S
Crossroads Mall
50 S. Main St.
Salt Lake City
801/521-8700
Mervyn's serves Salt Lake City well with its "big brands and small prices" mission, accompanied by a sale every week all year long. Other Salt Lake Valley stores are at Brickyard Plaza, 801/487-0671, and at Valley Fair Mall, 801/967-7228. (Downtown)

NORDSTROM
Crossroads Mall
50 S. Main St.
Salt Lake City
801/322-4200
The arrival of Nordstrom brought big-time, national chain, upscale shopping to Salt Lakers, and they have responded with immense gratitude by bringing a constant round of purchasing activity to the store. The downtown store is actually a smaller version of the Nordstrom found elsewhere in the Salt Lake Valley, but it manages to stock an excellent selection of shoes, business clothes, and most other sorts of apparel. Another Utah location is in Murray at the Fashion Place Mall, 801/261-4402. (Downtown)

ZCMI
ZCMI Center Mall
15 S. Main St.
Salt Lake City
801/579-6000
Zion's Cooperative Mercantile Institution's history is as long and storied as that of Salt Lake City. It was founded in 1868 and is generally regarded as the nation's first department store. Brigham Young wanted a local store where settlers could avoid buying from high-priced traveling salesmen. Today ZCMI continues to thrive, with 15 stores in Utah and Idaho, selling all manner of goods, from cookware to designer fashions to electronic equipment. The five-floor flagship store stands on the site of original ZCMI, anchoring the ZCMI Mall. (Downtown)

SHOPPING MALLS

COTTONWOOD MALL
4835 S. Highland Dr.
Holladay
801/278-0416
When it first opened in the 1960s, Cottonwood Mall was a vanguard in the enclosed shopping mall arena, and its advertisements boasted of "climatized" shopping year-round. The mall has withstood the test of time, and though its outdoor parking lot has become a bit odd-shaped, its solid and spacious layout remains hospitable to shoppers. Its anchor stores are ZCMI and JC Penney, and 140 other shops, restaurants, and movie theaters are found here as well. (Southeastern Valley)

CROSSROADS MALL
50 S. Main St.
Salt Lake City
801/531-1799
Not too long ago, Crossroads was the largest indoor mall in the United

States. It can no longer claim that distinction, but it is still big enough to impress the average shopper. The mall is located directly south of Temple Square and is one of the mainstays of a downtown shopping experience. Nordstrom and Mervyn's provide the anchor, and over 140 other shops and boutiques are spread throughout the four levels. A food court is on the lower level, and parking is accessed on the west end of each floor. Valet parking is available. Parking is free on Sunday and validated at all mall stores on other days. (Downtown)

FASHION PLACE MALL
6200 S. State St.
Murray
801/265-0504
Fashion Place's nice selection of major department stores qualifies it as one of the best malls in the Salt Lake Valley. Nordstrom, ZCMI, Dillard's, and Sears are slung at the far ends, and 110 other specialty stores fill in the long hallways between. Many of the popular, smaller national retail chains are here. The mall has a busy food court and is surrounded by free parking. (Cottonwood Canyons and Environs)

TROLLEY SQUARE
700 E. 600 South St.
Salt Lake City
801/521-9877
The huge, barnlike structures that enclose Trolley Square were once garages for Salt Lake City's fleet of trolley cars. The careful renovation that turned the buildings into a shopping center preserved the square's interesting architecture and retained its historical qualities. The result is a happy jumble of 80 odd-shaped shops, which often poke out from crazy-angled walls and interior cornices. The high, skylighted ceilings remain, as do the original brick floors. Trolley Square's landmark water tower stands three stories high on the front lawn. Two movie theaters are here, as well as a half-dozen restaurants, including the Hard Rock Café. (Downtown)

ZCMI CENTER MALL
35 S. Main St.

TIP

The clever Salt Lake City shopper can go almost a lifetime without paying for parking. The shopping centers and malls located outside the downtown area are mostly surrounded by asphalt seas of parking lots, and paid parking is rare. Downtown streets are lined with metered parking stalls, and private lots require payment. However, the two major downtown malls, ZCMI and Crossroads, have cavernous, multi-level parking lots, and purchases of five dollars or more earn a validation good for two hours. Savvy Salt Lake shoppers keep these validations even when they don't need them for that day's parking, collecting a stash for future use.

Salt Lake City
801/321-8745
The flagship ZCMI Department Store
anchors this downtown mall, and 80
shops and restaurants (and a mini–
post office) sprawl between its
multi-levels. A tourist information
service is found in the central public
area of the main level, and traveling
exhibits and local entertainment
often take the stage in the nearby
central court. An atrium food court
offers a wide selection of ethnic and
fast foods. To get a guided tour, visit
the customer service booth on the
main level. Parking is free with validation in the many-storied lot attached to the east end of the mall.
(Downtown)

FACTORY OUTLETS

FACTORY STORES OF AMERICA
12101 S. Factory Outlet Dr.
Draper
801/571-2933
This is a nice-sized outlet mall located just east of one of the busiest
sections of I-15. Its more than 30
stores sell everything any shopper
might expect to find at an outlet mall,
at 30 to 70 percent (it's a promise!) off
regular retail price. Some of the recognized brand names sold here are
Casual Corner, Izod, Adidas, Corning
Revere, and American Tourister. A
food court and restaurant are on-site.
(Cottonwood Canyons and Environs)

FACTORY STORES AT PARK CITY
Kimball Junction and I-15
Park City
435/645-7078
This outlet mall is located 30 minutes
outside the area covered elsewhere
in this book, but it merits a mention.
Busloads of outlet shoppers arrive

here daily, having heard of the great
buys on "real" designer and manufacturer's merchandise. Fifty shops
are housed in an open-air, U-shaped
configuration so large that most
shoppers are not able to complete it
in one day. Nike, Gap, Ralph Lauren,
Mikasa, and Eddie Bauer are just a
few of the outlet stores that sell
brand-name merchandise. (25 miles
south of Salt Lake City)

NORDSTROM'S RACK
2236 S. 1300 East St.
Salt Lake City
801/484-8880
The Rack is an adjunct of the Nordstrom chain, selling remaindered
goods from all of Nordstrom's depart-
ments as well as deeply discounted
clothing from various other sources.
(Southeastern Valley)

PATAGONIA OUTLET
3267 S. Highland Dr.
Holladay
801/466-2226
Patagonia is a manufacturer of sports
clothing and is perhaps best known
for its collections of fleece outerwear.
This smallish outlet store sells an
ever-changing array of seconds and
leftover items, including ski under-
wear, shorts, shirts, and pants—often
at bargain basement prices. (Southeastern Valley)

SUNDANCE CATALOG
OUTLET STORE
1460 Foothill Dr.
Salt Lake City
801/581-9711
Robert Redford's Sundance Resort,
located in nearby Provo Canyon,
started a small on-site retail operation a few years ago that has blos-
somed into a full-scale catalog
business. Salt Lakers are the bene-

ficiaries of the "leftovers" from the catalog sales, with a lovely store filled with incredible bargains. The merchandise leans to Southwest-inspired items, including ceramics, rugs, household ornaments, and clothing. The merchandise comes and goes at a fast clip, so bargain hunters are advised to shop often. (University Area)

Utah Travel Council/Frank Jensen

10

Stop 20 Salt Lakers on the street and ask them about the local sports scene, and the first 10 answers (as well as the second 10) will include the Utah Jazz. Salt Lake City is passionate about its NBA team, so much so that a major downtown arena, a TV station, retail shops, and even a car dealership support the team. Off season and on, media coverage is nonstop, and public discussion seemingly never ends. The Utah Jazz have repaid their hometown's loyalty with two NBA finals series in 1997 and 1998, and all-star status for Karl Malone.

Sports fans disperse their loyalty among Salt Lake City's other primary sports attractions, including the Womens' NBA Utah Starzz, the AAA baseball Salt Lake Buzz, the International Hockey League Utah Grizzlies, and a rabid subset of fans of University of Utah football, basketball, and gymnastics teams.

Recreationists have unequaled opportunities in the great outdoors. Hiking, biking, camping, hunting, fishing, and virtually anything else that can be accomplished in wide-open spaces for the pure fun of it are enjoyed here, with the backdrop of unparalleled scenic beauty. The canyons to the east of the city and the desert and lake to the west are made up almost entirely of public land, with trails, streams, and campsites ready and waiting for visitors.

PROFESSIONAL SPORTS

Auto Racing

BONNEVILLE SALT FLATS
Access road off I-80, Exit 4
Wendover
801/977-4300 (BLM office)

The Flats, 110 miles east of Salt Lake City, bring new definition to the word "unique." They are exotic and weird and unimaginably beautiful. This 30,000-acre bed of absolutely flat salt crystals is left over from Lake Bonneville, which in ancient times evaporated to become the Great Salt Lake, now the next-door neighbor of the Flats. Besides being a world-famous attraction, the Flats also are a favorite of race-car drivers, who like the natural straightaways and the salt's water content, which keeps car tires relatively cool. In the middle of the 1900s several speed records were broken here—the 300, then the 400 . . . 500 . . . and finally the 600-mile-per-hour records. In the 1960s vehicles equipped with jet engines took to the Flats; one rocket car reached 622.4 miles per hour.

There are several major speed events scheduled at the Bonneville Salt Flats throughout the summer and fall, the seasons when the salt and water content is best for racing. Two mainstays are July's Land Speed Opener and August's Speed Week, when professional racers from all over the world come to try their luck at breaking land speed records. Visitors are welcome to observe the racing events and also to visit the Flats any time of year. Drivers are cautioned to stay on designated roads, as the Flats, especially during a wet winter, can be dangerous. Temporary visitor facilities are set up for events, but no permanent services are available outside of Wendover. (Western Valley)

ROCKY MOUNTAIN RACEWAYS
6555 W. 2100 South St.
West Valley City

801/252-9557
Rocky Mountain Raceways consists of a 72-acre entertainment area that includes a 2,580-foot National Hot Rod Association–approved drag strip and a three-eighths–mile, figure-eight oval track. A family atmosphere is maintained, and a special section is reserved for those who choose not to smoke or drink alcohol. Regularly scheduled events throughout the warm weather months include street-legal drags, funny-car competitions, sprints, super stocks, street stocks, and mini stocks. June–Oct. Tickets cost $5–$10 adults, $3–$5 children. Family passes and pit passes are available. & (Western Valley)

Baseball

SALT LAKE BUZZ
Franklin Covey Field
77 W. 1300 South St.
Salt Lake City
801/485-3800
Salt Lake City has long had a love affair with its various minor league baseball teams, but only since the mid-1990s has the city been "this close" to the majors, with a Triple-A team all its own. The Salt Lake Buzz have had highly successful seasons since their move from Portland in 1994. The Buzz's name stems from Utah's nickname, "The Beehive State." The Buzz's home is the state-of-the-art Franklin Covey Field.

The stadium seats 15,000 but has managed to maintain a small-town, hot-dog-and-beer ambience. Its half-circle of double-decker bleachers opens to a perfectly framed view of the Wasatch Mountains, and at sunset (timed at about the third inning of most baseball games) the mountains turn a bright pink as their last act of the day. The Field's wide rim of green space accommodates picnickers and young families. The Field is also a popular venue for summer festivals and rock concerts. Tickets may be reserved by calling 801/467-8499; $5–$7 adults, $4 seniors, $3 children. & (Downtown)

Basketball

UTAH JAZZ
Delta Center
301 W. South Temple St.
801/325-2500
It doesn't take long for visitors to become aware of Utah's affection for its Jazz. During basketball season billboards, banners, bumper stickers, and endless discussion center on Utah's most successful sports team ever. The Jazz play their home games at the Delta Center, regularly selling out the 20,000-seat arena. The Delta Center is a landmark in downtown Salt Lake City. At night the mostly glass walls spill their light onto neigh-

boring blocks, and in the day the lovely, manicured grounds—especially the rose garden in front of the building—soften the building's sharp angles. Both the arena and the surrounding 44,000 square feet of multi-use space serve as the location for many other community events, including rock concerts, rodeos, ice shows, circuses, and large conventions. Tickets are $11–$75 per game. & (Downtown)

UNIVERSITY OF UTAH RUNNIN' UTES
Jon M. Huntsman Center
1825 E. South Campus Dr.
Salt Lake City
801/581-6641
The Utes have enjoyed fabulous success in the last half-decade, earning top-10 national rankings and producing All-American players. Coach Rick Majerus leads the team, which regularly fills the seats for its home games at the Huntsman Center. The Utes' colors of red and white dominate the arena, and its in-the-round seating accommodates 15,000 spectators. The arena is also a popular venue for concerts and community events. Tickets are $11 adults, $8 children. & (University Area)

UTAH STARZZ
Delta Center

TRIVIA

All of Utah's professional sports teams are proud to have a double "z" in their name. The tradition began innocently with the Utah Jazz, who brought the name with them when they moved from New Orleans in the 1970s. Subsequent teams have chosen to join the "z" club, including the Salt Lake Buzz AAA baseball team, the Utah Grizzlies hockey team, and most recently the WNBA Utah Starzz.

301 W. South Temple St.
801/325-2500 5-40
Salt Lake City's newest professional team is the Utah Starzz, who have been playing their home games in the Delta Center since 1997. The elite women's basketball team is one of only eight WNBA charter teams in the United States. Tickets are $5–$40 per game. ⅊ (Downtown)

Football

UNIVERSITY OF UTAH
RUNNIN' UTES
Rice-Eccles Stadium
1400 E. 500 South St.
Salt Lake City
801/581-6641
Ron McBride took over as head football coach of the Utes in 1990, and the team has showed steady improvement since, playing in National Bowl games for four out of the last five years. The Utes play in the Western Athletic League. Their home stadium was recently given a $52-million facelift and now ranks as a first-class facility, with seating for 46,500 rabid

Ute fans. The oval stadium is constructed of concrete and steel, surrounded by a concourse filled with concession stands and shops. The three stories of walled glass that rise to the west of the playing field hold luxury seating and press boxes. For the Olympic Winter Games of 2002, the Rice-Eccles Stadium will double as the venue for the Olympic opening and closing ceremonies, when seating will be expanded to accommodate more than 50,000 spectators. Runnin' Utes tickets are $10–$17 adults, $7 children. ⅊ (University Area)

Gymnastics

UNIVERSITY OF UTAH
GYMNASTICS
Huntsman Center
1825 E. South Campus Dr.
Salt Lake City
801/581-6641
The University of Utah's women's gymnastics team is consistently ranked as one of the top programs in intercollegiate sports. The Utes

Rocket Car at Bonneville Salt Flats, p. 144

Utah Travel Council/Frank Jensen

TRIVIA

What makes Salt Lake's snow so great? It has something to do with the arid desert that the snow clouds must cross to reach the mountains, and the collision that occurs when the storms meet the sudden, steep slopes of the Wasatch. The snow's water content is a mere four percent—some say it is closer in composition to sugar than the usual watery white stuff. The snow's depth is another phenomenon, with an average of 500 inches a year.

have won 10 NCAA Championships, five of them in the last decade. The team has a large and loyal following, and draws more spectators to home games at the Huntsman Center than any other women's program. & (University Area)

Hockey

UTAH GRIZZLIES
"E" Center
3200 S. Decker Lake Dr.
West Valley City
801/988-8000
The International Hockey League Grizzlies filled Utah's hockey void in 1996, and recently have moved to the shiny new "E" Center, which was built with special accommodations for the team and their screaming hordes of over 10,000 fans. The team has twice won IHL championships and continues to have winning seasons. Tickets are $8–$35. & (Western Valley)

OLYMPIC WINTER GAMES OF 2002 VENUES

Ice Skating

Several ice facilities are either constructed or in the works in anticipation of the Olympic Winter

Games of 2002. They are all located within an hour's drive of the Salt Lake Valley and are open to the public before and after the Olympics, either as spectator venues or skating rinks.

"E" CENTER
3200 S. Decker Lake Dr.
West Valley City
801/988-8000
This rink will be the setting for some of the men's ice hockey games. In the meantime, the center's 10,000 seats are regularly filled with fans of Utah's pro hockey team, the Utah Grizzlies, who make their home here.

ICE SHEET AT OGDEN
4390 Harrison Blvd.
Ogden
801/399-8750
The Ice Sheet, located on the campus of Weber State University, has wonderful mountain views from its wide windows, and invites the public for scheduled skating hours daily. Its 2,000 seats will most likely be filled during the Olympic games, when the men's and women's curling contests will be held here.

ICE SHEET AT PROVO
Provo's Ice Sheet is still in construction at this writing. It will be open to the public for scheduled skating

WINTER GAMES VENUES

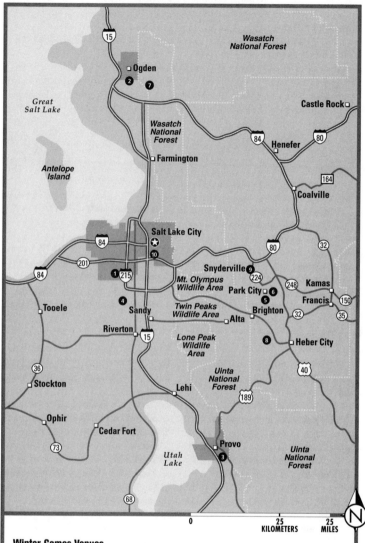

Winter Games Venues

1 "E" Center (Men's Ice Hockey)
2 Ice Sheet at Ogden (Men's and Women's Curling)
3 Ice Sheet at Provo (Men's and Women's Ice Hockey)
4 Oquirrh Speed Skating Oval Park (Long-Track Speed Skating)
5 Deer Valley Resort (Slalom, Freestyle, Aerial, and Mogul Skiing)
6 Park City Mountain Resort (Giant Slalom and Snowboarding)
7 Snowbasin Ski Area (Downhill and Super G)
8 Soldier Hollow (18 events including Cross Country, Nordic Combined, and Biathlon)
9 Utah Winter Sports Park (Ski Jumping, Bobsled, Luge)
10 Skating Arena at Salt Lake City (Ice Skating and Ice Dancing)

hours and will be the site of the men's and women's Olympic hockey games.

OQUIRRH PARK
SPEED SKATING OVAL
624 S. 4800 West St.
Kearns
801/966-5944
The 400-meter enclosed oval will host the 10 long-rack speed-skating events. In the meantime it is utilized by ice hockey teams, public skaters, and, in the off-season, by rollerbladers.

Skiing

The resorts closest to the Salt Lake Valley are located in canyons too fragile to accommodate the demands of the Olympic games. Big Cottonwood and Little Cottonwood Canyons would both require extensive gutting in order to develop the infrastructure needed for the games, and it was decided long ago that their narrow and pristine boundaries are off-limits. The larger, broader resorts just a bit farther up the road, easily accessible to Salt Lake City via major freeways, will host the Olympic downhill and cross-country action. Most of these venues are currently open to the public, and all of them will operate as public facilities after the Olympic games.

DEER VALLEY RESORT
Park City
435/649-1000
Deer Valley is famous for pampering its guests with excellent food, service, and groomed trails. Its gentle image will be shed for two weeks in February 2002, when hard-bodied athletes take on some of the toughest terrain in the world. Slalom races, as well as freestyle, aerial, and mogul

events will he held on existing black-diamond runs and newly constructed courses.

PARK CITY MOUNTAIN RESORT
Park City
435/649-8111
Race fans have enjoyed the World Cup at Park City for over 15 years, and the mountain is well-known to ski enthusiasts, both amateur and professional, from all over the world. Olympic giant slalom and snowboarding competitions will take place at the Eagle Race Arena.

SNOWBASIN SKI AREA
Ogden Canyon
Huntsville
801/399-1135
Snowbasin is being greatly expanded and renovated for its Olympic hosting duties. The once humble resort where families could ski at affordable rates will enlarge to accommodate downhill and super G races. A premiere course is in the works with a vertical drop of 2,770 feet, and it is estimated its skiers will reach speeds of 90 miles per hour.

SOLDIER HOLLOW
Wasatch Mountain State Park
Midway
435/654-1791
No less than 18 Olympic events are scheduled for this gorgeous expanse, located in a deep and forested pocket of a state park. Cross-country, Nordic combined, and biathlon tracks and stations are now in various stages of construction.

Ski Jumping/Bobsledding/ Luging

UTAH WINTER SPORTS PARK
3000 Bear Hollow Dr.

Tram at Snowbird Ski Resort, p. 153

Park City
435/658-4200

The general public is offered a rare opportunity to hurtle through the air in a variety of positions at the Utah Winter Sports Park, a world-class facility developed for the upcoming Olympic Winter Games of 2002. Ski jumping is reportedly taught in just two hours to mortals who dare a leap of faith from 18- or 38-meter launching stations. Bobsleds hurtle down a 1,335-meter refrigerated track at speeds up to 80 miles per hour, holding two speed-freak passengers (and a professional driver and brakeman). The bobsled ride costs $125 for an approximately one-minute ride, and open slots are hard to come by. A similar warm-weather experience is available for $27, called the Rocket Ride. The track is cement and the vehicle is a one-passenger, self-steering sled that reaches speeds of 45 miles per hour. Reservations are recommended for all park activities and should be made as far in advance as possible.

RECREATION

Alpine Skiing

Hundreds of books and tens of thousands of photographs testify to the brilliance of Utah skiing. Eleven resorts line up along the Wasatch Mountains, and all of them catch the famous fine white powder, the likes of which falls nowhere else. Salt Lakers like to boast that they can be sitting in their office one minute and 45 minutes later be boarding a ski lift. Skiing is not just a sport here—it is a passion and a way of life.

ALTA SKI AREA
Little Cottonwood Canyon
Sandy
801/359-1078

Some 140 years ago Alta was a mining boomtown, where silver miners made and lost fortunes. The resort's location, at the very top of Little Cottonwood Canyon, with a boxed, narrow base and steep, high surroundings, has limited development enough that Alta's Wild West

Cross-Country Skiing and Snowshoeing at Solitude's Nordic Center

The Nordic Center is located near Silver Lake, a small mountain lake with wide shores and an almost perfectly oval shape. In winter the lake freezes over, and its perimeter makes a perfect, groomed, flat ski trail. More-difficult trails branch up and outward from the main trail. A total of 20 kilometers are groomed for skiers and snowshoers of all abilities. Lessons, rentals, and guided backcountry tours are offered. Call 801/536-5774 for more information. Open Nov–spring. Tickets cost $10; half-day and workshop rates are available. Children under 10 ski free.

roots remain visible today. The tiny town has its own mayor and sheriff, and some of the old, rough-hewn buildings and mine shafts can still be seen from the road. The sport of skiing started here in the 1930s, and by 1940 Alta had become one of the first full-fledged ski resorts in the United States.

Today it is known for its stunning descents and expert-skier terrain, as well as for its many wide, groomed beginner hills. Eight lifts and five tow ropes carry 10,750 skiers an hour up Point Supreme, Baldy, and Sugarloaf Mountains. Alta's famous ski school is named after its founder, Alf Engen, who practically invented the sport of skiing in Utah. A number of lodges and restaurants dot the base of the resort, offering a range of facilities from dormitories to luxury suites (see Chapter 3, Where to Stay). Ski lifts operate from mid-November through mid-April. Lift tickets cost $22–$31 per day; half-day rates are available. (Cottonwood Canyons and Environs)

BRIGHTON SKI RESORT
Big Cottonwood Canyon
Sandy
800/873-5512
Not too long ago Brighton was considered the most gentle of Utah's ski hills, and proudly proclaimed itself as the resort where "Utahns learn to ski." The addition of the Great Western chairlift, which runs to the top of Clayton Peak, and the Crest chairlift, which runs to the saddle below Pioneer Peak ridgeline above Snake Creek Canyon, has elevated (literally) Brighton to the ranks of other steep and difficult ski mountains, and now there is as much machismo here as anywhere. Seven lifts carry skiers to 64 runs that span two mountains. Most lifts lead to separate runs for every ability level. Snowboarders are catered to with total mountain access, halfpipes, and a free first-time lesson. Ski lifts operate early Nov–late Apr. Tickets cost $31, kids under 10 ski free. (Cottonwood Canyons and Environs)

SNOWBIRD SKI AND SUMMER RESORT
Little Cottonwood Canyon
Sandy
801/742-2222

Snowbird's sophistication and chic are modeled after European resorts, but its granite canyons and sheer vertical drop are strictly from Utah. This is a classy, upscale resort that works hard to attract the out-of-town skier; however, it remains a steadfast favorite with locals as well. It offers 2,500 acres of skiable terrain, with a total vertical drop of 3,240 feet. Its high-speed aerial tram is world famous for its fantastic canyon views and thrilling ride to the 11,000-foot summit of Hidden Peak. Eight lifts carry skiers to hills ranging from bunny to double black diamond.

Special offerings include a sunrise tram program, which allows skiers an hour's head start on the mountain, guided snowcat skiing, and free lift tickets for kids ages 12 and under. Snowboarders are welcome. Lodging, restaurant services, a spa, and a pedestrian retail village are found within the resort. Ski lifts operate from November until as long as snow conditions permit (several seasons have lasted through mid-June). Tickets cost $36–$45 per day; half-day, group, and family rates and lifts-only tickets are available. (Cottonwood Canyons and Environs)

SOLITUDE RESORT
Big Cottonwood Canyon
Sandy
801/534-1400

Since 1959 Solitude has been a favorite with local skiers. Its recent major renovations, both on the mountain and at the base facilities, have elevated the resort to world-class status. Sixty-three runs and bowls cascade down from the resort's 10,035-foot summit, accessed by seven lifts. Fifty percent of Solitude's trails are ranked for beginner skiers, but the 30 percent saved for expert skiers are amazingly steep and beautiful. The full range of services is available inside the resort, including food, lodging, lessons, and special programs for kids. Lifts run early Nov–late Apr. Tickets cost $36; kids 10 and under ski free. (Cottonwood Canyons and Environs)

Bowling

FAIRMONT BOWL AND CAFÉ
1121 E. Ashton Ave.
Salt Lake City
801/487-0856

The Fairmont may be old and comfortable when compared with the neon and splash of some of the newer alleys, but it gets top marks from traditionalists who enjoy its well-kept lanes and low lights. The on-site café serves the best chili-and-

---

T I P

Public tennis facilities are available in many city and county parks, including Liberty Park, 500 E. 900 South St., 801/328-4711; the Dee Smith Tennis Courts, 1216 Wasatch Dr., 801/583-9451; and Cottonwood Heights Recreation Center, 7500 S. 2700 East St., 801/943-3190.

Public Swimming Pools

Some of Salt Lake City's public parks have swimming pools. They include the following: Fairmont Park, 2245 S. McClelland St., 801/272-2243; Jordan Park, 1000 S. 900 West St., 801/596-0072; and Liberty Park, 500 E. 900 South St., 801/538-2062. Two public facilities have both indoor and outdoor pools and offer classes and extensive training programs: Steiner Aquatic Center, 645 S. Guardsman Way, 801/583-9713; and Cottonwood Heights Recreation Center, 7500 S. 2700 East St., 801/943-9673.

cheese fries in town, and a special Sunday morning deal includes breakfast trays delivered to the scoring tables. A small bar serves ice-cold pitchers of beer. Mon–Sun 9 a.m.–midnight. 75 cents–$2.75 per game. ⟐ (Southeastern Valley)

OLYMPUS HILLS BOWL
4015 S. Wasatch Blvd.
Holladay
801/277-4444
Bowlers standing at one end of the building can barely see their colleagues at the other end. This huge and busy bowling alley is a hangout for the serious bowl aficionado. Daily 11–11, $1.50–$2.50 per game. ⟐ (Southeastern Valley)

UNION BOWLING LANES
University of Utah
142 Union Building
Salt Lake City
801/581-7440
This bowling alley could be the setting for an *Animal House* movie—funky and retro and really cool. Ten lanes have been updated by computerized scoring machines, but not much else has changed in the last few decades. The lanes are patronized by students and a fun-loving public. The snack bar features great nachos. Mon–Sun 8–10. $1.95 per game. ⟐ (University Area)

Cycling

From early spring to late fall, Salt Lake City's paved roads and mountain trails resound with the spinning of two-wheeled machines. Biking is an accepted means of transport here, with specially designed bike paths lining many of the secondary city roadways and paved canyon roads that specify safety rules for bicyclists and those with whom they share the road. Commuter routes are described in Chapter 2, Getting Around Salt Lake City. Recreationists have access to hundreds of miles of groomed (and not-so-groomed) mountain trails that accommodate bicyclists of all experience levels. The following is by no means a complete list but is intended as a "get acquainted" tour of a few of the most popular trails. Over 50 bicycle shops in Salt Lake City sell, rent, repair, and out-

fit bicycles, and most offer trail advice as well.

BIG COTTONWOOD CANYON
Both Brighton and Solitude ski areas, located near the top of the canyon, have trailheads at their parking lots. Solitude's five-mile Moonbeam loop heads straight up and past the Moonbeam ski hill to Lake Solitude and then straight back down again. Brighton's several trails are also steep; the trip to Snake Creek Pass is rewarded with a stellar view of Heber Valley and the surrounding Wasatch peaks.

CITY CREEK CANYON
City Creek Canyon is much appreciated by Salt Lakers, who travel just four minutes from the city center to enter its thick woods and steep-walled interior. The canyon is just above the state capitol, and its road is a mostly gentle climb, suitable for beginner riders. Bicyclists must share an every-other-day-off schedule with automobiles, and hikers are welcome every day.

EASTERN FOOTHILLS
The Bonneville Shoreline Trail is an ambitious project that at its completion will trace over 90 miles along the fossilized shoreline of the lake that covered this area over a million years ago. Parts of the trail are completed and heavily used, including a seven-mile section that rims the eastern border of Salt Lake City. It is accessed at Popperton Park (behind the Shriner's Hospital for Children on Virginia Street) and ends at Sunnyside Avenue. It is an intermediate ride; a map is recommended because the trail's maze of offshoots are not clearly marked.

JORDAN RIVER PARKWAY
It may be an impossible dream, but plans are in the works for a multi-recreational use path that follows along the Jordan River as it connects two of Utah's largest bodies of water, Utah Lake and Great Salt Lake. Several small sections of the parkway are complete; they make for a wonderful, easy family bike ride that can also include fishing, hiking, and wildlife watching. Three miles of parkway head north from the Utah State Fairpark (1000 West and North Temple Streets) to an intersection with Redwood Road, where a turnaround is recommended, as the continuing road is not always groomed. Another section begins at Winchester Park in

The National Forest Service administers four public campsites in the Salt Lake Valley, two in Big Cottonwood Canyon and two in Little Cottonwood Canyon. All are considered high-elevation campgrounds, and their seasons begin in May, June, or July and run to October. Services such as drinking water and flush toilets vary from site to site. Reservations may be made by calling 800/280-2267.

Murray (6400 South and approximately 1100 West) and travels two miles north to Walden Park.

LITTLE COTTONWOOD CANYON
Albion Basin is best known for its excellent skiing in winter, but it is also popular with locals for its overwhelming abundance of wildflowers in spring and summer. When the road is dry, the flowers can be enjoyed via a bicycle route that begins at the Albion Lodge parking lot and follows the Albion Basin Summer Road to the Albion Basin Campground, and then returns along the same route. The trail is easy to navigate, though its high elevation can leave city folks gasping for air.

MILLCREEK CANYON
The Pipeline Trail follows the cut of an actual pipeline that once served this canyon. It begins about six miles up Millcreek at Elbow Fork and makes a nice, but sometimes steep, descent to the bottom of the canyon, near the ranger's station. The trail offers scenic views of the canyon and surrounding peaks.

Big Water Trail's six round-trip miles begin at the top of Millcreek Canyon and travel a woodsy, steadily uphill path to Dog Lake, where the trail loops and begins its return trip. Intermediate to advanced riders love this trail—the only drawback is that it may be crowded. Upper Millcreek Canyon is accessible to cyclists only on even-numbered days of the month.

Hiking/Climbing

Salt Lake City is rimmed by gentle, rolling foothills that slowly graduate to some of the steepest and grand-est slopes of the Rocky Mountains. Ramblers and technical climbers alike take to the hills in droves during the warm-weather months, enjoying the views of wildflowers, rock canyons, and the valley below. Three of the major canyons that descend into the Salt Lake Valley hold some of the most popular and scenic trails. This list is just a tiny sampling of the designated hiking trails in the valley. Several excellent hiking guides that offer much greater detail are available in area bookstores.

BIG COTTONWOOD CANYON
The trail to Lake Blanche is extremely popular, and deservedly so. It is a fairly easy three-mile round trip, and the view of the lake, the valley, and the impressive Sundial Peak that rises just above the lake is absolutely gorgeous. From the general store at Brighton, Lake Solitude is a 1.5 mile hike leading under and over several chairlifts and ski runs, and featuring lovely walks through open fields and mountain forests.

Golfing near Salt Lake City, p. 158

Utah Travel Council/John Telford

Area Fishing

It is estimated that one out of every four Utahns has a fishing license, and it is an undisputed fact that fishing is Utah's most popular sport. Fishing is allowed on all public lands year-round. While opportunities in the Salt Lake Valley are scenic and fun, premiere fishing sites are found not too far away. In fact, some of the most sought-after rivers in the world are just an hour south on the Provo River and four hours east on the Green River near Vernal. The most popular areas near Salt Lake City are the high lakes of the Wasatch Mountains and the canyon streams of Millcreek, Little Cottonwood, and Big Cottonwood Canyons.

Fishing licenses are required of everyone over the age of 14. An annual license is $18 for ages 14 to 64, $9 for 65 and over. An additional Wildlife Habitat Authorization is required of all sportspeople in Utah, with an additional cost of $5.25. Licenses are available at most sporting goods stores. For more information on Utah's fishing regulations, contact the Utah Division of Wildlife Resources, 1596 W. North Temple, Salt Lake City, Utah 84116, 801/538-4700.

EASTERN FOOTHILLS

Mount Van Cott is more accurately described as a large hill rather than a mountain. Located behind the University of Utah campus, it provides a wonderful view of the entire Salt Lake Valley and beyond from its summit. The Twin Peaks, which rise just above the Avenues section of Salt Lake City, are reached from several different trails—mostly old jeep roads—that stem from residential streets in the high avenues. From the peaks is a view of the Salt Lake Valley and City Creek Canyon.

LITTLE COTTONWOOD CANYON

The Red Pine Canyon trail begins (along with several other hikes) at the White Pine Trailhead. It leads to both Lower and Upper Red Pine Lakes, as well as a great valley overlook that is just 1.5 miles from the trailhead. The trail to Cardiff Pass begins in the town of Alta, heads one mile up to beautiful views of surrounding peaks, and leads to summits of Flagstaff Mountain and Mount Superior.

MILLCREEK CANYON

The Desolation Trail runs a whopping 19 miles to Desolation Lake, but after just two miles hikers are rewarded with a great views of the Salt Lake Valley. The Elbow Fork Trail is so named because its trailhead is located at a sharp turn in Millcreek's paved road. An easy one-mile hike to

Mount Aire (great view!) is accessed here, as well as more difficult hikes to Burch Hollow and the Terrace campground.

Golfing

Salt Lakers are no less avid about the game of golf than foursomes anywhere else, and, statewide, golf is played 12 months of the year. In Salt Lake City's high mountain climate, courses are closed for much of the winter because of snow, but if ever the fairways are clear, many of the golf courses are open. A roster of Utah PGA events runs April through December. For reservations at all Salt Lake City public golf courses, call 801/484-3333.

BONNEVILLE GOLF COURSE
954 Connor Rd.
Salt Lake City
801/583-9513
Salt Lakers love their "Bonney" for its location in the middle of an upscale residential neighborhood and its serious challenge for all golfing levels. 18 holes, par 72. $10 for 9 holes, $20 for 18 holes. Mon–Sun. ♿ (University Area)

FOREST DALE
2375 S. 900 East St.
Salt Lake City
801/483-5420
Forest Dale is a good course for beginners, but its hazards and switchback layout seem to be attractive to advanced players as well. 9 holes, par 36. Mon–Thu $8, Fri–Sun $8.50. ♿ (Southeastern Valley)

MICK RILEY
421 E. Vine St.
Murray
801/266-8185
Mick's is a favorite with the golfer of middle-range skills, as its fairways are somewhat straightforward and its greens forgiving. A separate par 3 course is great for beginners. 9 holes, par 36. Mon–Thu $8, Fri–Sun $8.50. ♿ (Southeastern Valley)

MOUNTAIN DELL
Parley's Canyon
Salt Lake City

T I P

Hunters must be 14 years or older and must have completed a safety course in order to purchase a permit. Deer permits are $25 for a season, elk permits $50 for a season. An additional Wildlife Habitat Authorization is required of all sportspeople in Utah, with an additional cost of $5.25. Licenses are available at most sporting goods stores. For more information on Utah's hunting regulations, contact the Utah Division of Wildlife Resources, 1596 W. North Temple St., Salt Lake City, Utah 84116, 801/538-4700.

801/582-3812

The name is literal—all 36 holes are tucked into a dell, surrounded by the fabulous Wasatch Mountains. The course is beautiful, sometimes difficult, and often a good place for wildlife watching. 36 holes, par 71. $14 for 9 holes, $28 for 18 holes. & (University Area)

MURRAY PARKWAY GOLF COURSE
6345 S. Parkway Ave.
Murray
801/262-4653

This semi-friendly course has wide and forgiving fairways and large-sized greens that can eat up a par. 18 holes, par 72. $9.50 for 9 holes, $19 for 18 holes. & (Southeastern Valley)

NIBLEY PARK
2730 S. 700 East St.
Salt Lake City
801/483-5418

If there is any triumph during the fairway's long hauls, it is most likely vanquished by the killer water obstacle at the ninth hole. 9 holes, par 33. Mon–Thu $8, Fri–Sun $8.50. & (Southeastern Valley)

OLD MILL
6080 S. Wasatch Blvd.
Holladay
801/424-1302

Salt Lake City's newest golf course is located near the site of a former flour mill. The view upward is of the towering peaks of the Wasatch Mountains, and the view down is of a busy freeway. 18 holes, par 71. $11 for 9 holes, $22 for 18 holes. & (Southeastern Valley)

ROSE PARK
1386 N. Redwood Rd.

Skier taking time out for lunch in Park City, p. 150

Salt Lake City
801/596-5030

Golfers should not be fooled by the level playing field here. Even though there's little in the up-and-down aspects of this course, it is challenging nonetheless. 18 holes, par 72. Mon–Thu $8.50 for 9 holes, $17 for 18 holes, Fri–Sun $9 for 9 holes, $18 for 18 holes. & (Western Valley)

SOUTH MOUNTAIN GOLF CLUB
1247 E. Rambling Rd.
Draper
801/495-0500

The setting is so beautiful that many non-golfers choose to have parties and get married here, overlooking the lush and rolling hills. 18 holes, par 72. Mon–Thu $35 for 9 holes, $55 for 18 holes. Fri–Sun $45 for 9 holes, $75 for 18 holes. Prices include a cart. & (Cottonwood Canyons and Environs)

WINGPOINTE
3602 W. 100 North St.
Salt Lake City

801/575-2345

The course is a bobbing series of small hills and valleys, dotted with treacherous water and bunker hazards. It serves double duty as the landscaping for the entrance to Salt Lake City's International Airport. 18 holes, par 72. $10 for 9 holes, $20 for 18 holes. ♿ (Western Valley)

Horseback Riding

SALT LAKE EQUESTRIAN PARK
10800 S. 2200 West St.
South Jordan
801/254-0106

The Equestrian Park is a primary training venue for Salt Lakers who wish to practice jumping, barrel racing, and track skills. Horses are boarded here, and the arena can be rented for private practice and events. Many other regularly scheduled horsey events take place here as well, including springtime flat track racing, summer barrel racing, winter chariot races, and various rodeos and commercial shows. ♿ (Cottonwood Canyons and Environs)

Ice Skating

COTTONWOOD HEIGHTS RECREATION CENTER
7500 S. 2700 East St.
Holladay
801/943-3190

Among its other offerings, including swimming, track, racquetball, and basketball, the Cottonwood Heights Center has an excellent ice rink that's open for general public use. Hours vary and change seasonally. $4.50 adults, $3.25 seniors, $3.25 children. ♿ (Cottonwood Canyons and Environs)

GALLIVAN UTAH CENTER
36 E. 200 South St.
Salt Lake City
801/596-2874

In winter the center's small, attractive pond is frozen to a smooth finish, and skaters, most of whom are not too far advanced in skill level, take to the ice with relish. Mon–Sat 12–9, Sun 12–7. $4 adults, $3 children, for 2-hour sessions. ♿ (Downtown)

Sailing

For a landlocked, desert state, Utah has the surprising ranking of number six in the nation for surface acres of boatable waters. Dozens of reservoirs rim the downslopes just outside the Salt Lake Valley, and it is less than an hour's drive to myriad motorboating adventures. Within the confines of the valley, motorboating is almost nonexistent, but sailing takes over as the primary boating experience.

GREAT SALT LAKE

The Great Salt Lake is regarded as one of the best sailing lakes in the West, for its wind power and expanse, but mostly for its highly unusual (in fact, unique in all the world) water conditions and mountain/island geography. Marinas are found at both the south shore at Great Salt Lake State Park and on Antelope Island State Park, reached via freeway from the town of Syracuse. Several major sailing events are held on the lake each year that draw hundreds of sailors and spectators. Sail Fest is a weeklong extravaganza with races, clinics, water fights, and potluck dinners. Year-round. (Western Valley)

11

PERFORMING ARTS

Salt Lake City is enormously proud of its performing arts companies: The Utah Symphony, Ballet West, Utah Opera Company, and Repertory Dance Theatre are all first-rate organizations known worldwide. The talents of the individual artists in these companies cannot be underestimated, but without the full and enthusiastic support of a devoted community, arts organizations in Salt Lake City would not enjoy the success that they do.

Public support of the arts was proven when Utahns voted to use tax dollars for a "Zoo, Arts, and Parks" bill, which earmarks cash dollars for arts organizations. The city has an acoustically perfect symphony hall, a renovated theater that serves as home to dance and opera companies, a rehearsal/performance space dedicated to modern dance, and several major live theater venues. The Utah Legislature, usually extremely conservative when it comes to public expenditures, almost always finds the money needed to fund major arts projects.

THEATER

BABCOCK THEATER
University of Utah
300 S. 1340 East St.
Salt Lake City
801/581-6961
The University of Utah gave Maud May Babcock a fitting honor by naming its cozy, lab-style student theater

after her. Babcock was the undisputed grande dame of Utah's early theatrical life, traveling to Utah from Harvard University in 1892 to teach at the then University of Deseret. She stayed for almost five decades and trained many actors who went on to important careers. The Babcock is used for student productions, and its winter series offers an inexpensive

Buying Tickets

ArtTix, *801/355-2787 or 888/451-2787, is the primary vendor for tickets to cultural events in Salt Lake City, and it does the huge bulk of its business via telephone. Downtown ticket offices are in the lobby of the Capitol Theatre, 50 W. 200 South St., open Mon–Fri 10–6, Sat 10–2; and at Abravanel Hall, 128 W. South Temple St., open Mon–Sat 10–6. Kingsbury Hall on the University of Utah campus handles ArtTix services only for its own performances. Additional ArtTix ticket offices are found in most Albertson's grocery stores in the Salt Lake Valley, at the customer service booth, open Mon–Sat 9–8.*

Smith's Tix, 801/467-8499 or 800/888-8499, is another major ticketing agency in Salt Lake City, with tickets sold by phone or from the customer service booths at most Smith's Food and Drug Center stores. Smith's Tix offices are open Mon–Sat 10–8, Sun 10–5.

*Several outlets sell tickets to cultural events: **Pioneer Theatre Box Office**, 300 S. 1340 East St., 801/581-6961; **Ticket Exchange**, 165 S. West Temple St., 801/328-8490; **Utah Symphony Tickets**, 123 W. South Temple St., 801/533-6683. In addition to the above vendors, many venues sell tickets directly.*

opportunity to see often excellent theater close-up and personal. ♿ (University Area)

GRAND THEATRE
Salt Lake Community College
1575 S. State St.
Salt Lake City
801/957-3322
For a decade the Grand has provided Utahns with wholesome productions of mostly well-known dramas, comedies, and musicals. Plays in the last few years have included *Joseph and the Amazing Technicolor Dreamcoat*, *The Sound*

of Music, and *Sweet Charity*. The plays attain excellent production qualities while managing to keep a fun, family-oriented, community theater atmosphere. The cast is drawn not only from students at the community college but also from local citizens of all ages and various theatrical backgrounds. ♿ (Downtown)

HALE CENTER THEATER
3333 S. Decker Lake Blvd.
West Valley City
801/484-9257
The Hale family has provided family and values-based entertainment for

over 15 years. The theater has an extensive repertoire of plays, with over 80 of them written by family matriarch Ruth (Grandma) Hale. Fans of the Hale Centre love the center-stage experience, which seats the audience directly next to the stage and in a total circle around it, offering a more intimate experience with the cast members. They also love the familiarity of the actors, many of whom are Hale family members. In 1998 the theater moved to its current, grand space in West Valley City, which seats 820 patrons. ⅋ (Western Valley)

OFF BROADWAY THEATRE
272 S. Main St.
Salt Lake City
801/355-4628
It's a laff-riot-a-minute at the Off Broadway, Salt Lake City's only full-time live comedy theater. Spoofs make gentle fun of both local and national events, and major Broadway productions and TV shows are parodied. An popular improv troupe known as the Quick Wits performs every Fri and Sat night at 10. A second theater location is in Murray at 4900 South State St. (801/262-6219), where the Quick Wits perform Wed at 7:30. ⅋ (Downtown)

PIONEER THEATRE COMPANY
University of Utah
300 S. 1340 East St.
Salt Lake City
801/581-6961
For 35 years the professional company-in-residence at the University of Utah has provided entertainment for the community, as well as a theatrical education for university students. From its home in the 1,000-seat Pioneer Theatre, the company mounts a season of seven plays running from September through May.

Plays run the gamut in styles and subject matter, and production is ambitious, with major musicals such as *Into the Woods* as well as classics such as *A Tale of Two Cities*. An annual audience of about 100,000 theatergoers enjoys the performances of this company, which has a well-deserved reputation for excellence. ⅋ (University Area)

SALT LAKE ACTING COMPANY
168 W. 500 North St.
Salt Lake City
801/363-0526
The Salt Lake Acting Company is beloved by theater patrons who want entertainment that is hip, bold, and sometimes risky. The professional company performs mostly contemporary dramas, comedies, and small musicals, and features new plays from award-winning writers and newcomers. Its two theaters are housed in a historic church in Salt Lake City's Marmalade Hill district. SLAC regularly sells out its season of plays, and its annual summer produc-

Utah Opera's performance
of Helen of Troy, *p. 165*

Utah Travel Council/Frank Jensen

Ballet West, p. 166

tion of *Saturday's Voyeur* is hugely popular with Salt Lakers, who enjoy its in-jokes and parodies of local events. & (Downtown)

STAGERIGHT THEATER
1140 S. 900 East St.
Salt Lake City
801/485-8038
StageRight is a lively volunteer company with a mission of serving Everyman by offering classical theater at low prices and appealing to not only regular theatergoers but nontraditional audiences as well. Its repertoire spans the classics from Shakespeare to the modern age. For six years it has served as resident company for Realms of Inquiry private school, and many of the productions feature student involvement. Community participation is encouraged as well. & (Downtown)

MUSIC AND OPERA

CHASE HOME MUSEUM OF UTAH FOLK ART

Liberty Park
900 S. 700 East St.
Salt Lake City
801/533-5760
The Utah Arts Council's Folk Arts division hosts a weekly series of concerts each August in the large, grassy area that makes up the front yard of the Folk Art Museum. The concerts are meant to showcase Utah's lesser-known folk artists, and the music featured is wide-ranging and unusual and a lot of fun. A typical Monday night might bring Japanese taiko drumming, Tongan singers, or a Scottish drum corps and pipers. Concerts are free and begin at 7 every Monday night. Many patrons bring lawn chairs and snacks. & (Downtown)

GINA BACHAUER INTERNATIONAL PIANO COMPETITION
Abravanel Hall
123 W. South Temple St.
801/521-9200
Named after pianist Gina Bachauer, this 22-year-old piano competition is one of the most prestigious in the world, often spinning its winners and non-winners alike on to performance careers. The competition is held every fourth year in June and offers prize money of over $100,000. Approximately 50 contestants are accepted from a field of applicants five times that size. Pianists come from all over the world, and while in Utah they stay with host families—an unusual situation that makes the Bachauer one of the more popular competitions. The public is invited to attend many of the juried concerts. & (Downtown)

JAZZ CONCERT SERIES AT THE HILTON
150 W. 500 South St.

Salt Lake City
801/278-0411
From September through June the Hilton hosts 11 jazz concerts in its 1,200-capacity Seasons Ballroom. Most of the performers are huge names in the world of jazz, although some local musicians play as well. Call the above number for the upcoming season's schedule and information on individual and season tickets. (Downtown)

MORMON TABERNACLE CHOIR
Tabernacle at Temple Square
South Temple and State Sts.
801/240-1000
After the Great Salt Lake, the Mormon Tabernacle Choir may be Utah's most famous attraction. The 320-member choir, an official division of the Mormon Church, and is named after its performance home in the Tabernacle at Temple Square. The choir's weekly rehearsals and performances are free and open to the public, and seats are much coveted and nearly always filled. The choir's Sunday morning radio/TV program, *Music and the Spoken Word*, is the longest-running radio program ever, carried live by over 500 stations around the world. The singing group has become a national symbol of patriotism, and has performed at four presidential inaugurations as well as many historic national events. Recordings are sold all over the world, and annual tours have included many of the world's major concert halls.

Rehearsals for the radio broadcast are held each Thursday from 8 to 9:30 p.m. Broadcasts are each Sunday from 9:30 to 10 a.m.; the audience is asked to be seated by 9:15. The organ that accompanies the choir is famous in its own right, as one of the largest pipe organs in the world. Thirty-minute organ concerts, sans choir, are offered every day in the summer at 12 and 2 p.m. (2 p.m. only on Sunday) and less often during the winter. ♿ (Downtown)

TEMPLE SQUARE CONCERT SERIES
Assembly Hall at Temple Square
South Temple and State Sts.
Salt Lake City
801/240-1000
The Mormon Church hosts a year-round series of classical concerts each Friday and Saturday night from its Assembly Hall on Temple Square. The smallish hall has a formal surround and excellent acoustics and is a perfect venue for the mostly local performers. Typical concerts might feature an opera selection, a piano quartet, a choir, or an army band. Concerts are free. (Downtown)

UTAH OPERA COMPANY
Capitol Theatre
50 W. 200 South St.
Salt Lake City
801/323-6868

TRIVIA

Established by the state legislature in 1899 to "stimulate and encourage the arts," the Utah Arts Council is the oldest publicly subsidized arts council in the country.

People may have scoffed when Utah Opera Company performed its first season in 1978. Productions were somewhat uneven, and many of the artists were known only locally. Founder Glade Peterson had a vision, however, and in just a few years he had turned Utah's resident opera company into a classy, professional operation. A work commissioned in 1996 for Utah's Centennial, *Dreamkeepers*, was written and produced by Utahans and received national rave reviews. The opera currently sells out almost all of its four productions each year, performing for over 130,000 people during its season. Its "Opera In The Schools" program instills appreciation in the next generation of opera lovers. Utah Opera's director is Anne Ewers. ♿ (Downtown)

UTAH SYMPHONY
Abravanel Hall
123 W. S. Temple St.
801/533-6683
The Utah Symphony's stature as one of the country's leading professional orchestra is, quite frankly, surprising, given Salt Lake City's smallish population and Utah's rural roots. The symphony's success is generally credited to conductor Maurice Abravanel, who was hired in the mid-1940s and not only saved the symphony from bankruptcy but turned it into a world-class organization. The symphony records extensively (its recordings of all 10 Mahler symphonies is notable), tours internationally, performs regularly in Utah schools, and stages a full winter season as well as several outdoor summer concert series. Utah Symphony's conductor is Keith Lockhart. ♿ (Downtown)

WESTMINSTER COLLEGE CONCERT SERIES
1840 S. 1300 East St.
Salt Lake City
801/484-7651
This small liberal-arts college in the heart of Salt Lake City serves its community with several excellent series. The Anne Newman Sutton Weeks Poetry Series brings some of the most acclaimed poets in the country to the campus for readings and workshops. Dramas and comedies are offered by the college's very own Westminster Players, and an eclectic series of musical concerts features local performers. Most presentations take place in Westminster's Jewett Center. ♿ (Downtown)

DANCE

BALLET WEST
Capitol Theatre
50 W. 200 South St.
Salt Lake City
801/323-6900
Ballet West is another of Salt Lake City's cultural jewels and a considerable source of community pride. It is one of the premiere ballet companies in the country, with a reputation well-known in the dance world. Founded over 30 years ago, the company now has a 40-week season with a company of approximately 40 dancers and a full-time support staff that includes exclusive costume and scenery shops. The company has performed virtually all of the classical ballets, as well as original and modern works that have sometimes raised the eyebrows of Salt Lake City's more traditional arts patrons. Company founder Willam F. Christensen also created the University of Utah's ballet department (the first at

an American university), which continues to profit from its association with Ballet West. The Ballet West Conservatory is the official company dance school for children ages 12 to 17. Ballet West's outreach programs include lecture/performances in Utah's elementary schools and specially priced student matinees. The company is currently directed by Jonas Kage and performs over 100 productions each year, mostly in the Capitol Theatre, but also in venues in other Utah cities. ⅃ (Downtown)

CHILDREN'S DANCE THEATRE
University of Utah
230 S. Wasatch Dr.
Salt Lake City
801/581-7374
The dancers are schoolchildren from third grade through high school who are accepted through a competitive process. They meet for classes twice a week during the school year and create an original, full-length program—complete with costumes,

sets, and live music—which is performed each spring in the Capitol Theatre. The company has received rave national reviews for its professionalism and high quality of performance. ⅃ (University Area)

KISMET DANCE COMPANY
1760 S. 1100 East St.
Salt Lake City
801/486-7780
Kismet is the biggest and best producer of the art of danse oriental (aka belly dancing) in the West. Company founders Jason and Yasamina Roque offer a year-round plethora of shows, festivals, and seminars, which over the last 20 years have earned a stellar reputation. Kismet hosts the Utah Belly Dance Festival in Liberty Park each August, purportedly the largest such festival in the nation, with a hundred or so dancers performing for a crowd of thousands. ⅃ (Downtown)

REPERTORY DANCE THEATRE
Rose Wagner Performing Arts

Vaudeville Days

Completed in 1861, the Salt Lake Theatre was one of the first major buildings in the Salt Lake Valley, when the population of Salt Lake City was a mere 12,000. It stood on the corner of what is now State Street and 100 South Street, and played host to a number of theatrical performances and musicals. The theater's heyday was during the vaudeville era, when nearly all of the major acts of the time passed through Salt Lake City. Those who graced the stage include P.T. Barnum, the Barrymores, Buffalo Bill Cody, Sarah Bernhardt, Al Jolson, and Lillian Russell. Oscar Wilde gave one of his famous elocutionary recitals on the small stage. During the Depression, hard times fell on the theater, and it was finally razed in the late 1930s.

Abravanel Hall

Center
138 W. 300 South St.
Salt Lake City
801/534-1000
RDT, as it is known locally, is a pioneer in the history of modern dance in the West. When it was formed in 1966, modern dance, especially a professional company that employed full-time dancers, was relatively rare anywhere in the country. Its goals back then were the same as today—to create meaningful artistic projects, to inspire artistic creation, and to explore a broad range of cultural and artistic topics. Besides its primary season of concerts, RDT hosts small, often cutting-edge "black box" performances featuring new and emerging choreographers (named for the intimate, black-walled studio where they are performed). The company is currently engaged in a five-year "Millennium" series that celebrates Salt Lake City's hosting of the Olympic Winter Games of 2002 with guest artists from five different continents. ⅍ (Downtown)

RIRIE-WOODBURY
DANCE COMPANY
Capitol Theatre
50 W. 200 South St.
Salt Lake City
801/323-6801
Shirley Ririe and Joan Woodbury formed their modern dance company in 1964 with the goal of combining formal performances and community residencies. In the three decades since, the company has become not only a dance institution in Utah but a leader in "Artists in Schools" projects, performing for students and assisting teachers in creating fine-arts curriculums. Its six dancers (three men and three women) perform an at-home season of dances from September through May, tour extensively throughout the United States, and teach and perform at a number of rural Utah schools. ⅍ (Downtown)

CONCERT VENUES

ABRAVANEL HALL
123 W. South Temple St.
Salt Lake City
801/323-6800
This grand symphony hall is named after a former maestro, Maurice Abravanel. It was built in 1979 as part of Utah's Bicentennial Arts Center at a cost of $10 million. Its exterior is an ultramodern cliff wall of cement and glass, and its wide, sweeping interior is splashed with gold leaf and crystal chandeliers. The wood-lined concert hall is famous for superior acoustics. The Utah Symphony makes its performance home here, and a number of classical and popular concerts are performed throughout the year. ⅍ (Downtown)

CAPITOL THEATRE
50 W. 200 South St.
Salt Lake City
801/323-6800

Salt Lakers love their gaudy, opulent Capitol Theatre. It was built in 1913, and its stage has played host to vaudeville entertainers as well as silent movies accompanied by a Wurlitzer organ. After a renovation in the middle of the century, the theater served for decades as Salt Lake City's fanciest movie theater. In 1975 Salt Lakers voted for an $8.6-million bond to renovate the run-down building, resulting in the present state-of-the-art (but still baroquely flamboyant) theater for the performing arts. It is the performance home of Ballet West, Utah Opera Company, Ririe-Woodbury Dance Company, and Children's Dance Theatre. A host of other local and touring performers use the stage as well, including major Broadway shows. ☈ (Downtown)

DELTA CENTER
301 W. South Temple St.
Salt Lake City
801/325-2000

The huge arena at the Delta Center is home turf for both of Utah's pro basketball teams—the NBA Utah Jazz and the WNBA Utah Starzz. On non-basketball nights the Delta Center is often the scene of major rock shows, rodeos, and other community events. (See also Chapter 10, Sports and Recreation.) ☈ (Downtown)

KINGSBURY HALL
Presidents Circle,
University of Utah
Salt Lake City
801/581-7100

Fresh from a $13-million facelift, Kingsbury is enjoying the benefits of lush 70-year-old architecture and state-of-the art production equipment. Its new seven-story stage fronts a mechanized orchestra pit, while the hall's walls are covered with gilt and murals from a time when hand decoration was an art. Kingsbury is one of the older buildings on the campus of the University of Utah, the home of the U's first "Dramatic Club." In its present reincarnation, its primary purpose is as a venue for student productions and academic activities. National touring shows and musicals are also performed here, as well as numerous community dramatic and musical programs. ☈ (University Area)

SALTAIR
Access road off I-80, Exit 104
Magna
801/250-1308

This resort 17 miles west of Salt Lake City on the south shores of the Great Salt Lake has a voluminous central lobby that is fairly often the scene of alternative concerts. High school and college-age people love this impossible-to-damage floorspace far away from civilization. ☈ (Western Valley)

Utah Travel Council

12

NIGHTLIFE

Yes, it's true. Salt Lake City is not the center of the universe when it comes to nightlife or clubbing or partying in general. The city's straightlaced reputation is perhaps deserved when compared with other same-size metropolitan areas, and it can be said truthfully that the streets do not burst with noise and gaiety in the hours after dark. However, it absolutely is possible to venture out on any night of the week and find all sorts of live music, dancing, and socializing opportunities. The choices, though perhaps limited, are wide-ranging and eclectic.

Excellent country-western bars are found in the south end of town, with arena-sized dance floors and top-name touring performers. Swing and line dancing are the favored steps, and even first-timers can navigate the floor after a short practice session.

Pricey places-to-be-seen are found in the city center, where clothes and companions are rated on an invisible style meter. Even the less glamorous among us can appreciate the truly lovely architecture and furnishings found in some of these places, as well as the excellent food and drink.

A major university found inside Salt Lake City's borders ensure a raucous bar scene, infused with alternative music and dance. These nightspots are generally found in not-yet-renovated buildings and fringe areas of town, and often the music and socializing don't begin until well into the night.

Note:The nightspots listed below are designated as "private clubs" or "taverns" where applicable. These labels refer to legal licenses to sell mixed drinks and/or beer (see "Booze News" sidebar, page 172, for more information). Listings without either of these designations do not sell liquor on the premises.

DANCE CLUBS

THE BAY
404 S. West Temple St.
Salt Lake City
801/532-9114
Serious teenage action is found here on the weekends, as the under-21 crowd lines up around the block in an attempt to get inside. There is no smoking or drinking, but excruciatingly loud dance music and multitudes of writhing bodies contribute to a semi-adult atmosphere. In summer an outdoor patio and swimming pool contribute to the frenzy, and all year the multileveled dance floors feature karaoke, top-40, and all-request and country nights. (Downtown)

MANHATTAN CLUB
5 E. 400 South St.
Salt Lake City
801/364-7651
For decades the Manhattan was an insiders' club, and its totally glammed out '50s decor was known only to a fortunate few. That has all changed during the last few years as the college crowd began to discover this gem of a hangout, dressing up in droves on the weekends to listen to the live combo and dance on the tiny, perfect dance floor. From its kitschy exterior sign to its curved leather banquettes to its pink powder room, the Manhattan is the real thing, and it is hoped that its current renaissance will not herald an update in decor. Private club. (Downtown)

RASKALS
832 E. 3900 South St.
Salt Lake City
801/269-8383
Raskals found a good thing with the '80s-style dance scene, and it has continued to fill this niche through the end of the 20th century. Partying and preening are recognized pastimes, but steppin' out on the brightly lit, center-stage dance floor takes precedence over everything else. Alternative lifestylers and their friends are part of the regular clientele, and a strict dress code is enforced that prohibits, among other things, collarless shirts. Private club. (Southeastern Valley)

SANDY'S STATION
8925 S. 255 West St.
Sandy
801/255-2289
The Station's huge, barnlike interior accommodates a variety of concurrent activities, including pool, TV watching, and loud drinking contests; however, line dancing to country-western music is the most popular of all. Some big-name country-western bands stop here on road tours, and live entertainment is a staple. Partiers of all ages pack this place most nights, and the single room is so large that patrons are advised to establish a meeting place if they lose sight of each other. Private club. (Cottonwood Canyons and Environs)

THE TRAPP
102 S. 600 West St.
Salt Lake City
801/531-8727
The Trapp may be Utah's only gay country-western bar, and the scene here may not be truly country, but it is openly gay. The corner location is surrounded by an industrial area, which is lucky, because most nights the recorded singing of various country-music stars can be heard for blocks away. Notable is the large patio, which the owners have managed to make into a true garden spot, and the rhinestone boots that

Booze News

Utah liquor laws are much-maligned and often misunderstood. It is not difficult to purchase alcohol in Salt Lake City; however, a description of the rules and regulations is helpful.

1. Liquor is sold in two ways: by the bottle or by the drink. Bottles may be purchased only at state-affiliated liquor stores or package agencies. Liquor store locations are listed in the blue pages of the phone book under "State Government, Alcoholic Beverage Control."

2. Hard-liquor drinks are sold only at restaurants with special permits, at "private clubs," and at the airport.

3. In restaurants with special permits, food must be purchased in order to buy an alcoholic drink. In private clubs, drinks may be bought without a food order.

4. Private clubs require a membership fee for entrance. You can buy an annual membership or a five-dollar temporary membership, good for two weeks, on-site at any private club.

5. "Taverns" have not been granted private club licenses—they can sell beer and wine spritzers only.

take the place of a disco ball on the ceiling of the dance floor. Private club. (Western Valley)

THE WESTERNER CLUB
3360 S. Redwood Rd.
West Valley City
801/972-5447
It's almost impossible to miss The Westerner, with its faux Wild West exterior created to look like a set from *Gunsmoke*. There is nothing faux, however, about its country-western appeal. Some of the biggest acts in the country-western business perform here, and on weekend nights the place is packed

with cowboys and cowgirls looking for a good time. The dance floor is huge, and the live music flows on most nights. Mondays are saved for karoake and open mike, and free swing and line dance lessons are offered on Mon, Tue, and Wed nights. Private club. (Western Valley)

MUSIC CLUBS

BARBARY COAST
4242 S. State St.
Murray
801/265-9889

Sometimes called "the best biker bar in the state," the Barbary Coast cements its reputation with an ever-present row of fancy motorcycles by the door and a clientele that favors leather and tattoos. The exterior has seen better days, but the bar is clean and well-aired and pleasant. Danceable live music is presented on Friday and Saturday nights (a house band is called Roadkill), and the people-watching is worth the price of admission. Private club. (Southeastern Valley)

BRICK'S
579 W. 200 South St.
Salt Lake City
801/328-0255

This place is huge—both in size and popularity. Brick's takes up close to a city block, and the 30-and-under-crowd waits outside in long lines, late into the night, for a chance to be granted entrance. Once inside they find a kaleidoscope of hip offerings in five (at last count—Brick's keeps adding on) huge rooms and several outside decks and patios, all of which feature different styles of music and ambience. Every night of the week has a rotating theme: techno-pop, live DJ, swing, and gay nights are among the choices. Brick's has a good ear for music and the live, touring bands that play here often launch to the big time. Beware the noise level; the sound system in one room alone cost over $1 million. Private club. (Downtown)

BURT'S TIKI LOUNGE
726 S. State St.
Salt Lake City
801/521-0572

Burt's is small and shabby and beloved by crowds of alternatively dressed and colorfully coiffed young adults. Decor is true tiki; palm fronds on the ceiling and a surfboard mounted on the wall. The unmatched chairs and tables are strewn about the room, the beer is not quite cold enough, and "No cover ever!" is the rallying theme. Live bands with shocking names play regularly, cranking up at about 10 o'clock and playing into the night. Tavern. (Downtown)

CANYON INN
3700 E. 7000 South St.
Holladay
801/942-9801

The Inn has been in the same place and served the same function for decades—a wild, cowboy, kick-up-your-heels sort of place. It has become a private club to accommodate patrons who want well drinks, but it keeps a firm hold on its tavern roots and ambience, with rough-hewn pine decor, well-used tables and chairs, and a television screen that fills an entire wall. Live music starts at about 9 p.m. on weekends, and dancing takes precedence over

Oyster Bar, p. 179

Tom Anastasian

other activities. A full-service menu features steak and potatoes. Private club. (Cottonwood Canyons and Environs)

CLUB DV8
115 S. West Temple St.
Salt Lake City
801/539-8400
Alternative is the rule here, in all of its glorious manifestations. The music is loud and percussive-based, and the clientele is dressed either in peacock colors or totally in black. There are two levels, and while they share the same music, the upper level, where drinks are served, is reserved for 21 years and older only. Live music is a staple here, and some big-name bands have graced the stage. Private club. (Downtown)

CROCODILE LOUNGE
60 E. 800 South St.
Salt Lake City
801/575-6900
A huge metal crocodile slithers across the exterior of this building, making it one of the most identifiable clubs in town. The Cajun food is more than respectable, and the menu is one of the few in town that regularly lists crocodile. The decor is upscale swamp, with trees and vines undulating between the 30 or so tables. It is possible to get a seat in the evening hours, so diners should arrive early. Most nights, especially on weekends, a band begins to set up about 10 o'clock, and the place fills up fast. Private club. (Downtown)

DIMITRI'S
6121 S. Highland Dr.
Holladay
801/277-7776

This big club is filled with lots of smaller spaces designated for different activities. The dance floor is surrounded by small, romantically lit tables. Live music, mostly of the classic rock variety, is performed on weekends. A corridor lined with big booths is perfect for dinner and conversation. A backlit bar surrounds the busy bartenders and provides a seating area from which to watch the other patrons. Big-screen TVs draw a sports-watching crowd who flock here on Monday nights during the fall for dollar spaghetti dinners. Private club. (Southeastern Valley)

HOLY COW
241 S. 500 East St.
Salt Lake City
801/531-8259
The live music is the thing here, with almost-weekly presentations by some of the best local and touring bands in the country. The oeuvre is mostly alternative rock and blues, and the crowd is mostly college kids. The origin of Holy Cow's name is not clear; however, it may stem from the wall mural, which features a bovine reenactment of the Last Supper. Music and cows aside, this huge, single room has the ambience of a basement rec room, fitted with uncomfortable chairs and a half-dozen televisions. Private club. (Downtown)

LIQUID JOE'S
1249 E. 3300 South St.
Salt Lake City
801/467-5637
Patrons seeking a cozy atmosphere should be advised to go somewhere else. This warehouse-style expanse of a club skimped on the wall decor, but made up for it in a

Iggy's Sports Grill, p. 178

huge sound system that envelopes the room. Live music is played most nights, and some serious dancing takes place on the large dance floor. Dress is casual. Private club. (Southeastern Valley)

OLYMPIC CLUB
1193 E. Wilmington Ave.
Salt Lake City
801/466-1796
It is always nighttime inside the Olympic, with mood lighting below and a faux starry sky above. For eyes that do manage to adjust to the low wattage, the leatherette bar and comfy booths are shadowy places for a drink and conversation. Live music is sometimes imported, but most nights the piped music is perfect for a slow turn around the dance floor. Private club. (Southeastern Valley)

THE ZEPHYR CLUB
301 S. W. Temple St.
Salt Lake City
801/355-2582
Often cited as Salt Lake City's best club for live music, the Zephyr features emerging and already-famous bands every night of the week. Seating on both levels of the club is directed at the stage and the dance floor, and music is the focus here, not food or conversation. Music styles run the gamut from grunge to disco to soul, and the large billboard posted outside acts as a calendar listing. The age of patrons varies with the program, but if you're a music lover who can tolerate noise and crowds, this is a comfortable place any night of the week. Private club. (Downtown)

PUBS AND BARS

BAR X
155 E. 200 South St.
Salt Lake City
801/532-9114
Bar X's history is as interesting as its present. For years it was a down-at-the-heels haven for men only, and women were not only turned away at the door, they were unceremoniously

disconnected when they attempted to phone any of the patrons. In the 1970s an ardent female television reporter burst into the bar on live TV, loudly renouncing the illegality of its exclusive policy. Since then, the X has gone through several rotations of clients (all of which include females), and currently it is favored by college kids. The house specialty is tap beer served in 32-ounce glass tankards, and the primary activities are flirting and pool. Tavern. (Downtown)

BEL AIR LOUNGE
161 E. Broadway
Salt Lake City
801/532-5254
Beware the badly drawn velvet paintings of nudes and the sliced-up Naugahyde booths. This bar has not yielded to the recent gentrification of the surrounding neighborhood, and remains the same dark and seedy bar it has been for decades. The clientele is distant but friendly. Snacks include pickled eggs. Tavern. (Downtown)

BONGO LOUNGE
2965 S. Highland Dr.
Salt Lake City
801/466-1577
The Bongo is a mere shadow of its former self, when its comfy booths and old-fashioned decor attracted a full house of revelers almost every night. Attempts at modernization have left it colorless, and the current clientele consists mostly of devoted regulars. Tavern. (Southeastern Valley)

COTTON BOTTOM
2820 E. 6200 South St.
Holladay
801/273-9830
The primary action at this small, neighborhood-type bar centers

around the kitchen doorway, from which emerge incredibly fabulous garlic burgers. Order one for yourself and one for your friends, because the burger's piquance will remain with you for some time. The burgers are well worth a visit; however, dense cigarette smoke is a perpetual annoyance here. Nonsmoking patrons will do well to come here in warm weather, when a large outdoor patio is open. Tavern. (Cottonwood Canyons and Environs)

HOG WALLOW PUB
3200 E. Big Cottonwood
Canyon Rd.
Holladay
801/733-5567
Perhaps this area held a pig farm at one time, but the tavern's present setting, tucked between old creek banks with an upward view of the Wasatch Mountains, is lovely. The grounds are filled with river rocks and native grasses; the interior is updated rustic lodge. A highlight is the tiered outdoor patio, with tables hidden among the rock-and-plant nooks. Indoors, there is a long bar and a pool table. The beer list is long, and the menu is short, with pizza being the best choice. Acoustic-type rock is played live four nights a week. Tavern. (Cottonwood Canyons and Environs)

JUNIOR'S TAVERN
202 E. 500 South St.
Salt Lake City
801/322-0318
Junior's is a place for long philosophical discussions and games of chess, as long as you don't mind the decades-old smell of stale beer and the withered pine decor. It is dark and friendly and quiet—and best of all, the library is just across the street. Tavern. (Downtown)

Port O' Call Social Club, p. 179

TAP ROOM
2168 S. Highland Dr.
Salt Lake City
801/466-0974
Famous for being Utah's smallest bar, the Tap Room has a cute log exterior that can barely be seen between the pushy strip malls that have sprung up on all sides. The tiny interior may be charming, but once a few patrons crowd into the place, it is hard to tell where the seats are or what is on the walls. The snacks consist pretty much of nuts and jerky, but the beer is always ice cold. Tavern. (Southeastern Valley)

SOCIAL CLUBS

D.B. COOPERS SOCIAL CLUB
19 E. 200 South St.
Salt Lake City
801/532-2948
D.B.'s is like an old, reliable friend, occupying the same below-street-level space for several decades. Thankfully, no one has felt the need to rearrange the seating or change the decor, and it remains a manly sort of place, good for business lunches and late-night dates. The club is named after the once-infamous Cooper, who stole a fortune and got away with it. A small stage is occasionally set up for live music. Private club. (Downtown)

FATS GRILL & POOL
2182 S. Highland Dr.
Salt Lake City
801/484-9467
The emphasis is more on the pool than on the grill. Fats' large and well-lit room comfortably holds eight full-sized pool tables, most of which are constantly in service on weekend nights. A big-screen sports TV entertains the crowd of cue-holders waiting for a free table. The grill portion of Fats' service consists of sandwiches and pizza. (Southeastern Valley)

FIDDLER'S ELBOW
1063 ½ 2100 South St.
Salt Lake City
801/463-9393

The ½ part of the address means it is hard to find, and a journey down a narrow alley is required to reach the front door. Once inside, patrons find a large, well-lit room with several dozen booths and tables, a wall-length bar, pool tables, and (weather permitting) a pleasant patio. Microbrewed beer from several local makers is featured, and 32 (count 'em) beers are always on tap. The menu includes great meat loaf and fish-and-chips. Bands tend toward the acoustic bluegrass and folk varieties, and their audio level rarely discounts conversation. Tavern. (Southeastern Valley)

GREEN STREET SOCIAL CLUB
Trolley Square
600 E. 500 South St.
Salt Lake City
801/532-4200
Green Street was ousted from its decades-old home by Salt Lake City's new Hard Rock Café, but has successfully relocated to the west end of Trolley Square. The new digs are airy and spacious, but retain the familiar Green Street cozy, private-conversation, back-booth sort of ambience. A lovely bar and two levels of seating accommodate Green Street's throng of regulars, and live music is usually performed on weekends. A full-service menu includes a very good pot roast dinner. Well drinks are recommended, as the beer and wine lists are ordinary. Private club. (Downtown)

IGGY'S SPORTS GRILL
677 S. 200 West St.
Salt Lake City
801/532-9999
A jovial crowd is always found here—eating, drinking from Go-liath-sized mugs, and watching one of the giant TV screens that drop from the walls like basketball nets. The decor, not surprisingly, consists solely of sports memorabilia. But even the most rabid sports fans will pause to notice the food here, which is excellent—the menu is lineman-sized, with about 70 items from which to choose. The beer list includes two Iggy's specialties that celebrate a local rivalry—Crimson ale is dedicated to University of Utah fans, while Blueberry interprets the colors of nearby Brigham Young University. Iggy's rooms are large, clean, and smoke-free. Private club. (Downtown)

LUMPY'S
3000 S. Highland Dr.
Holladay
801/484-5597
Lumpy's patrons are loyal and legion. On big (and small) game nights this place is packed with serious sports fans who prefer cheering en masse. The bar holds at least four separate viewing areas, and often fans of various sports set up camp throughout. A younger crowd tends to dominate the lower level, while the upstairs is saved for the over-30s. The menu is excellent, and the prime-rib sandwiches are famous. Private club. (Southeastern Valley)

MULBOON'S 13TH FLOOR AT THE OLYMPUS HOTEL
161 W. 600 South St.
Salt Lake City
801/530-1313
The killer view of the city from this restaurant/bar is unfortunately eclipsed by mediocre food and an indifferent waitstaff. To further muck things up, the owners have placed

various visual barriers throughout the room, making an unimpeded valley view impossible. What can be seen is still worth a trip, especially at night, and drinks and snacks to begin or end an evening are recommended. (Downtown)

OYSTER BAR
54 W. Market St.
Salt Lake City
801/531-6044

This is one of the few always-on, truly hip spots in town. Upscale folks of all ages fill this place from lunchtime until the wee hours. The decor is marble and glass and original art, the food is excellent, the drinks are perfectly served, and the waitstaff could model for a Gap ad. The setup is perfect for people-watching, with large windows looking onto the street, and interior booths graduated so everyone can be seen by everyone else. Yes—fresh oysters of all kinds, both raw and cooked, are always on the menu. Private club. (Downtown)

PORT O' CALL SOCIAL CLUB
400 S. West Temple St.
Salt Lake City
801/521-0589

The blowsy, beery decor seems to make everybody feel at home. Partiers of all ages and inclinations pack the Port almost every night of the week. Live music is played most nights on the main floor, and occasionally on the patio as well. The huge game room downstairs features eight pool tables, pinball machines, video games, and music from a jukebox. Private club. (Downtown)

TOTEM'S PRIVATE CLUB AND STEAKHOUSE
538 S. Redwood Rd.

Salt Lake City
801/975-0401

If a log cabin took steroids, it might turn into Totem's—a huge, faux-pine affair built to feed and water a thousand working-class folks at a time. One side of the building has been isolated as a restaurant, while the much bigger and friendlier space is outfitted as a drinking, dancing, and dining club. Private club. (Western Valley)

WIDOW McCOY'S
3928 S. Highland Dr.
Holladay
801/277-4233

Widow's is a big, wheeler-dealer sort of place, with schmaltzy decor and disco-ball lighting. The fab environs would seem to encourage dressing up and drinking colorful cocktails, and a dress code is posted, but most nights the clientele doesn't seem up to the task. A further anomaly is provided by midweek evenings of entertainment featuring female mud wrestlers. A live DJ spins the vinyl on weekends. Private club. (Southeastern Valley)

MOVIE HOUSES OF NOTE

BREWVIES CINEMA CLUB
677 S. 200 West St.
Salt Lake City
801/355-5500

For those who like the comforts of home video-watching but want more of a social experience, Brewvies is the answer. The setting is theater-like, but equipped with café tables and spacious, comfortable seating. The movies are first-runs, and the audiovisuals are first-rate. The menu is filled with perfect movie-watching food: pizza and hamburgers and spicy sandwiches. Pitchers of

microbrewed beer complete the experience. Tavern. (Downtown)

TOWER THEATER
1100 E. 900 South St.
Salt Lake City
801/297-4040
The Tower is Salt Lake City's last,
best hope for a cinema art house.
The seats may be funky and the
screen has seen better days, but
the theater is beloved by movie
afficionados for its cutting-edge
agenda. The marquee offerings
are far-ranging, eclectic, and
sometimes weird, but the movies
are dependably worth seeing.
Recuts of classics, independents,
foreign films, and winners of small
film festivals are shown, along with
anything else that catches the
management's fancy. The Tower
also has an excellent lending
library, alphabetized by director,
featuring titles found nowhere else
in town. (Downtown)

13

DAY TRIPS FROM SALT LAKE CITY

DAY TRIP: Antelope Island State Park

Distance from Salt Lake City: 40 miles or about 45 minutes by car

Antelope Island, the largest island in the Great Salt Lake, is just a short drive from a heavily populated metropolitan area, but worlds away in terms of solitude and natural beauty. Antelope's 28,000 acres of low, rolling hills support a bison herd of 600 as well as bighorn sheep, deer, and coyote. Recently antelope were reintroduced to life on the island after a many-year absence. The unique-in-the-world ecosystem provided by the salty lake attracts millions of migrating fowl and shorebirds, and birdwatchers flock here from all over the world. No fish can survive the salty water of the lake, but brine flies and brine shrimp thrive.

The island is reached by crossing a 7.5-mile causeway, and while most visitors prefer to travel in cars, bike-riding across this flat, narrow span (built with especially wide bike lanes) is great fun. Once on the island, 20 miles of backcountry trails are set aside for biking and hiking, and rollerblading is popular on paved roads. An outfitter offers guided horseback rides. An eight-mile loop road provides pullouts and overlooks for stellar lake and island views; the sunset hours are an ideal time to explore the island, as the light on the lake is especially beautiful.

Take note, swimmers! The rumors about flotation in the Great Salt Lake are mostly true. If the lake level is not too high and the salinity level is adequate, it is almost impossible to sink in this water. You can bob and float for as long as you wish. The best swimming area on Antelope is **Bridger Beach**. Its wide expanses are covered with ultra-fine sand, and it

SALT LAKE CITY REGION

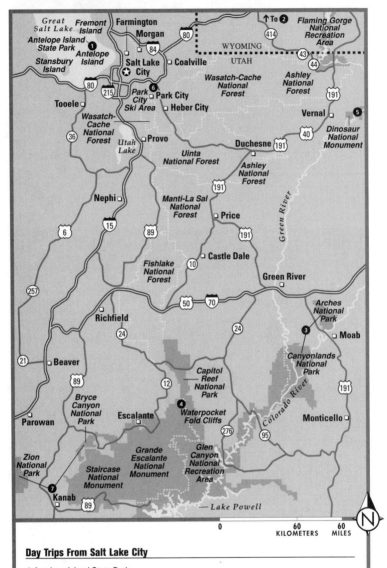

Great Salt Lake
Fremont Island
Farmington
Morgan
↑ To ②
Flaming Gorge National Recreation Area
Antelope Island State Park
Antelope Island ①
Stansbury Island
80
84
WYOMING
414
43
UTAH
44
Salt Lake City ✪
Coalville
Wasatch-Cache National Forest
Ashley National Forest
191
215
Park City Ski Area ⑥ Park City
Tooele
Heber City
Vernal
⑤
Wasatch-Cache National Forest
Utah Lake
Provo
Duchesne
191
40
Dinosaur National Monument
36
Uinta National Forest
Ashley National Forest
Nephi
Manti-La Sal National Forest
191
Green River
15
89
Price
Fishlake National Forest
10
Castle Dale
191
Green River
50
70
Arches National Park
257
Richfield
24
③
Moab
21
Beaver
24
Canyonlands National Park
89
Capitol Reef National Park
12
④
Waterpocket Fold Cliffs
191
Parowan
Bryce Canyon National Park
Escalante
276
Colorado River
Monticello
95
Zion National Park
Grande Staircase Escalante National Monument
Glen Canyon National Recreation Area
Staircase National Monument
⑦
Kanab
89
— Lake Powell

0   60   60
KILOMETERS   MILES

N

Day Trips From Salt Lake City

1 Antelope Island State Park
2 Bear Lake
3 Canyonlands and Arches National Parks
4 Capitol Reef National Park and Grand Staircase/Escalante National Monuments
5 Dinosaurland
6 Park City
7 Zion and Bryce Canyon National Parks

is outfitted with changing cabanas and picnic tables. Outdoor showers are necessary for bathers, who emerge from the water encrusted with salt.

An overnight parking lot is available for RVs, and two campsites are located at Bridger Beach and **White Rock Bay**. Both campsites are primitive, which means there is no on-site running water, no restrooms, and no open fires allowed.

Picnic areas are found along the northern end of the island, and all feature wonderful views of the surrounding lake. **Buffalo Point's** 4,700-foot elevation not only has some of the best views on the island, but also a visitors center and rest rooms. A restaurant near the Buffalo Point Overlook offers buffalo burgers and buffalo bratwurst along with other short-order entrees.

One of the oldest homes in Utah is located on the eastern shore of the island. The **Fielding Garr Ranch House** was built in 1848 and occupied by the seven-member Garr family. Beginning in the spring of 1999 it will be open daily for public tours.

Each autumn for over 100 years a **Bison Roundup** has been held on the island. The entire population of buffalo is rounded up by a volunteer group of hundreds of horsemen and -women. Once the buffalo are penned, they are checked for disease—the phase of the operation that is most popular with the public. You can get rare, close-up views of the mighty beasts as they are worked through a series of corrals; a guide explains the vaccination process.

Getting there from Salt Lake City: Take I-15 north of Salt Lake City to Syracuse, Exit 335. Head west on State Road 108 for seven miles to the causeway entrance.

DAY TRIP: Bear Lake

Distance from Salt Lake City: 130 miles or about 2½ hours by car

Bear Lake straddles the Utah/Idaho border, and the perimeter of its 172 square miles are dotted with parks, lodging facilities, and recreation opportunities. The lake is famous for its vibrant turquoise color and beautiful setting and perhaps lesser known for its depth, which keeps the lake cold even in the hottest summers. Boating and swimming are the preferred activities in summer. In autumn, visitors come from far and wide to witness the spectacular leaf colors in the hills and canyons surrounding the lake. Ice fishers enjoy a unique sport in winter; netting a fish called the Bonneville cisco—a species found only in Bear Lake's unique habitat. The hills surrounding the lake are popular snowmobiling areas, and a small family ski resort called **Beaver Mountain** is 12 miles from the lake, heading west up Logan Canyon.

Garden City is the hub of commercial activity on the lake. Motels ranging from deluxe to spartan are here, as well as campgrounds, a variety of restaurants, shops, and recreation rental businesses. Summer visitors will notice the plethora of signage advertising the area's most famous crop: raspberries. Several stands in town serve excellent raspberry shakes, and other for-sale items include pies, fettuccine, syrup, T-shirts, and silly hats. The raspberry crop is harvested during the first two weeks of August, and Garden City celebrates with an annual **Raspberry Days** event, featuring a craft fair, parade, fun run, rodeo, fireworks, and Western dance.

A fun bicycle path skirts the lake from the **Marina State Park** at the northern end of Garden City to the **Ideal Beach** area four miles south. Nighttime entertainment includes melodrama-style plays at the **Pickleville Playhouse**.

Rendezvous Beach State Park, near the small burg of Laketown, has fine expanses of sandy beach, as well as boat launches and food concessions. The park hosts a **Mountain Man Rendezvous** the second weekend in September, celebrating the lifestyles and activities of the mountain men who tracked and mapped this area 175 years ago.

The **Bear Lake National Wildlife Refuge** is found on the north shores of the lake. Marshes, bogs, and a huge mud lake totaling over 17,600 acres attract sandhill cranes, herons, pelicans, egrets, and myriad species of ducks.

A few miles north of Bear Lake, across the Idaho border, is the town of St. Charles. A canyon here leads to **Minnetonka Cave**, a half-mile geologic wonder. Ranger-led tours of the cave are available in summer for a nominal fee. The tours fill up fast on weekends, however, and there's no phone at the cave, so visitors must drive the 10.5 miles from the main road without assurance they'll be able to get inside.

For more information on the Bear Lake area, call 435/752-2161.

Getting there from Salt Lake City: Drive north on I-15 to Brigham City Exit 364. From Brigham City, take Highway 89 to Logan. From Logan, continue on Highway 89 through Logan Canyon to Garden City, which is located on the west shores of Bear Lake.

DAY TRIP: Park City

Distance from Salt Lake City: 31 miles or about 45 minutes by car

Park City is Salt Lake City's sophisticated sister to the east. Its setting is thoroughly Utahan, but its lifestyle is closer to southern California. The population is young, energetic, and upwardly mobile. Park City's real estate and income levels are often ranked at the top of Utah's money lists.

The city's heart is its historic **Main Street**, a long stretch of Victorian storefronts that have been renovated to maintain their quaint facades. The street originally served thousands of rowdy miners who made Park City a boomtown in the 1800s, flocking here to profit from the massive silver lodes discovered in the surrounding mountains. Main Street is now a tony collection of elegant boutiques, cafés, microbreweries, and trend-setting art galleries and gift shops. Some of Utah's best restaurants are found here, including the super upscale **Grappa Italian Restaurant** and **Zoom Roadhouse Grill**, which is owned by local celebrity Robert Redford. The **Park City Museum**, at 528 Main St., interprets the mining and skiing history of the town and also disburses tourism information. The 75-year-old **Egyptian Theater**, at 328 Main St., serves as the town's community theater, offering family-appropriate comedies and musicals. The **Kimball Art Center** at the bottom of Main St. is famous for its fine exhibits and arts and crafts shows. On summer Saturdays musicians often stroll the street as part of a Performing Arts Series.

Skiers at Park City

Utah Travel Council/Frank Jensen

Park City is perhaps most fa-mous for its world-famous resorts. Four separate recreation areas surround the town, each with their own distinct qualities. **Park City Resort** rises directly above the town, its 3,000 acres of steep terrain culminating at a 10,000-foot summit. The mountain offer challenges for hikers and mountain bikers in summer, and in winter 14 lifts carry 27,000 skiers an hour up the mountainside. The resort has a shopping center as well as several popular restaurants. In summer its base turns into a playground, with miniature golf, children's carnival rides, and an alpine slide that thrills all ages. **The Canyons** resort is found just a few miles north of Park City, with nine major ski runs (snowboarders are welcomed with their own halfpipe and tube runs), three restaurants, and mountain biking in the summer. **Utah Winter Sports Park** is the West's premiere bobsled/luge and Nordic jumping facility. Visitors can watch from a day lodge as athletes train for professional events, and on scheduled days of the week can actually participate in these Olympic sports. Ski jumpers land in a training pool, and luge rides propel novices down a 1,335-meter ice or concrete run, depending on the season. **Deer Valley** is the queen bee of Utah's resorts, where celebrities and other glitterati go to be pampered. In winter the ski runs are meticulously groomed, in summer the trails are well-tended, and all year long the lodging and restaurant facilities are world-class. Lift-served mountain biking is offered during the summer, and the Slopeside Concert Series hosts classical and popular music events in an outdoor theater.

The Park City Silver Mine Adventure is a working mine that offers a unique look at an underground operation. An elevator carries visitors 1,500 feet down a mine shaft (farther underground than the Empire State Building rises aboveground) to a tunnel, where a train is boarded for a two-mile tour of both historic and modern mining techniques. Displays and a gift shop are located above ground.

Shoppers come from far and wide to visit the **Factory Stores at Park City**, a 50-store collections of designer outlets including Mikasa, Gap, Nike, and Ralph Lauren.

For more on Park City's activities and events, call 801/649-6100.

Getting there from Salt Lake City: *Drive east on I-80 to the Kimball Junction/Park City turnoff.*

WEEKEND TRIP: Dinosaurland

Distance from Salt Lake City: 175 miles or about 4 hours by car

"Dinosaurland" did not come by its nickname lightly: The northeastern corner of Utah is seriously old and fossilized. Some of the oldest formations in the world raise their rocky heads in view of passersby, exposing billions of years of geological history. Scientists have recorded over 600 million years of life forms in these hills and mountains, ranging from primitive algae to highly advanced mammals. In the town of Jensen is the **Dinosaur National Monument Quarry**, a building that has been fitted over a 160-foot-long ancient sandbar. Dozens of dinosaurs were trapped in its mire, and their excavated, full skeletons remain in their natural state. In the town of Vernal the **Utah Field House of Natural History State Park** has exhibits of plant, mammal, and human life that once thrived in the area. The adjacent outdoor **Dinosaur Gardens** is home to 18 life-size dinosaur replicas, which are placed in settings that re-create their original homes. Up the road is **Red Fleet State Park**, where the footprints of ancient dinosaurs have been immortalized.

Dinosaur National Monument Quarry

Utah Travel Council/Tom Till

More recent ancient history can be viewed in **Dry Fork Canyon**, about 10 miles outside of Vernal. A thousand-year-old Native American winter camp is now the privately owned McConkie Ranch, and its present owners graciously allow visitors to hike on designated trails and view some of the most outstanding petroglyphs in the world. Yet more petroglyphs can be seen from the **Harper's Corner Road**, accessed from the Quarry, which also showcases the life forms of a mere hundred years ago at the **Homestead of Cowgirl Josie Morris**.

The incredible **Split Mountain Gorge** is best seen from a raft floating the Green River. **Hatch River Expeditions** (800/342-8243) and **Adrift Adventures** (800/824-0150) offer day trips.

In July, Vernal hosts one of the top pro rodeos in the country, the 50-year-old **Dinosaur Round-Up**, as well as the **Outlaw Trail Festival**, which features an amphitheater play re-creating Vernal's infamous cowboy past.

For more information on Dinosaurland call 435/789-6932.

Getting there from Salt Lake City: Drive east on I-80 to Silver Creek Junction, then southeast on State Road 40 through Heber City and on to Vernal.

WEEKEND TRIPS: Southern Utah's National Parks and Monuments

The southern half of Utah is a wide sweep of desert canyons and impossible rock formations. Its geography is so phenomenal and unique that almost the entire lower end of the state has been set aside as six separate national parks and monuments. These public lands, recognized as national treasures, can most easily be divided into three separate, multi-day outings.

ZION AND BRYCE CANYON

Distance from Salt Lake City: 310 miles or about 5–6 hours by car

Zion National Park and Bryce Canyon National Park are in close proximity and have vastly different characteristics, making a visit to both a perfect single vacation. Zion has over 147,000 acres; however, its most popular, much smaller area is called Zion Canyon. Crowded monolithic rocks form the canyon's walls, reflecting rainbows of color all hours of the day, while the Virgin River creates a series of waterfalls and fern gardens. There is a wonderful lodge in the canyon, and the nearby town of Springdale has dozens of lodging, dining, and shopping opportunities. Bryce offers a wonderful contrast to Zion's quiet majesty. Often compared to a fairyland, Bryce's delicate, pastel formations are viewed thousands of acres at a time from a series of viewpoints along the canyon rim. Trails head straight down (and straight back up) into the canyon, offering a close-up view of the rock hoodoos and goblins. There are two full-service lodges within the park, and a number of hotels are located at its entrance. For more information call 435/628-4171.

Getting there from Salt Lake City: Drive south on I-15 for almost 250 miles to Exit 27, near Toquerville. Turn east onto State Road 17/9 to Springdale and the entrance to Zion National Park. From Zion, head east on State Road 9 to the Mt. Carmel Junction, then head north on Highway 89 to its junction with State Road 12 and the turnoff to Bryce Canyon National Park.

CAPITOL REEF AND GRAND STAIRCASE/ESCALANTE

Distance from Salt Lake City: 225 miles or about 4½ hours by car

Capitol Reef National Park and Grand Staircase/Escalante National Monument are both sprawling panoramas of yellow and red and white rock mountains that look as if they have been poured onto a cookie sheet landscape from a huge mixer in the sky. The two are on opposite sides of 11,000-foot **Boulder Mountain** and connected by a beautiful scenic road. Capitol Reef is part of a formation called the Waterpocket Fold, so named because its mesa flattops catch the rain in nature-carved buckets. State Road 24 runs directly through the park and accesses some of its best hikes. An offshoot scenic road passes the park's visitor center, its campgrounds, and then a fee station, which leads to several narrow canyon gorges, historic sites, and incredible view areas. Food and lodging are available in the nearby town of Torrey. Grand Staircase/Escalante National Monument is a whopping 1.7 million acres of multicolored plateaus, descending in a staircase visible only from heaven. Each successive "step" is a separate strata of rock that has weathered the ages according to its density. Calf Creek Falls is a wonderful hike, and its signage is easily seen on the road. Most of the monument, however, is not mapped for visitors, so directions and guide services, available in the towns of Escalante or Boulder, are recommended. For more information on Capitol Reef, call 800/858-7951; for Grand Staircase/Escalante, 435/676-1160.

Zion National Park, p. 187

Utah Travel Council/John Telford

Getting there from Salt Lake City: Drive south on I-15 to Nephi Exit 222. Continue south on State Road 28 to Salina, then head east on I-80 for a short stretch to Exit 85. Take State Road 72 south to its connection to State Road 24, which leads to Torrey and the entrance to Capitol Reef National Park. From Capitol Reef, take State Road 12 to the towns of Boulder and Escalante, which border Grand Staircase/Escalante National Monument.

CANYONLANDS AND ARCHES

Distance from Salt Lake City: 305 miles or about 5½ hours by car

Canyonlands National Park is a land mass that has been sliced neatly into thirds by the tenacious Green and Colorado Rivers. The park's three sections are **The Maze** (aptly named for its zigzag of canyons and known as one of the most inaccessible places in the United States), **The Needles** (named for its piercing spires of rock), and **Island in the Sky** (a stand-alone plateau with unbelievable scenic views). Although they are relatively close as the crow flies, the water and rock that separates them is formidable and they are reached by separate, distant roads. The Maze is accessible only with an off-road vehicle. Arches National Park is just to the north but in a more easily accessed area. Almost the entire park can be reached from a central road, which affords views of hundreds of the 2,000 stone openings that give Arches its name. Many hikes start from the road, offering a closer look at such formations as The Windows and Delicate Arch. Food and lodging for both Canyonlands and Arches is available in the nearby town of Moab. For more information call 435-259-1370.

Getting there from Salt Lake City: Take I-15 south to Spanish Fork Exit, head southeast on State Road 6 to Green River Exit 156. Head east on I-70 to Crescent Junction Exit 180, then south on U.S. 191 to Moab.

APPENDIX: CITY·SMART BASICS

EMERGENCY PHONE NUMBERS

Police/ Fire/ Ambulance—911
Poison Control Center
    801/581-2151
Crisis/Suicide Prevention Hotline
    801/483-5444
Highway Patrol Emergency
    Assistance
    801/965-4505

HOSPITALS AND EMERGENCY MEDICAL CENTERS

Alta View Hospital
9660 S. 1300 East St.
801/576-2600
Columbia St. Mark's Hospital
1200 E. 3900 South St.
801/268-7111
Cottonwood Hospital
5770 S. 300 East St.
801/262-3461
LDS Hospital
Eighth Ave. and C St.
801/321-1100
Primary Children's Medical Center
100 N. Medical Dr.
801/588-2000
Salt Lake Regional Medical Center
1050 E. South Temple St.
801/350-4111
Shriner's Hospital for Children
Fairfax Rd. and Virginia St.
801/536-3500
University Hospital
50 N. Medical Dr.
801/581-2121
Veterans' Hospital
500 Foothill Dr.
801/582-1565

VISITOR INFORMATION

AAA
    800/541-9902
Chamber of Commerce
    801/364-3631
Salt Lake Convention &
    Visitors Bureau
    801/521-2868
Utah Travel Council
    800-200-1160

RECORDED INFORMATION

Airport Information
    801/575-2400
Area Entertainment
    801/466-8788
I-15 Freeway Renovation Hotline
    888/463-6415
Road Conditions
    801/964-6000
Time and Temperature
    801/467-8463
Weather Report
    801/575-7669

SKI INFORMATION

Avalanche Forecast Center
    801/364-1581
Ski Utah
    801/534-1779
Utah Snow Conditions
    801/521-8102
Utah Transit Authority/
Ski Bus Information
    801/287-4636
Utah-Lift Rideshare
    801/533-7433

CITY TOURS

Gray Line Motor Tours
  801/521-7060
Innsbrook Tours
  801/534-1001
Passage To Utah
  801/519-2400
Rocky Mountain Wild West Tours
  800/392-3759
Sample Salt Lake, Inc.
  801/278-9212

CAR RENTAL

Advantage, 800/777-5500
Avis, 800/331-1212
Budget, 800/237-7251
Dollar, 800/421-9849
Enterprise, 800/736-8227
Hertz, 800/654-3131
National, 800/227-7368
Payless, 800/327-3631
Thrifty, 800/367-2277

RESOURCES FOR NEW RESIDENTS

Newcomers Club of Salt Lake
  801/261-5656
Welcome Neighbor of Utah
  801/553-1003
Welcome Utah
  801/967-7818

MULTICULTURAL RESOURCES

Asian Association of Utah
  801/486-5987
Native American Services
  801/486-4877
New Hope Multicultural Association
  801/363-4955
Utah Division of Indian Affairs
  801/538-8808
Utah Office of Asian Affairs
  801/538-8883

Utah Office of Black Affairs
  801/538-8829
Utah Office of Hispanic Affairs
  801/538-8850
Utah Office of Polynesian Affairs
  801/538-8691

DISABLED SERVICES

Access Utah Network
  800/333-8824
The Arc of Utah
  801/364-5060
Governor's Committee on Employment of People with Disabilities
  801/538-7781
Learning Disabilities Association of Utah
  801/355-2881
Murray B. Allen Blind Center
  801/323-4343

OTHER COMMUNITY ORGANIZATIONS

Child Care Resource and Referral
  801/537-1044
Salt Lake City Health Department
  801/468-2750
Salt Lake County Aging Services
  801/468-2454
Salt Lake Public Libraries
  801/524-8200
Utah Legal Services
  801/328-8891

MAIN POST OFFICE

U.S. Postal Service
1760 W. 2100 South St.
801/974-2200

CITY MEDIA

Daily Newspapers

Deseret News
  801/237-2800

The Salt Lake Tribune
801/237-2075

Periodicals

Ad News
801/532-1325
Catalyst Magazine
801/363-1505
City Weekly
801/575-7003
The Event
801/487-4556
The Enterprise
801/533-0556
Salt Lake City Magazine
801/975-1927
Utah Business
801/568-0114

Radio Stations

88.3 FM, KPCW, community
90.1 FM, KUER, classical
90.9 FM, KRCL, community
93.3 FM, KUBL, country
94.1 FM, KODJ, oldies
94.9 FM, KZHT, rock
96.1 FM, KXRK, rock
97.1 FM, KISN, soft rock
97.9 FM, KBZN, jazz
98.7 FM, KBEE, rock
99.5 FM, KUTQ, rock
100.3 FM, KSFI, soft rock
101.1 FM, KBER, rock
101.9 FM, KKAT country
102.7 FM, KQMB, rock
103.5 FM, KRSP, rock
104.3 FM, KSOP, country
105.7 FM, KUMT, rock
106.5 FM, KOSY, adult contemporary
106.9 FM, KLZX, rock
107.5 FM, KENZ, rock

570 AM, KISN, soft rock
860 AM, KCNR, kids
910 AM, KALL, news, talk, sports
1010 AM, KTUR, news

1060 AM, KKDS, adult contemporary
1120 AM, KANN, religious
1160 AM, KSL, news
1280 AM, KDYL, adult contemporary
1320 AM, KFNZ, sports
1370 AM, KSOP, country

Television Stations

Channel 2, KUTV, CBS
Channel 4, KTVX, ABC
Channel 5, KSL, NBC
Channel 7, KUED, PBS
Channel 9, KULC, educational
Channel 11, KBYU, PBS
Channel 13, KSTU, Fox
Channel 14, KJZZ, UPN
Channel 30, KOOG, WB
Channel 48, KEJ, Spanish

BOOKSTORES

B. Dalton Bookseller
Cottonwood Mall
801/278-2624
South Towne Mall
801/571-6077
Trolley Square
801/532-7107
Valley Fair Mall
801/967-3361

Barnes & Noble Booksellers
612 E. 400 South St.
801/524-0089
2100 S. 1100 East St.
801/463-2610
7119 S. 1300 East St., Midvale
801/565-0086
5928 S. State St., Murray
801/266-0075
10180 S. State St., Sandy
801/233-0203

Bibliotect
329 W. Pierpont Ave.
801/236-1010

Borders Books and Music
Crossroads Mall
801/355-6899

Deseret Book Company (LDS)
40 E. South Temple St.
801/534-1515
Cottonwood Mall
801/278-2661
South Towne Mall
801/572-6050
Sugarhouse Center
801/466-2669
Valley Fair Mall
801/969-6288
ZCMI Center
801/328-8191
3843 W. 5400 South St., Kearns
801/967-3884
1110 E. Fort Union Blvd., Midvale
801/561-8777

Frost Bookstore
1320 Foothill Blvd.
801/582-8426

Genesis Books
248 E. 3900 South St.
801/268-1919

Golden Braid Books
151 S. 500 East St.
801/322-1162

King's English
1511 S. 1500 East St.
801/484-9100

Media Play
1198 E. Brickyard Rd.
801/486-5161
7170 S. 1000 East St., Midvale
801/568-0220
5546 S. Redwood Rd., Taylorsville
801/968-6404

Seagull Book & Tape (LDS)
1720 S. Redwood Rd.
801/972-2429
1961 Murray-Holladay Blvd.
801/424-0918
242 E. 6400 South St., Murray
801/261-5434
5730 S. Redwood Rd., Taylorsville
801/969-7747
1629 W. 9000 South St., West Jordan
801/568-0444

Waking Owl Books
208 S. 1300 East St.
801/582-7323

Waldenbooks
Crossroads Mall
801/363-1271
Fashion Place Mall
801/262-9921
South Towne Mall
801/572-1952

INDEX

Abravanel Hall, 79, 168
Alta Ski Area, 151
Antelope Island State Park, 181

Babcock Theater, 161
Ballet West, 166
Beehive House, 79, 112
Big Cottonwood Canyon, 99, 110, 121
Bonneville Salt Flats, 97, 144
Bonneville Shoreline Trail, 155
Brigham Young Gravesite, 79
Brigham Young Historic Park, 122
Brigham Young Monument, 107
Brighton Ski Resort, 152

Capitol Building, 79
Capitol Grounds, 108
Capitol Theatre, 169
Cathedral Church of St. Mark, 80
Cathedral of the Madeleine, 81
Chase Home Museum of Utah Folk Art, 103, 164
Children's Dance Theatre, 116, 167
Children's Museum of Utah, 113
Christmas Box Angel Monument, 81
City and County Building, 92
City Creek Canyon, 88, 122
City Creek Park, 123
City Rep's Family Theater, 116
Council Hall, 84

Delta Center, 169
Desert Star Playhouse, 117
Dimple Dell Regional Park, 123

Eagle Gate, 84
Emigration Canyon, 123
Exchange Place Historic District, 84

Fairmont Park, 124
Family History Library, 84
Finch Lane Gallery/Art Barn, 100
First Presbyterian Church, 85
First Tree Monument, 85
Fort Douglas, 93, 104

Gallivan Utah Center Plaza, 85
Gilgal Gardens, 108
Gina Bachauer Int'l Piano Competition, 164
Glacio Park, 124
Glendinning Gallery, 101
Grande Theatre, 162
Great Salt Lake, 97

Great Salt Lake State Park, 124

Hale Center Theater, 162
Hansen Planetarium, 86, 114
Hellenic Cultural Museum, 104
Hogle Zoological Gardens, 93, 111

International Peace Gardens, 124

Jazz Concert Series at the Hilton, 164
Jordan Park, 124
Jordan River Parkway, 155
Jordan River State Park, 125
Joseph Smith Memorial Building, 86

Kearns Mansion, 87
Kennecott Copper Mine, 97
Kingsbury Hall, 169
Kismet Dance Company, 167

Lady of Guadalupe icon, 87
Lagoon Amusement Park, 119
LDS Church Office Bldg Observation Deck, 87
Liberty Park, 111, 125
Lion House, 79
Little Cottonwood Canyon, 99, 110, 125

McCune Mansion, 88
Memory Grove, 88, 126
Millcreek Canyon, 126, 156
Mormon Historic Trail (inside the valley), 88
Mormon Tabernacle Choir, 165
Mt. Olympus Wilderness Area, 126
Museum of LDS Church History and Art, 105

Off Broadway Theatre, 163
Old Deseret Village, 93, 114
Olympic Games of 2002 (venue sites), 148

Pioneer Memorial Museum, 102
Pioneer Park, 127
Pioneer Theatre Company, 163

Red Butte Garden and Arboretum, 127
Repertory Dance Theatre, 167
Rio Grande Depot (Amtrak), 89
Ririe-Woodbury Dance Company, 168

Salt Lake Acting Company, 163
Salt Lake Art Center, 101

Salt Lake Art Center Kids' Space, 115
Salt Lake Buzz, 145
Salt Lake City Libraries, 115
Salt Lake Community College, 92
Salt Palace Convention Center, 89, 108
Saltair Resort, 98, 169
Sandy City Historic District and
    Museum, 99
Snowbird Ski and Summer Resort, 153
Social Hall Museum, 90
Solitude Resort, 153
Solitude's Nordic Center, 152
Stageright Theater, 164
Sugarhouse Park, 128

Temple Square, 75
Temple Square Concert Series, 165
This Is the Place Heritage Park, 93
Tracy Aviary, 112
Tree of Life, 109
Triad Center, 90
Trolley Square, 90
Twin Peaks Wilderness Area, 128

Union Pacific Depot, 91
University of Utah, 96
Utah Grizzlies, 148
Utah Jazz, 146
Utah Museum of Fine Arts, 101
Utah Museum of Natural History, 102,
    116
Utah Opera Company, 165
Utah Starzz, 147
Utah State Fairpark, 98
Utah State Historical Society Museum,
    103
Utah Symphony, 166

Washington Square, 92
Welfare Square, 98
Westminster College, 92
Wheeler Historic Farm, 92, 116
White Memorial Chapel, 92

ABOUT THE AUTHOR

Margaret Sandberg Godfrey has lived the better part of her life in Salt Lake City, and her explorations of her hometown have included stints as a restaurant reviewer, fine arts reviewer, local-history columnist, business writer, and marketer of tourism. She has written dozens of travel articles for local and national magazines, and is a regular contributor to the *Salt Lake Tribune* and *Enterprise* newspapers.

JOHN MUIR PUBLICATIONS and its City•Smart Guidebook authors are dedicated to building community awareness within City•Smart cities. We are proud to work with Literacy Action Center as we publish this guide to Salt Lake City .

Literacy Action Center, a non-profit organization established in 1984, offers literacy education to beginning adult readers who have been unable to master basic reading skills. Our staff and volunteers have served over 2,000 adults, whose lives have been greatly enhanced through one-on-one reading help from volunteer tutors.

Based on methodology developed by Laubach Literacy Action, the nation's largest volunteer literacy program, Literacy Action further enriches the learning process with computers and other technological tools in our efforts to meet the enormous challenge of reaching the 70,000 adults in the greater Salt Lake area who need basic reading skills.

For more information, please contact:
Literacy Action Center
Horizonte Center, Room 240
1234 S. Main St.
Salt Lake City, UT 84101-3117
801-521-9050